To A

From

Merry Christmas
12/25/12

To

_____

From

_____

*Be of good courage,*
*and He shall strengthen your heart,*
*all you who hope in the Lord.*
—

Psalm 31:24 NKJV

# Courage
## *for my*
# Daily Walk

Freeman-Smith, a division of Worthy Media, Inc.
134 Franklin Road, Suite 200, Brentwood, Tennessee 37027

*The quoted ideas expressed in this book (but not Scripture verses) are not, in all cases, exact quotations, as some have been edited for clarity and brevity. In all cases, the author has attempted to maintain the speaker's original intent. In some cases, quoted material for this book was obtained from secondary sources, primarily print media. While every effort was made to ensure the accuracy of these sources, the accuracy cannot be guaranteed. For additions, deletions, corrections, or clarifications in future editions of this text, please write Freeman-Smith.*

The Holy Bible, King James Version

The Holy Bible, New King James Version (NKJV) Copyright © 1982 by Thomas Nelson, Inc. Used by permission.

New Century Version®. (NCV) Copyright © 1987, 1988, 1991 by Word Publishing, a division of Thomas Nelson, Inc. All rights reserved. Used by permission.

The Holman Christian Standard Bible™ (HCSB) Copyright © 1999, 2000, 2001 by Holman Bible Publishers. Used by permission.

The Holy Bible, New International Version®. (NIV) Copyright © 1973, 1978, 1984 International Bible Society. Used by permission of Zondervan. All rights reserved.

The Holy Bible. New Living Translation (NLT) copyright © 1996 Tyndale Charitable Trust. Used by permission of Tyndale House Publishers.

Scripture taken from The Message. (MSG) Copyright © 1993, 1994, 1995, 1996, 2000, 2001, 2002. Used by permission of NavPress Publishing Group.

Cover Design by Kim Russell / Wahoo Designs
Page Layout by Bart Dawson

ISBN 978-1-60587-321-3

365 devotions for women

Courage *for my* Daily Walk

# Introduction

Your life here on earth is an all-too-brief journey from the cradle to the grave. When you make that journey with God—and when you walk with Him each day and encourage your family members to do the same—you will avail yourself of the peace and abundance that God offers to those who invite Him into their hearts.

In your hands, you hold a book that contains 365 devotional readings for women. During the next year, please try this experiment: read a page from this book each day. If you're already committed to a daily time of worship, this book will enrich that experience. If you are not, the simple act of giving God a few minutes each morning will change the direction and the quality of your life.

Each day provides opportunities to put the Creator where He belongs: at the center of your life. When you do, you will worship Him, not just with words, but with deeds. And you will be richly rewarded.

This book is intended to remind you of the eternal promises that are found in God's Holy Word and of God's never-ending love for you. May these pages be a blessing to you, and may you, in turn, be a blessing to those whom God has seen fit to place along your path.

# Courage for the Storms of Life

*Immediately Jesus spoke to them. "Have courage! It is I. Don't be afraid."*

Matthew 14:27 HCSB

A storm rose quickly on the Sea of Galilee, and the disciples were afraid. Although they had seen Jesus perform many miracles, the disciples feared for their lives, so they turned to their Savior, and He calmed the waters and the wind.

Sometimes, we, like the disciples, feel threatened by the inevitable storms of life. And when we are fearful, we, too, can turn to Christ for courage and for comfort.

The next time you're afraid, remember that the One who calmed the wind and the waves is also your personal Savior. And remember that the ultimate battle has already been won at Calvary. We, as believers, can live courageously in the promises of our Lord . . . and we should.

## — A Prayer for Today —

Dear Lord, sometimes I face disappointments and challenges that leave me worried and afraid. Keep me mindful, Lord, that You are my God. With You by my side, Lord, I have nothing to fear. Help me to be Your grateful and courageous servant this day and every day. Amen

# A Daily Walk with God

*For I have given you an example that you also should do just as I have done for you.*

*John 13:15 HCSB*

Each day, we are confronted with countless opportunities to serve God and to follow in the footsteps of His Son. When we do, our Heavenly Father guides our steps and blesses our endeavors. As citizens of a fast-changing world, we face challenges that sometimes leave us feeling overworked, over-committed, and overwhelmed. But God has different plans for us. He intends that we slow down long enough to praise Him and to glorify His Son. When we do, He lifts our spirits and enriches our lives.

Today provides a glorious opportunity to place yourself in the service of the One who is the Giver of all blessings. May you seek His will, may you trust His Word, and may you walk in the footsteps of His Son.

Will you, with a glad and eager surrender, hand yourself and all that concerns you over into His hands? If you will do this, your soul will begin to know something of the joy of union with Christ.

*Hannah Whitall Smith*

## — A Prayer for Today —

Dear Jesus, because I am Your disciple, I will trust You, I will obey Your teachings, and I will share Your Good News. You have given me life abundant and life eternal, and I will follow You today and forever. Amen

# Your Journey with God

*For it is God who is working among you both the willing and the working for His good purpose.*

Philippians 2:13 HCSB

Your life is a journey, and every step of the way, God is with you. If you seek to live in accordance with God's will for your life—and you should—then you will live in accordance with His commandments. You will study God's Word, and you will be watchful for His signs. You will associate with fellow Christians who will encourage your spiritual growth, and you will listen to that inner voice that speaks to you in the quiet moments of your daily devotionals.

Sometimes, God's plans seem unmistakably clear to you. But other times, He may lead you through the wilderness before He directs you to the Promised Land. So be patient and keep seeking His will for your life. When you do, you'll be amazed at the marvelous things that an all-powerful, all-knowing God can do.

God intends to use you in wonderful, unexpected ways if you let Him. The decision to seek God's plan and to follow it is yours and yours alone. The consequences of that decision have implications that are both profound and eternal, so choose carefully.

## — A Prayer for Today —

Dear Lord, You created me for a reason. Let me do Your work here on earth by seeking Your will and living it, knowing that when I trust in You, Father, I am eternally blessed. Amen

# A Love That Changes Everything

*Your old life is dead. Your new life, which is your real life—*
*even though invisible to spectators—is with Christ in God.*
*He is your life.*

Colossians 3:3 MSG

What does the love of Christ mean to His believers? It changes everything. His love is perfect and steadfast. Even though we are fallible, and wayward, the Good Shepherd cares for us still. Even though we have fallen far short of the Father's commandments, Christ loves us with a power and depth that is beyond our understanding. And, as we accept Christ's love and walk in Christ's footsteps, our lives bear testimony to His power and to His grace. Yes, Christ's love changes everything; may we invite Him into our hearts so it can then change everything in us.

This hard place in which you perhaps find yourself is the very place in which God is giving you opportunity to look only to Him, to spend time in prayer, and to learn long-suffering, gentleness, meekness—in short, to learn the depths of the love that Christ Himself has poured out on all of us.

*Elisabeth Elliot*

## — A Prayer for Today —

Dear Jesus, my life has been changed forever by Your love and sacrifice. Today I will praise You, I will honor You, and I will walk with You. Amen

# The Importance of Prayer

*Be anxious for nothing, but in everything by prayer and supplication, with thanksgiving, let your requests be made known to God.*

*Philippians 4:6 NKJV*

Prayer is a powerful tool for communicating with our Creator; it is an opportunity to commune with the Giver of all things good. Prayer is not a thing to be taken lightly or to be used infrequently. Prayer should never be reserved for mealtimes or for bedtimes; it should be an ever-present focus in our daily lives.

Daily prayer and meditation is a matter of will and habit. You must willingly organize your time by carving out quiet moments with God, and you must form the habit of daily worship. When you do, you'll discover that no time is more precious than the silent moments you spend with your Heavenly Father.

A prayerful heart and an obedient heart will learn, very slowly and not without sorrow, to stake everything on God Himself.

*Elisabeth Elliot*

## — A Prayer for Today —

Dear Lord, I will open my heart to You. I will take my concerns, my fears, and my hopes to You in prayer. And, then, I will trust the answers that You give. You are my loving Father, and I will accept Your will for my life today and every day that I live. Amen

# A Fresh Opportunity

*Therefore we were buried with Him by baptism into death, in order that, just as Christ was raised from the dead by the glory of the Father, so we too may walk in a new way of life.*
*Romans 6:4 HCSB*

God's Word is clear: When we genuinely invite Him to reign over our hearts, and when we accept His transforming love, we are forever changed. When we welcome Christ into our hearts, an old life ends and a new way of living—along with a completely new way of viewing the world—begins.

Each morning offers a fresh opportunity to invite Christ, once again, to rule over our hearts and our days. Each morning presents yet another opportunity to take up His cross and follow in His footsteps. Today, let us rejoice in the new life that is ours through Christ, and let us follow Him, step by step, on the path that He first walked.

If you are God's child, you are no longer bound to your past or to what you were. You are a brand new creature in Christ Jesus.

*Kay Arthur*

## — A Prayer for Today —

Heavenly Father, renew in me the passion to share the Good News of Jesus Christ. Make the experience of my conversion real and fresh so that I might be an effective witness for You. Amen

# Beyond the Daily Grind

*Come to Me, all you who are weary and burdened, and I will give you rest. Take My yoke upon you and learn from Me, because I am gentle and humble in heart, and you will find rest for your souls. For My yoke is easy and My burden is light.*

*Matthew 11:28-30 HCSB*

Even the most inspired women can, from time to time, find themselves running on empty. Why? Because the inevitable demands of daily life can drain us of our strength and rob us of the joy that is rightfully ours in Christ. Thankfully, God stands ready to renew our spirits, even on the darkest of days. God's Word is clear: When we genuinely lift our hearts and prayers to Him, He renews our strength.

Are you seeking a renewed sense of purpose? Turn your heart toward God in prayer. Are you weak or worried? Take the time to delve deeply into God's Holy Word. Are you spiritually depleted? Call upon fellow believers to support you, and call upon Christ to renew your spirit and your life. When you do, you'll discover that the Creator of the universe stands always ready and always able to create a new sense of wonderment and joy in you.

## — A Prayer for Today —

Dear Lord, every day of my life is a journey with You. Guide my steps today, Father, and keep me mindful that today offers yet another opportunity to celebrate Your blessings, Your love, and Your Son. Amen

# Enthusiastic Service

*Do your work with enthusiasm. Work as if you were serving the Lord, not as if you were serving only men and women.*
*Ephesians 6:7 NCV*

Do you see each day as a glorious opportunity to serve God and to do His will? Are you enthused about life, or do you struggle through each day giving scarcely a thought to God's blessings? Are you constantly praising God for His gifts, and are you sharing His Good News with the world? And are you excited about the possibilities for service that God has placed before you, whether at home, at work, at church, or at school? You should be.

You are the recipient of Christ's sacrificial love. Accept it enthusiastically and share it fervently. Jesus deserves your enthusiasm; the world deserves it; and you deserve the experience of sharing it.

The proper perspective creates within us a spirit of reaching outside of ourselves with joy and enthusiasm.
*Luci Swindoll*

## — A Prayer for Today —

Dear Lord, the Christian life is a glorious adventure— let me share my excitement with others. Let me be an enthusiastic believer, Father, and let me share my enthusiasm today and every day. Amen

# You Are Blessed

*I will make them and the area around My hill a blessing: I will send down showers in their season—showers of blessing.*
*Ezekiel 34:26 HCSB*

If you sat down and began counting your blessings, how long would it take? A very, very long time! Your blessings include life, freedom, family, friends, talents, and possessions, for starters. But, your greatest blessing—a gift that is yours for the asking—is God's gift of salvation through Christ Jesus.

Today, begin making a list of your blessings. You most certainly will not be able to make a complete list, but take a few moments and jot down as many blessings as you can. Then give thanks to the giver of all good things: God. His love for you is eternal, as are His gifts. And it's never too soon—or too late—to offer Him thanks.

Oh! what a Savior, gracious to all, / Oh! how His blessings round us fall, / Gently to comfort, kindly to cheer, / Sleeping or waking, God is near.

*Fanny Crosby*

## — A Prayer for Today —

Lord, I have more blessings than I can possibly count; make me mindful of Your precious gifts. You have cared for me, Lord, and You have saved me. I will give thanks and praise You always. Today, let me share Your blessings with others, just as You first shared them with me. Amen

# Courage for Your Daily Walk

*What time I am afraid, I will trust in thee.*

*Psalm 56:3 KJV*

God has promised to protect us, and He intends to fulfill His promise. In a world filled with dangers and temptations, God is the ultimate armor. In a world filled with misleading messages, God's Word is the ultimate truth. In a world filled with more frustrations than we can count, God's Son offers the ultimate peace.

Will you accept God's peace and wear God's armor against the dangers of our world? Hopefully so, because when you do, you can live courageously, knowing that you possess the ultimate protection: God's unfailing love for you.

Our future may look fearfully intimidating, yet we can look up to the Engineer of the Universe, confident that nothing escapes His attention or slips out of the control of those strong hands.

*Elisabeth Elliot*

## — A Prayer for Today —

Lord, You have promised to protect me, and I will trust You. Today, I will live courageously as I place my hopes, my faith, and my life in Your hands. Let my life be a testimony to the transforming power of Your love, Your grace, and Your Son. Amen

# The Power of Faith

*Believe in the Lord your God, and you will be established; believe in His prophets, and you will succeed.*

2 Chronicles 20:20 HCSB

Every life—including yours—is a series of successes and failures, celebrations and disappointments, joys and sorrows. Every step of the way, through every triumph and tragedy, God will stand by your side and strengthen you . . . if you have faith in Him. Jesus taught His disciples that if they had faith, they could move mountains. You can too.

When you place your faith, your trust, indeed your life in the hands of Christ Jesus, you'll be amazed at the marvelous things He can do with you and through you. So strengthen your faith through praise, through worship, through Bible study, and through prayer. And trust God's plans. With Him, all things are possible, and He stands ready to open a world of possibilities to you . . . if you have faith.

## — A Prayer for Today —

Dear God, sometimes this world can be a fearful place, full of uncertainty and doubt. But You are always near and You can overcome any challenge. Give me faith, and let me remember always that with Your love and Your power, I can live courageously and faithfully today and every day. Amen

# New Beginnings

*Do not remember the former things, nor consider the things of old. Behold, I will do a new thing.*

*Isaiah 43:18-19 NKJV*

Each day offers countless opportunities to serve God, to seek His will, and to obey His teachings. But each day also offers countless opportunities to stray from God's commandments and to wander from His path.

Sometimes, we wander aimlessly in a wilderness of our own making, but God has better plans for us. And, whenever we ask Him to renew our strength and guide our steps, He does so.

Consider this day a new beginning. Consider it a fresh start, a renewed opportunity to serve your Creator with willing hands and a loving heart. Ask God to renew your sense of purpose as He guides your steps. Today is a glorious opportunity to serve your Father in heaven. Seize that opportunity while you can; tomorrow may indeed be too late.

## — A Prayer for Today —

Dear Lord, conform me to Your image. Create in me a clean heart, a new heart that reflects Your love for me. When I need to change, change me, Lord, and make me new. Amen

# Optimism Now!

*And now, dear brothers and sisters, let me say one more thing as I close this letter. Fix your thoughts on what is true and honorable and right. Think about things that are pure and lovely and admirable. Think about things that are excellent and worthy of praise.*

*Philippians 4:8 NLT*

As Christian women, we have every reason to rejoice. God is in His heaven; Christ has risen, and we are the sheep of His flock. But, when the demands of life seem great and our resources seem small by comparison, we may find ourselves exhausted, discouraged, or both.

What's your attitude today? Are you fearful, angry, or worried. Are you confused, bitter, or pessimistic? If so, God wants to have a little chat with you.

God wants you to experience His joy and abundance. But, God will not force His joy upon you; you must claim it for yourself. So today, and every day thereafter, celebrate this life that God has given you. Think optimistically about yourself and your future. Give thanks to the One who has given you everything, and trust in your heart that He wants to give you so much more.

## — A Prayer for Today —

Lord, I have so many reasons to be thankful; let my attitude be a reflection of the many blessings I have received. Make me a woman whose thoughts are Christlike and whose hopes are worthy of the One who has given me so much. Amen

# Celebrating Others

*Therefore encourage one another and build each other up as you are already doing.*

*1 Thessalonians 5:11 HCSB*

Do you delight in the victories of others? You should. Each day provides countless opportunities to encourage others and to praise their good works. When you do so, you not only spread seeds of joy and happiness, you also obey the commandments of God's Holy Word.

As Christians, we are called upon to spread the Good News of Christ, and we are also called to spread a message of encouragement and hope to the world. So, let us be cheerful Christians with smiles on our faces and encouraging words on our lips. By blessing others, we also bless ourselves, and, at the same time, we do honor to the One who gave His life for us.

A single word, if spoken in a friendly spirit, may be sufficient to turn one from dangerous error.

*Fanny Crosby*

— A Prayer for Today —

Dear Lord, let me celebrate the accomplishments of others. Make me a source of genuine, lasting encouragement to my family and friends. And let my words and deeds be worthy of Your Son, the One who gives me strength and salvation, this day and for all eternity. Amen

# What Doesn't Change

*Jesus Christ is the same yesterday, today, and forever.*
*Hebrews 13:8 HCSB*

Our world is in a state of constant change. God is not. At times, the world seems to be trembling beneath our feet. But we can be comforted in the knowledge that our Heavenly Father is the rock that cannot be shaken. His Word promises, "I am the Lord, I do not change" (Malachi 3:6 NKJV).

Every day that we live, we mortals encounter a multitude of changes—some good, some not so good, some downright disheartening. On those occasions when us must endure life-changing personal losses that leave us breathless, there is a place we can turn for comfort and assurance—we can turn to God. When we do, our loving Heavenly Father stands ready to protect us, to comfort us, to guide us, and, in time, to heal us.

Conditions are always changing; therefore, I must not be dependent upon conditions. What matters supremely is my soul and my relationship to God.

*Corrie ten Boom*

## — A Prayer for Today —

Dear Lord, our world changes, but You are unchanging. When I face challenges that leave me discouraged or fearful, I will turn to You for strength and assurance. Let my trust in You—like Your love for me—be unchanging and everlasting. Amen

# Claiming the Joy

*A cheerful heart has a continual feast.*

*Proverbs 15:15 HCSB*

On some days, as every woman knows, it's hard to be cheerful. Sometimes, as the demands of the world increase and our energy sags, we feel less like "cheering up" and more like "tearing up." But even in our darkest hours, we can turn to God, and He will give us comfort.

Few things in life are more sad, or, for that matter, more absurd, than a grumpy Christian. Christ promises us lives of abundance and joy, but He does not force His joy upon us. We must claim His joy for ourselves, and when we do, Jesus, in turn, fills our spirits with His power and His love.

When we place Jesus at the center of our lives and trust Him as our personal Savior, He will transform us, not just for today, but for all eternity. Then we, as God's children, can share Christ's joy and His message with a world that needs both.

God is good, and heaven is forever. And if those two facts don't cheer you up, nothing will.

*Marie T. Freeman*

## — A Prayer for Today —

Dear Lord, You have given me so many reasons to celebrate life. Today, let me be a joyful Christian— quick to smile and quick to laugh. And, let Your love shine in me and through me, this day and forever. Amen

# Making Time for God

*He said to him, "You shall love the Lord your God with all your heart, with all your soul, and with all your mind. This is the greatest and most important commandment."*

Matthew 22:37-38 HCSB

When it comes to spending time with God, are you a "squeezer" or a "pleaser"? Do you squeeze God into your schedule with a prayer before meals (and maybe, if you've got the time, with a quick visit to church on Sunday)? Or do you please God by talking to Him far more often than that? If you're wise, you'll form the habit of spending time with God every day. When you do, it will change your life.

This book asks that you give your undivided attention to God for at least five minutes each day. And make no mistake about it: the emphasis in the previous sentence should be placed on the words "at least." In truth, you should give God lots more time than a couple of minutes a day, but hey, it's a start.

Even if you're the busiest person on Planet Earth, you can still carve out a little time for God. And when you think about it, isn't that the very least you should do?

## — A Prayer for Today —

Lord, let Your priorities be my priorities. Let Your will be my will. Let Your Word be my guide, and let me grow in faith and in wisdom this day and every day. Amen

# The Master's Touch

*Everything is possible to the one who believes.*
*Mark 9:23 HCSB*

When a suffering woman sought healing by simply touching the hem of His garment, Jesus turned and said, "Daughter, be of good comfort; thy faith hath made thee whole" (Matthew 9:22 KJV). We, too, can be made whole when we place our faith completely and unwaveringly in the person of Jesus Christ.

Concentration camp survivor Corrie ten Boom relied on faith during her ten months of imprisonment and torture. Later, despite the fact that four of her family members had died in Nazi death camps, Corrie's faith was unshaken. She wrote, "There is no pit so deep that God's love is not deeper still." Christians take note: Genuine faith in God means faith in all circumstances, happy or sad, joyful or tragic.

If your faith is being tested to the point of breaking, know that your Savior is near. If you reach out to Him in faith, He will give you peace and heal your broken spirit. Be content to touch even the smallest fragment of the Master's garment, and He will make you whole.

## — A Prayer for Today —

Dear Lord, help me to be a woman of faith. Help me to remember that You are always near and that You can overcome any challenge. With Your love and Your power, Lord, I can live courageously and faithfully today and every day. Amen

# When the Journey Is Difficult

*For whatever is born of God overcomes the world. And this is the victory that has overcome the world—our faith.*

1 John 5:4 NKJV

All of us face times of adversity. On occasion, we all must endure the disappointments and tragedies that befall believers and nonbelievers alike. The reassuring words of 1 John 5:4 remind us that when we accept God's grace, we overcome the passing hardships of this world by relying upon His strength, His love, and His promise of eternal life.

When we face the inevitable difficulties of life-here-on-earth, God stands ready to protect us. Our responsibility, of course, is to ask Him for protection. When we call upon Him in heartfelt prayer, He will answer—in His own time and according to His own plan—and He will heal us. And while we are waiting for God's plans to unfold and for His healing touch to restore us, we can be comforted in the knowledge that our Creator can overcome any obstacle, even if we cannot. Let us take God at His word, and let us trust Him.

## — A Prayer for Today —

Dear Lord, when I am troubled, You heal me. When I am discouraged, You lift me up. In times of adversity, let me trust Your plan and Your will for my life. And whatever my circumstances, Lord, let me always give the thanks and the glory to You. Amen

# Discipline Yourself

*Discipline yourself for the purpose of godliness.*
1 Timothy 4:7 NASB

Are you a self-disciplined woman? If so, congratulations . . . your disciplined approach to life can help you build a more meaningful relationship with God. Why? Because God expects all His believers (including you) to lead lives of disciplined obedience to Him . . . and He rewards those believers who do.

Sometimes, it's hard to be dignified and disciplined. Why? Because you live in a world where many prominent people want you to believe that dignified, self-disciplined behavior is going out of style. But don't deceive yourself: self-discipline never goes out of style.

Your greatest accomplishments will probably require heaping helpings of self-discipline—which, by the way, is perfectly fine with God. After all, He knows that you're up to the task, and He has big plans for you. God will do His part to fulfill those plans, and the rest, of course, depends upon you.

Work is doing it. Discipline is doing it every day. Diligence is doing it well every day.

*Dave Ramsey*

## — A Prayer for Today —
Dear Lord, I want to be a disciplined believer. Let me use my time wisely, let me obey Your commandments faithfully, and let me worship you joyfully, today and every day. Amen

# Pats on the Back

*So then, we must pursue what promotes peace and what builds up one another.*

Romans 14:19 HCSB

Life is a team sport, and all of us need occasional pats on the back from our teammates. In the book of Ephesians, Paul writes, "Do not let any unwholesome talk come out of your mouths, but only what is helpful for building others up according to their needs, that it may benefit those who listen" (4:29 NIV). Paul reminds us that when we choose our words carefully, we can have a powerful impact on those around us.

Since we don't always know who needs our help, the best strategy is to encourage all the people who cross our paths. So today, be a world-class source of encouragement to everyone you meet. Never has the need been greater.

Don't forget that a single sentence, spoken at the right moment, can change somebody's whole perspective on life. A little encouragement can go a long, long way.

Marie T. Freeman

— A Prayer for Today —

Dear Heavenly Father, just as You have lifted me up, let me lift up others in a spirit of encouragement and hope. And if I can help a fellow traveler, even in a small way, Dear Lord, may the glory be Yours. Amen

# Your Shining Light

*While ye have light, believe in the light, that ye may be the children of light.*

John 12:36 KJV

The Bible says that you are "the light that gives light to the world." What kind of light have you been giving off? Hopefully, you've been a good example for everybody to see. Why? Because the world needs all the light it can get, and that includes your light, too!

Christ showed enduring love for you by willingly sacrificing His own life so that you might have eternal life. As a response to His sacrifice, you should love Him, praise Him, and share His message of salvation with your neighbors and with the world. So let your light shine today and every day. When you do, God will bless you now and forever.

Light is stronger than darkness—darkness cannot "comprehend" or "overcome" it.

*Anne Graham Lotz*

## — A Prayer for Today —

Dear Lord, You are the way and the truth and the light. Today—as I follow Your way and share Your Good News—let me be a worthy example to others and a worthy servant to You. Amen

# In His Hands

*For whatever is born of God overcomes the world. And this is the victory that has overcome the world—our faith.*

1 John 5:4 NKJV

The first element of a successful life is faith: faith in God, faith in His Son, and faith in His promises. If we place our lives in God's hands, our faith is rewarded in ways that we—as human beings with clouded vision and limited understanding—can scarcely comprehend. But, if we seek to rely solely upon our own resources, or if we seek earthly success outside the boundaries of God's commandments, we reap a bitter harvest for ourselves and for our loved ones.

Do you desire the abundance and success that God has promised? Then trust Him today and every day that you live. Then, when you have entrusted your future to the Giver of all things good, rest assured that your future is secure, not only for today, but also for all eternity.

Faith is seeing light with the eyes of your heart, when the eyes of your body see only darkness.

*Barbara Johnson*

## — A Prayer for Today —

Father, in the dark moments of my life, help me to remember that You are always near and that You can overcome any challenge. Keep me mindful of Your love and Your power, so that I may live courageously and faithfully today and every day. Amen

# The Last Word

*For God has not given us a spirit of fearfulness, but one of power, love, and sound judgment. So don't be ashamed of the testimony about our Lord, or of me His prisoner. Instead, share in suffering for the gospel, relying on the power of God.*

2 Timothy 1:7-8 HCSB

All of us may find our courage tested by the inevitable disappointments and tragedies of life. After all, ours is a world filled with uncertainty, hardship, sickness, and danger. Old Man Trouble, it seems, is never too far from the front door.

When we focus upon our fears and our doubts, we may find many reasons to lie awake at night and fret about the uncertainties of the coming day. A better strategy, of course, is to focus not upon our fears, but instead upon our God.

God is your shield and your strength; you are His forever. So don't focus your thoughts upon the fears of the day. Instead, trust God's plan and His eternal love for you. And remember: God is good, and He has the last word.

## — A Prayer for Today —

Father, even when I walk through the valley of the shadow of death, I will fear no evil because You are with me. Thank You, Lord, for Your perfect love, a love that casts out fear and gives me strength and courage to meet the challenges of this world. Amen

# In the Footsteps of the Savior

*The one who loves his life will lose it, and the one who hates his life in this world will keep it for eternal life. If anyone serves Me, he must follow Me. Where I am, there My servant also will be. If anyone serves Me, the Father will honor him.*

John 12:25-26 HCSB

With whom will you walk today? Will you walk with people who worship the ways of the world? Or will you walk with the Son of God? Jesus walks with you. Are you walking with Him? Hopefully, you will choose to walk with Him today and every day of your life. God's Word promises that when you follow in Christ's footsteps, you will learn how to live freely and lightly (Matthew 11:28-30).

Are you worried about the day ahead? Be confident in God's power. He will never desert you. Are you concerned about the future? Be courageous and call upon God. He will protect you. Are you confused? Listen to the quiet voice of your Heavenly Father. He is not a God of confusion. So talk with God; listen to Him; and walk with His Son—starting now.

## — A Prayer for Today —

Dear Lord, You sent Your Son so that I might have abundant life and eternal life. Thank You, Father, for my Savior, Christ Jesus. I will follow Him, honor Him, and share His Good News, this day and every day. Amen

# Perfect Wisdom

*Therefore, everyone who hears these words of Mine and acts on them will be like a sensible man who built his house on the rock. The rain fell, the rivers rose, and the winds blew and pounded that house. Yet it didn't collapse, because its foundation was on the rock.*

*Matthew 7:24-25 HCSB*

Where will you place your trust today? Will you trust in the wisdom of fallible men and women, or will you place your faith in God's perfect wisdom? Where you choose to place your trust will determine the direction and quality of your life.

Are you tired? Discouraged? Fearful? Be comforted and trust God. Are you worried or anxious? Be confident in God's power and trust His Holy Word. Are you confused? Listen to the quiet voice of your Heavenly Father. He is not a God of confusion. Talk with Him; listen to Him; trust Him. He is steadfast, and He is your protector . . . forever.

Decisions which are made in the light of God's Word are stable and show wisdom.

*Vonette Bright*

## — A Prayer for Today —

Dear Lord, You are my wise Teacher. Help me to learn from You. And then, let me show others what it means to be a kind, generous, loving Christian. Amen

# Using Your Gifts

*I remind you to keep ablaze the gift of God that is in you.*
2 Timothy 1:6 HCSB

All women possess special gifts and talents; you are no exception. But, your gift is no guarantee of success; it must be cultivated and nurtured; otherwise, it will go unused . . . and God's gift to you will be squandered.

Today, accept this challenge: value the talent that God has given you, nourish it, make it grow, and share it with the world. After all, the best way to say "Thank You" for God's gift is to use it.

What we are is God's gift to us. What we become is our gift to God.

*Anonymous*

— A Prayer for Today —

Heavenly Father, Your gifts to me are priceless and eternal. I praise You and give thanks for Your creation, for Your Son, and for the unique talents and opportunities that You have given me. Let me use my gifts for the glory of Your kingdom, this day and every day. Amen

# Why He Sent His Son

*For all have sinned, and fall short of the glory of God, being justified freely by His grace through the redemption that is in Christ Jesus . . . .*

Romans 3:23-24 NKJV

Despite our shortcomings, God sent His Son so that we might be redeemed from our sins. In doing so, our Heavenly Father demonstrated His infinite mercy and His infinite love. We have received countless gifts from God, but none can compare with the gift of salvation. God's grace is the ultimate gift, and we owe Him the ultimate in thanksgiving.

Christ sacrificed His life on the cross so that we might have eternal life. This gift, freely given from God's only begotten Son, is the priceless possession of everyone who accepts Him as Lord and Savior. We return our Savior's love by welcoming Him into our hearts and sharing His message and His love. When we do so, we are blessed here on earth and throughout all eternity.

## — A Prayer for Today —

Dear Lord, You have offered Your grace freely through Christ Jesus. I praise You for that priceless gift. Let me share the good news of Your Son with a world that desperately needs His peace, His abundance, His love, and His salvation. Amen

# Our Actions and Our Beliefs

*As you have therefore received Christ Jesus the Lord, so walk in Him, rooted and built up in Him and established in the faith, as you have been taught, abounding in it with thanksgiving.*

*Colossians 2:6-7 NKJV*

As Christians, we must do our best to make sure that our actions are accurate reflections of our beliefs. Our theology must be demonstrated, not only by our words but, more importantly, by our actions. In short, we should be practical believers, quick to act whenever we see an opportunity to serve God.

We may proclaim our beliefs to our hearts' content, but our proclamations will mean nothing—to others or to ourselves—unless we accompany our words with deeds that match. The sermons that we live are far more compelling than the ones we preach. So remember this: whether you like it or not, your life is an accurate reflection of your creed. If this fact gives you cause for concern, don't bother talking about the changes that you intend to make—make them. And then, when your good deeds speak for themselves—as they most certainly will—don't interrupt.

## — A Prayer for Today —

Lord, it is so much easier to speak of the righteous life than it is to live it. Let me live righteously, and let my actions be consistent with my beliefs. May every step that I take reflect Your truth and Your love, and may I live a life that is worthy of Your grace. Amen

# Life's Roadmap

*All Scripture is inspired by God and is profitable for teaching, for rebuking, for correcting, for training in righteousness, so that the man of God may be complete, equipped for every good work.*

*2 Timothy 3:16-17 HCSB*

God's Word is unlike any other book. The Bible is a roadmap for life here on earth and for life eternal. As Christians, we are called upon to study God's Holy Word, to trust its promises, to follow its commandments, and to share its Good News with the world.

As women who seek to follow in the footsteps of the One from Galilee, we must study the Bible and meditate upon its meaning for our lives. Otherwise, we deprive ourselves of a priceless gift from our Creator. God's Holy Word is, indeed, a life-changing, one-of-a-kind treasure. And, a passing acquaintance with the Good Book is insufficient for Christians who seek to obey God's Word and to understand His will.

The Reference Point for the Christian is the Bible. All values, judgments, and attitudes must be gauged in relationship to this Reference Point.

*Ruth Bell Graham*

## — A Prayer for Today —

Dear Lord, the Bible is Your gift to me; thank You. When I place Your Word at the very center of my life, I am protected and blessed. Make me a faithful student of Your Word. Amen

# This Is His Day

*This is the day the Lord has made; let us rejoice and be glad in it.*

*Psalm 118:24 HCSB*

The 118th Psalm reminds us that today, like every other day, is a cause for celebration. God gives us this day; He fills it to the brim with possibilities, and He challenges us to use it for His purposes. The day is presented to us fresh and clean at midnight, free of charge, but we must beware: Today is a non-renewable resource—once it's gone, it's gone forever. Our responsibility, of course, is to use this day in the service of God's will and according to His commandments.

Today, treasure the time that God has given you. Give Him the glory and the praise and the thanksgiving that He deserves. And search for the hidden possibilities that God has placed along your path. This day is a priceless gift from God, so use it joyfully and encourage others to do likewise. After all, this is the day the Lord has made.

## — A Prayer for Today —

Dear Lord, You have given me so many blessings, and as a way of saying "Thank You," I will celebrate. I will be a joyful Christian, Lord, and I will share my joy with my family, with my friends, and with my neighbors, this day and every day. Amen

# Character-building Takes Time

*For this very reason, make every effort to supplement your faith with goodness, goodness with knowledge, knowledge with self-control, self-control with endurance, endurance with godliness.*

*2 Peter 1:5-6 HCSB*

Character is built slowly over a lifetime. It is the sum of every right decision, every honest word, every noble thought, and every heartfelt prayer. It is forged on the anvil of honorable work and polished by the twin virtues of generosity and humility. Character is a precious thing—difficult to build but easy to tear down.

As believers in Christ, we must seek to live each day with discipline, honesty, and faith. When we do, integrity becomes a habit. And God smiles.

There is something about having endured great loss that brings purity of purpose and strength of character.

*Barbara Johnson*

### — A Prayer for Today —

Heavenly Father, Your Word instructs me to walk in righteousness and in truth. Make me Your worthy servant, Lord. Let my words be true, and let my actions lead others to You. Amen

# Choices That Please God

*I have set before you life and death, blessing and curse.*
*Choose life so that you and your descendants may live, love*
*the Lord your God, obey Him, and remain faithful to Him.*
*For He is your life, and He will prolong your life in the land*
*the Lord swore to give to your fathers Abraham, Isaac, and*
*Jacob.*

*Deuteronomy 30:19-20 HCSB*

Sometimes, because you're an imperfect being, you may become so wrapped up in meeting society's expectations that you fail to focus on God's expectations. To do so is a mistake of major proportions—don't make it. Instead, seek God's guidance as you focus your energies on becoming the best "you" that you can possibly be. And, when it comes to matters of conscience, seek approval not from your peers, but from your Creator.

Whom will you try to please today: God or man? Your primary obligation is not to please imperfect men and women. Your obligation is to strive diligently to meet the expectations of an all-knowing and perfect God. Trust Him always. Love Him always. Praise Him always. And make choices that please Him. Always.

— A Prayer for Today —

Dear Lord, today, I will choose to please You and only You. I will obey Your commandments, and I will praise You for Your gifts, for Your love, and for Your Son. Amen

# Building Fellowship

*It is good and pleasant when God's people live together in peace!*

*Psalms 133:1 NCV*

Fellowship with other believers should be an integral part of your everyday life. Your association with fellow Christians should be uplifting, enlightening, encouraging, and consistent.

Are you an active member of your own fellowship? Are you a builder of bridges inside the four walls of your church and outside it? Do you contribute to God's glory by contributing your time and your talents to a close-knit band of believers? Hopefully so. The fellowship of believers is intended to be a powerful tool for spreading God's Good News and uplifting His children. And God intends for you to be a fully contributing member of that fellowship. Your intentions should be the same.

Be united with other Christians. A wall with loose bricks is not good. The bricks must be cemented together.

*Corrie ten Boom*

— A Prayer for Today —

Heavenly Father, You have given me a community of supporters called the church. Let our fellowship be a refection of the love we feel for each other and the love we feel for You. Amen

# Extreme Changes

*Then He said to them all, "If anyone wants to come with Me, he must deny himself, take up his cross daily, and follow Me."*

Luke 9:23 HCSB

Jesus made an extreme sacrifice for you. Are you willing to make extreme changes in your life for Him? Can you honestly say that you're passionate about your faith and that you're really following Jesus? Hopefully so. But if you're preoccupied with other things—or if you're strictly a one-day-a-week Christian—then you're in need of an extreme spiritual makeover!

Nothing is more important than your wholehearted commitment to your Creator and to His only begotten Son. Your faith must never be an afterthought; it must be your ultimate priority, your ultimate possession, and your ultimate passion. You are the recipient of Christ's love. Accept it enthusiastically and share it passionately. Jesus deserves your extreme enthusiasm; the world deserves it; and you deserve the experience of sharing it.

To walk out of His will is to walk into nowhere.

C. S. Lewis

## — A Prayer for Today —

Dear Lord, You sent Jesus to save the world and to save me. I thank You for Jesus, and I will do my best to follow Him, today and forever. Amen

# Friendships
# That Honor God

*If your life honors the name of Jesus, he will honor you.*
*2 Thessalonians 1:12 MSG*

Some friendships help us honor God; these friendships should be nurtured. Other friendships place us in situations where we are tempted to dishonor God by disobeying His commandments; friendships such as these have the potential to do us great harm.

Because we tend to become like our friends, we must choose our friends carefully. Because our friends influence us in ways that are both subtle and powerful, we must ensure that our friendships are pleasing to God. When we spend our days in the presence of godly believers, we are blessed, not only by those friends, but also by our Creator.

Insomuch as any one pushes you nearer to God, he or she is your friend.

*Anonymous*

## — A Prayer for Today —

Dear Lord, let my friendships honor You. Keep me mindful that I am Your servant in every aspect of my life. Let me be a worthy servant, Lord, and a worthy friend. And, may the love of Jesus shine in me and through me today and forever. Amen

# The Miracle Worker

*Jesus said to them, "I have shown you many great miracles from the Father."*

John 10:32 NIV

God is a miracle worker. Throughout history He has intervened in the course of human events in ways that cannot be explained by science or human rationale. And He's still doing so today.

God's miracles are not limited to special occasions, nor are they witnessed by a select few. God is crafting His wonders all around us: the miracle of the birth of a new baby; the miracle of a world renewing itself with every sunrise; the miracle of lives transformed by God's love and grace. Each day, God's handiwork is evident for all to see and experience.

Today, seize the opportunity to inspect God's hand at work. His miracles come in a variety of shapes and sizes, so keep your eyes and your heart open. Be watchful, and you'll soon be amazed.

## — A Prayer for Today —

Dear Lord, absolutely nothing is impossible for You. Let me trust in Your power and in Your miracles. When I lose hope, give me faith; when others lose hope, let me tell them of Your glorious works. Today, Lord, keep me mindful that You are a God of infinite possibilities and infinite love. Amen

# The Ultimate Instruction Manual

*The one who has contempt for instruction will pay the penalty, but the one who respects a command will be rewarded.*

*Proverbs 13:13 HCSB*

The Holy Bible contains thorough instructions which, if followed, lead to fulfillment, righteousness, and salvation. But, if we choose to ignore God's commandments, the results are as predictable as they are tragic.

A righteous life has many components: faith, honesty, generosity, love, kindness, humility, gratitude, and worship, to name but a few. If we seek to follow the steps of our Savior, Jesus Christ, we must seek to live according to His commandments. Let us follow God's commandments, and let us conduct our lives in such a way that we might be shining examples for those who have not yet found Christ.

To yield to God means to belong to God, and to belong to God means to have all His infinite power. To belong to God means to have all.

*Hannah Whitall Smith*

## — A Prayer for Today —

Lord, Your commandments are a perfect guide for my life. Give me the wisdom to walk righteously in Your way, Father, trusting always in You. Amen

# The Lord Is Near

*Draw near to God, and He will draw near to you.*
James 4:8 HCSB

Since God is everywhere, we are free to sense His presence whenever we take the time to quiet our souls and turn our prayers to Him. But sometimes, amid the incessant demands of everyday life, we turn our thoughts far from God; when we do, we suffer.

Do you set aside quiet moments each day to offer praise to your Creator? As a woman who has received the gift of God's grace, you most certainly should. Silence is a gift that you give to yourself and to God. During these moments of stillness, you will often sense the infinite love and power of your Creator—and He, in turn, will speak directly to your heart.

The familiar words of Psalm 46:10 remind us to "Be still, and know that I am God." When we do so, we encounter the awesome presence of our loving Heavenly Father, and we are comforted in the knowledge that God is not just near. He is here.

## — A Prayer for Today —

Dear Lord, You are always near. Yet I sometimes feel so far from You. During those times, help me to sense Your presence . . . and Your love. Amen

# Seeking His Will

*Teach me to do Your will, for You are my God; Your Spirit is good. Lead me in the land of uprightness.*

Psalm 143:10 NKJV

God has a plan for our world and our lives. God does not do things by accident; He is willful and intentional. Unfortunately for us, we cannot always understand the will of God. Why? Because we are mortal beings with limited understanding. Although we cannot fully comprehend the will of God, we should always trust the will of God.

As this day unfolds, seek God's will and obey His Word. When you entrust your life to Him without reservation, He will give you the courage to meet any challenge, the strength to endure any trial, and the wisdom to live in His righteousness and in His peace.

The only safe place is in the center of God's will. It is not only the safest place. It is also the most rewarding and the most satisfying place to be.

*Gigi Graham Tchividjian*

## — A Prayer for Today —

Heavenly Father, I will study Your Word and seek Your guidance. Give me the wisdom to know Your will for my life and the courage to follow wherever You may lead me, today and forever. Amen

# Good Habits, Bad Habits

*Do not be deceived: "Evil company corrupts good habits."*
1 Corinthians 15:33 NKJV

It's an old saying and a true one: First, you make your habits, and then your habits make you. Some habits will inevitably bring you closer to God; other habits will lead you away from the path He has chosen for you. If you sincerely desire to improve your spiritual health, you must honestly examine the habits that make up the fabric of your day. And you must abandon those habits that are displeasing to God.

If you trust God, and if you keep asking for His help, He can transform your life. If you sincerely ask Him to help you, the same God who created the universe will help you defeat the harmful habits that have heretofore defeated you. So, if at first you don't succeed, keep praying. God is listening, and He's ready to help you become a better person if you ask Him . . . so ask today.

If you want to form a new habit, get to work. If you want to break a bad habit, get on your knees.

*Marie T. Freeman*

## — A Prayer for Today —

Dear Lord, help me break bad habits and form good ones. And let my actions be pleasing to You, today and every day. Amen

# Choosing the Good Life

*And in that day you will ask Me nothing. Most assuredly, I say to you, whatever you ask the Father in My name He will give you. Until now you have asked nothing in My name. Ask, and you will receive, that your joy may be full.*
John 16:23-24 NKJV

God offers us abundance through His Son, Jesus. Whether or not we accept God's abundance is, of course, up to each of us. When we entrust our hearts and our days to the One who created us, we experience abundance through the grace and sacrifice of His Son, Jesus. But, when we turn our thoughts and our energies away from God's commandments, we inevitably forfeit the spiritual abundance that might otherwise be ours.

What is your focus today? Are you focused on God's Word and His will for your life? Or are you focused on the distractions and temptations of a difficult world. The answer to this question will, to a surprising extent, determine the quality and the direction of your day.

If you sincerely seek the spiritual abundance that your Savior offers, then follow Him completely and without reservation. When you do, you will receive the love, the life, and the abundance that He has promised.

## — A Prayer for Today —
Dear Lord, thank You for the abundant life that is mine through Christ Jesus. Give me courage to claim the spiritual riches that You have promised, and lead me according to Your plan for my life, today and always. Amen

# To Judge or Not to Judge

*When they persisted in questioning Him, He stood up and said to them, "The one without sin among you should be the first to throw a stone at her."*

*John 8:7 HCSB*

The warning of Matthew 7:1 is clear: "Judge not, that ye be not judged" (KJV). Yet even the most devoted Christians may fall prey to a powerful yet subtle temptation: the temptation to judge others. But as obedient followers of Christ, we are commanded to refrain from such behavior.

As Jesus came upon a young woman who had been condemned by the Pharisees, He spoke not only to the crowd that was gathered there, but also to all generations when He warned, "He that is without sin among you, let him first cast a stone at her" (John 8:7 KJV). Christ's message is clear, and it applies not only to the Pharisees of ancient times, but also to us.

Judging draws the judgment of others.

*Catherine Marshall*

## — A Prayer for Today —

Dear Lord, sometimes I am quick to judge others. But, You have commanded me not to judge. Keep me mindful, Father, that when I judge others, I am living outside of Your will for my life. You have forgiven me, Lord. Let me forgive others, let me love them, and let me help them . . . without judging them. Amen

# Never-ending Love

*And we have this command from Him: the one who loves God must also love his brother.*

*1 John 4:21 HCSB*

C. S. Lewis observed, "A man's spiritual health is exactly proportional to his love for God." If we are to enjoy the spiritual health that God intends for us, we must praise Him, we must love Him, and we must obey Him.

When we worship God faithfully and obediently, we invite His love into our hearts. When we truly worship God, we allow Him to rule over our days and our lives. In turn, we grow to love God even more deeply as we sense His love for us.

Today, open your heart to the Father. And let your obedience be a fitting response to His never-ending love.

When we develop an authentic love relationship with God, we will not be able to keep Him compartmentalized in "churchy," religious categories.

*Beth Moore*

## — A Prayer for Today —

Dear Heavenly Father, You have blessed me with a love that is infinite and eternal. Let me love You, Lord, more and more each day. Make me a loving servant, Father, today and throughout eternity. And, let me show my love for You by sharing Your message and Your love with others. Amen

# Living Righteously

*Flee from youthful passions, and pursue righteousness, faith, love, and peace, along with those who call on the Lord from a pure heart.*

*2 Timothy 2:22 HCSB*

A life of righteousness is lived in accordance with God's commandments. A righteous woman strives to be faithful, honest, generous, disciplined, loving, kind, humble, and grateful, to name only a few of the more obvious qualities which are described in God's Word.

If we seek to follow the steps of Jesus, we must seek to live according to His teachings. In short, we must, to the best of our abilities, live according to the principles contained in the Holy Bible. When we do, we become powerful examples to our families and friends of the blessings that God bestows upon righteous women.

A life lived in God is not lived on the plane of feelings, but of the will.

*Elisabeth Elliot*

## — A Prayer for Today —

Dear Lord, this world is filled with so many temptations, distractions, and frustrations. When I turn my thoughts away from You and Your Word, I suffer. But when I turn my thoughts, my faith, and my prayers to You, I am safe. Direct my path, Father, and let me discover Your will for me today and every day that I live. Amen

# Give Me Patience . . . NOW!

*Rest in the Lord, and wait patiently for Him.*

*Psalm 37:7 NKJV*

Psalm 37:7 commands us to wait patiently for God. But as busy women in a fast-paced world, many of us find that waiting quietly for God is difficult. Why? Because we are fallible human beings seeking to live according to our own timetables, not God's. In our better moments, we realize that patience is not only a virtue; it is also a commandment from God.

We human beings are impatient by nature. We know what we want, and we know exactly when we want it: NOW! But, God knows better. He has created a world that unfolds according to His plans, not our own. As believers, we must trust His wisdom and His goodness.

God instructs us to be patient in all things. We must be patient with our families, our friends, and our associates. We must also be patient with our Creator as He unfolds His plan for our lives. And that's as it should be. After all, think how patient God has been with us.

## — A Prayer for Today —

Lord, make me a woman of patience. When I am hurried, give me peace. When I am frustrated, give me perspective. When I am angry, let me turn my heart to You. Today, let me be a patient Christian, Dear Lord, as I trust in You and in Your master plan for my life. Amen

# Maintaining Perspective

*It is important to look at things from God's point of view.*
*1 Corinthians 4:6 MSG*

If a temporary loss of perspective has left you worried, exhausted, or both, it's time to readjust your thought patterns. Negative thoughts are habit-forming; thankfully, so are positive ones. With practice, you can form the habit of focusing on God's priorities and your possibilities. When you do, you'll soon discover that you will spend less time fretting about your challenges and more time praising God for His gifts.

When you call upon the Lord and prayerfully seek His will, He will give you wisdom and perspective. When you make God's priorities your priorities, He will direct your steps and calm your fears. So today and every day hereafter, pray for a sense of balance and perspective. And remember: no problems are too big for God—and that includes yours.

## — A Prayer for Today —

Lord, sometimes, the world's perspective can lead me astray. Help me, Lord, to see the world through Your eyes. Give me guidance and wisdom. And keep me ever mindful, Father, that Your reality is the ultimate reality, and that Your truth is the ultimate truth, now and forever. Amen

# A Life of Abundance

*I have come that they may have life, and that they may have it more abundantly.*

*John 10:10 NKJV*

The 10th chapter of John tells us that Christ came to earth so that our lives might be filled with abundance. But what, exactly, did Jesus mean when He promised "life . . . more abundantly"? Was He referring to material possessions or financial wealth? Hardly. Jesus offers a different kind of abundance: a spiritual richness that extends beyond the temporal boundaries of this world. This everlasting abundance is available to all who seek it and claim it. May we, as believers, claim the riches of Christ Jesus every day that we live, and may we share His blessings with all who cross our path.

The gift of God is eternal life, spiritual life, abundant life through faith in Jesus Christ, the Living Word of God.

*Anne Graham Lotz*

## — A Prayer for Today —

Dear Lord, You have offered me the gift of abundance through Your Son. Thank You, Father, for the abundant life that is mine through Christ Jesus. Let me accept His gifts and use them always to glorify You. Amen

# Today's Opportunities

*But encourage each other daily, while it is still called today,
so that none of you is hardened by sin's deception.*

Hebrews 3:13 HCSB

The 118th Psalm reminds us, "This is the day which the Lord hath made; we will rejoice and be glad in it" (v. 24 KJV). As we rejoice in this day that the Lord has given us, let us remember that an important part of today's celebration is the time we spend celebrating others. Each day provides countless opportunities to encourage others and to praise their good works. When we do, we not only spread seeds of joy and happiness, we also follow the commandments of God's Holy Word.

How can we build others up? By celebrating their victories and their accomplishments. So look for the good in others and celebrate the good that you find. When you do, you'll be a powerful force of encouragement in the world . . . and a worthy servant to your God.

Encouragement starts at home, but it should never end there.

Marie T. Freeman

## — A Prayer for Today —

Dear Lord, You have blessed all of Your children with special gifts and talents. Today, help me to use the talents You have given me, and in turn, let me help others find the strength and courage to use their gifts according to Your master plan. Amen

# Humbled by His Sacrifice

*But as for me, I will never boast about anything except the cross of our Lord Jesus Christ, through whom the world has been crucified to me, and I to the world.*

Galatians 6:14 HCSB

As we consider Christ's sacrifice on the cross, we should be profoundly humbled. And today, as we come to Christ in prayer, we should do so in a spirit of humble devotion.

Christ humbled Himself on a cross—for you. He shed His blood—for you. He has offered to walk with you through this life and throughout all eternity. As you approach Him today in prayer, think about His sacrifice and His grace. And be humble.

The sacrifice of the Lamb is absolutely sufficient in itself to take away our sin and reconcile us to God.

*Anne Graham Lotz*

## — A Prayer for Today —

Dear Lord, when I am called upon to make sacrifices for causes that are just, give me courage. Let my words and deeds be pleasing to You, and let my service to others be worthy of the One who sacrificed His life for mine. Amen

# Eternal Perspective

*Our Savior Jesus poured out new life so generously. God's gift has restored our relationship with him and given us back our lives. And there's more life to come—an eternity of life!*
Titus 3:6-7 MSG

As mere mortals, our vision for the future, like our lives here on earth, is limited. God's vision is not burdened by such limitations: His plans extend throughout all eternity. Thus, God's plans for you are not limited to the ups and downs of everyday life. Your Heavenly Father has bigger things in mind . . . much bigger things. Christ sacrificed His life on the cross so that we might have eternal life. This gift, freely given by God's only begotten Son, is the priceless possession of everyone who accepts Him as Lord and Savior.

As you struggle with the inevitable hardships and occasional disappointments of everyday life, remember that God has invited you to accept His abundance not only for today but also for all eternity. So keep things in perspective. Although you will inevitably encounter occasional defeats in this world, you'll have all eternity to celebrate the ultimate victory in the next.

## — A Prayer for Today —

I know, Lord, this world is not my home; I am only here for a short time. You have given me the priceless gift of eternal life through Your Son Jesus. Keep the promise of heaven in my heart, and help me to pass through this world with joy, with perspective, with thanksgiving, and with praise on my lips for You. Amen

# God and Family

*Let the Word of Christ—the Message—have the run of the house. Give it plenty of room in your lives.*

Colossians 3:16 MSG

These are difficult days for our nation and for our families. But, thankfully, God is bigger than all of our challenges. God loves us and protects us. In times of trouble, He comforts us; in times of sorrow, He dries our tears. When we are troubled or weak or sorrowful, God is as near as our next breath.

Are you concerned for the well-being of your family? You are not alone. We live in a world where temptation and danger seem to lurk on every street corner. Parents and children alike have good reason to be watchful. But, despite the evils of our time, God remains steadfast. Even in these difficult days, no problem is too big for God.

Living life with a consistent spiritual walk deeply influences those we love most.

*Vonette Bright*

## — A Prayer for Today —

Dear Lord, I am blessed to be part of the family of God where I find love and acceptance. You have also blessed me with my earthly family. Let me show love and acceptance for my own family so that through me, they might come to know You. Amen

# Blessed Beyond Measure

*We always thank God, the Father of our Lord Jesus Christ,*
*when we pray for you.*

*Colossians 1:3 HCSB*

As believing Christians, we are blessed beyond measure. God sent His only Son to die for our sins. And, God has given us the priceless gifts of eternal love and eternal life. We, in turn, are instructed to approach our Heavenly Father with reverence and thanksgiving. But, as busy women caught up in the inevitable demands of everyday life, we sometimes fail to pause and thank our Creator for the countless blessings He has bestowed upon us. When we slow down and express our gratitude to the One who made us, we enrich our own lives and the lives of those around us. Thanksgiving should become a habit, a regular part of our daily routines. Yes, God has blessed us beyond measure, and we owe Him everything, including our eternal praise.

Do we not continually pass by blessings innumerable without notice, and instead fix our eyes on what we feel to be our trials and our losses, and think and talk about these until our whole horizon is filled with them, and we almost begin to think we have no blessings at all?

*Hannah Whitall Smith*

## — A Prayer for Today —

Lord, let me be a thankful Christian. Your blessings are priceless and eternal. I praise You, Lord, for Your gifts and, most of all, for Your Son. Amen

# Gentleness of Spirit

*Your beauty should not be the outer beauty of elaborate hairstyles and the wearing of gold ornaments or of fine clothes; rather, it should be an inner beauty with the imperishability of a gentle and quiet spirit, which is very valuable in God's eyes.*

1 Peter 3:3-4 HCSB

In a letter to the Christians at Philippi, Paul instructed his friends to make their gentleness evident to all. But, even for the most dedicated Christians, it is sometimes difficult to be gentle. As fallible human beings, we are subject to the normal frustrations of daily life, and when we are, we are tempted to strike out in anger.

As long as you live here on earth, you will face countless opportunities to lose your temper over small, relatively insignificant events: a traffic jam, a spilled cup of coffee, an inconsiderate comment, a broken promise. When you are tempted to lose your temper over the minor inconveniences of life, don't. Turn away from anger and turn instead to God; when you do, He will fill you with a loving spirit that will help you deal gently and generously with others.

## — A Prayer for Today —

In moments of weakness, Lord, I am tempted to strike out at those who have hurt me. Keep me mindful, Father, that gentleness is Your commandment. You have forgiven me, Lord; let me show my thankfulness to You by forgiving others. Amen

# The Choice to Forgive

*You have heard that it was said, You shall love your neighbor and hate your enemy. But I tell you, love your enemies, and pray for those who persecute you.*

*Matthew 5:43-44 HCSB*

Forgiveness is a choice. We can either choose to forgive those who have injured us, or not. When we obey God by offering forgiveness to His children, we are blessed. But when we allow bitterness and resentment to poison our hearts, we are tortured by our own shortsightedness.

Do you harbor resentment against anyone? If so, you are faced with an important decision: whether or not to forgive the person who has hurt you. God's instructions are clear: He commands you to forgive. And the time to forgive is now because tomorrow may be too late . . . for you.

Forgiveness is actually the best revenge because it not only sets us free from the person we forgive, but it frees us to move into all that God has in store for us.

*Stormie Omartian*

## — A Prayer for Today —

Dear Lord, today I will choose to forgive those who have hurt me. I will empty my heart of bitterness, and I will obey Your Word by offering love and mercy to others, just as You have offered mercy and love to me. Amen

# The Seeds of Generosity

*Freely you have received, freely give.*

*Matthew 10:8 NKJV*

Paul reminds us that when we sow the seeds of generosity, we reap bountiful rewards in accordance with God's plan for our lives. Thus, we are instructed to give cheerfully and without reservation: "But this I say, He which soweth sparingly shall reap also sparingly; and he which soweth bountifully shall reap also bountifully. Every man according as he purposeth in his heart, so let him give; not grudgingly, or of necessity: for God loveth a cheerful giver" (2 Corinthians 9:6-7 KJV).

Today, make this pledge and keep it: Be a cheerful, generous, courageous giver. The world needs your help, and you need the spiritual rewards that will be yours when you give it.

As faithful stewards of what we have, ought we not to give earnest thought to our staggering surplus?

*Elisabeth Elliot*

## — A Prayer for Today —

Lord, You have given me so much. Let me share my blessings with those in need. Make me a generous, humble Christian, Lord, and let the glory be Yours and Yours alone. Amen

# Transcendent Love

*Who can separate us from the love of Christ? Can affliction or anguish or persecution or famine or nakedness or danger or sword? . . . No, in all these things we are more than victorious through Him who loved us.*

Romans 8:35,37 HCSB

Where can we find God's love? Everywhere. God's love transcends space and time. It reaches beyond the heavens, and it touches the darkest, smallest corner of every human heart. When we become passionate in our devotion to the Father, when we sincerely open our minds and hearts to Him, His love does not arrive "some day"—it arrives immediately.

Today, take God at His word and welcome His Son into your heart. When you do, God's transcendent love will surround you and transform you, now and forever.

There is no pit so deep that God's love is not deeper still.

Corrie ten Boom

## — A Prayer for Today —

Thank You, Lord, for Your love. Your love is boundless, infinite, and eternal. Today, let me pause and reflect upon Your love for me, and let me share that love with all those who cross my path. Amen

# A Prescription for Panic

*Anxiety in the heart of man causes depression, but a good word makes it glad.*

*Proverbs 12:25 NKJV*

We are members of an anxious society, a society in which the changes we face threaten to outpace our abilities to make adjustments. No wonder we sometimes find ourselves beset by feelings of anxiety and panic.

At times, our anxieties may stem from physical causes—chemical imbalances in the brain that result in severe emotional distress or relentless panic attacks. In such cases, modern medicine offers hope to those who suffer. But oftentimes, our anxieties result from spiritual deficits, not physical ones. And when we're spiritually depleted, the best prescription is found not in the medicine cabinet but deep inside the human heart. What we need is a higher daily dose of God's love, God's peace, God's assurance, and God's presence. And how do we acquire these blessings from our Creator? Through prayer, through meditation, through worship, and through trust.

## — A Prayer for Today —

Lord, when I am tempted to lose faith in the future, touch my heart with Your enduring love. And, keep me mindful, Lord, that nothing, absolutely nothing, will happen this day that You and I cannot handle together. Amen

# Facing Up to Trouble

*I will be with you when you pass through the waters . . . when you walk through the fire . . . the flame will not burn you. For I the Lord your God, the Holy One of Israel, and your Savior.*

*Isaiah 43:2-3 HCSB*

As life-here-on-earth unfolds, all of us encounter occasional setbacks: Those occasional visits from Old Man Trouble are simply a fact of life, and none of us are exempt. When tough times arrive, we may be forced to rearrange our plans and our priorities. But even on our darkest days, we must remember that God's love remains constant.

The fact that we encounter adversity is not nearly so important as the way we choose to deal with it. When tough times arrive, we have a clear choice: we can begin the difficult work of tackling our troubles . . . or not. When we summon the courage to look Old Man Trouble squarely in the eye, an amazing thing usually happens: he blinks.

## — A Prayer for Today —

Heavenly Father, You are my refuge. As I journey through this day, I know that I may encounter disappointments and losses. When I am troubled, let me turn to You. Keep me steady, Lord, and renew a right spirit inside of me this day and forever. Amen

# Taking Time to Ask

*He granted their request because they trusted in Him.*
1 Chronicles 5:20 HCSB

Sometimes, amid the demands and the frustrations of everyday life, we forget to slow ourselves down long enough to talk with God. Instead of turning our thoughts and prayers to Him, we rely upon our own resources. Instead of praying for strength and courage, we seek to manufacture it within ourselves. Instead of asking God for guidance, we depend only upon our own limited wisdom. The results of such behaviors are unfortunate and, on occasion, tragic.

Are you in need? Ask God to sustain you. Are you troubled? Take your worries to Him in prayer. Are you weary? Seek God's strength. In all things great and small, seek God's wisdom and His grace. He hears your prayers, and He will answer. All you must do is ask.

God will help us become the people we are meant to be, if only we will ask Him.

*Hannah Whitall Smith*

## — A Prayer for Today —

Lord, when I have questions or fears, let me turn to You. When I am weak, let me seek Your strength. When I am discouraged, Father, keep me mindful of Your love and Your grace. In all things, let me seek Your will and Your way, Dear Lord, today and forever. Amen

# Beyond Our Regrets

*All bitterness, anger and wrath, insult and slander must be removed from you, along with all wickedness. And be kind and compassionate to one another, forgiving one another, just as God also forgave you in Christ.*

*Ephesians 4:31-32 HCSB*

Are you mired in the quicksand of bitterness or regret? If so, you are not only disobeying God's Word; you are also wasting your time. The world holds few if any rewards for those who remain angrily focused upon the past. Still, the act of forgiveness is difficult for all but the most saintly men and women.

Being frail, fallible, imperfect human beings, most of us are quick to anger, quick to blame, slow to forgive, and even slower to forget. Yet as Christians, we are commanded to forgive others, just as we, too, have been forgiven.

If there exists even one person—alive or dead—against whom you hold bitter feelings, it's time to forgive. Or, if you are embittered against yourself for some past mistake or shortcoming, it's finally time to forgive yourself and move on. Hatred, bitterness, and regret are not part of God's plan for your life. Forgiveness, however, is.

## — A Prayer for Today —

Heavenly Father, You are my refuge. As I journey through this day, I know that I may encounter disappointments and losses. Keep me steady, Lord, and renew a right spirit inside of me this day and forever. Amen

# Blessings from Above

*I said to myself, "Relax and rest. God has showered you with blessings."*

Psalm 116:7 MSG

Psalm 145 makes this promise: "The LORD is gracious and compassionate, slow to anger and rich in love. The LORD is good to all; he has compassion on all he has made" (vv. 8-9 NIV). As God's children, we are blessed beyond measure, but sometimes, as busy women in a demanding world, we are slow to count our gifts and even slower to give thanks to the Giver. Our blessings include life and health, family and friends, freedom and possessions—for starters. And, the gifts we receive from God are multiplied when we share them with others. May we always give thanks to God for our blessings, and may we always demonstrate our gratitude by sharing them.

Jesus intended for us to be overwhelmed by the blessings of regular days. He said it was the reason He had come: "I am come that they might have life, and that they might have it more abundantly."

*Gloria Gaither*

## — A Prayer for Today —

Lord, let me be a woman who counts her blessings, and let me be Your faithful servant as I give praise to the Giver of all things good. You have richly blessed my life, Lord. Let me, in turn, be a blessing to all those who cross my path, and may the glory be Yours forever. Amen

# Our Priceless Treasures

*For the promise is for you and for your children.*
Acts 2:39 HCSB

We are aware that God has entrusted us with price-less treasures from above—our children. Every child is a glorious gift from the Father. And, with the Father's gift comes profound responsibilities. Thoughtful parents understand the critical importance of raising their children with love, with family, with discipline, and with God.

If you're lucky enough to be a mother, give thanks to God for the gift of your child. Whether you're the mother of a newborn or a seasoned grandmother, remember this: your child—like every child—is a child of God. May you, as a responsible parent, behave accordingly.

Children are not so different from kites. Children were created to fly. But, they need wind, the undergirding, and strength that comes from unconditional love, encouragement, and prayer.

*Gigi Graham Tchividjian*

## — A Prayer for Today —

Lord, the children of the world are Your children. Let me love them, care for them, nurture them, teach them, and lead them to You. Let my words and deeds demonstrate the love that I feel for children . . . and for You. Amen

# Measuring Your Words

*A wise heart instructs its mouth and increases learning with its speech.*

*Proverbs 16:23 HCSB*

God's Word reminds us that "Reckless words pierce like a sword, but the tongue of the wise brings healing" (Proverbs 12:18 NIV). If you seek to be a source of encouragement to friends, to family members, and to coworkers, then you must measure your words carefully. And that's exactly what God wants you to do.

Today, make this promise to yourself: vow to be an honest, effective, encouraging communicator at work, at home, and everyplace in between. Speak wisely, not impulsively. Use words of kindness and praise, not words of anger or derision. Learn how to be truthful without being cruel. Remember that you have the power to heal others or to injure them, to lift others up or to hold them back. And when you learn how to lift them up, you'll soon discover that you've lifted yourself up, too.

We should ask ourselves three things before we speak: Is it true? Is it kind? Does it glorify God?

*Billy Graham*

## — A Prayer for Today —

Lord, You have warned me that I will be judged by the words I speak. Keep me mindful, Lord, that I have influence on many people; make me an influence for good. And, may the words that I speak today be worthy of the One who has saved me forever. Amen

# God's Assurance

*I have told you these things so that in Me you may have peace. In the world you have suffering. But take courage! I have conquered the world.*

John 16:33 HCSB

Are you a confident believer, or do you live under a cloud of uncertainty and doubt? As a Christian, you have many reasons to be confident. After all, God is in His heaven; Christ has risen; and you are the recipient of God's grace. Despite these blessings, you may, from time to time, find yourself being tormented by negative emotions—and you are certainly not alone.

Even the most faithful Christians are overcome by occasional bouts of fear and doubt. You are no different.

But even when you feel very distant from God, remember that God is never distant from you. When you sincerely seek His presence, He will touch your heart, calm your fears, and restore your confidence.

Believe and do what God says. The life-changing consequences will be limitless, and the results will be confidence and peace of mind.

*Franklin Graham*

## — A Prayer for Today —

Lord, You are my Savior and my Sustainer. I will be safe with You in heaven, and I am safe with You here on earth. Today, I will trust in Your promises, and I will be a confident, obedient, purposeful servant to Your Son. Amen

# Letting God Decide

*We can make our plans, but the LORD determines our steps.*

*Proverbs 16:9 NLT*

Are you facing a difficult decision, a troubling circumstance, or a powerful temptation? If so, it's time to step back, to stop focusing on the world, and to focus, instead, on the will of your Father in heaven. The world will often lead you astray, but God will not. His counsel leads you to Himself, which, of course, is the path He has always intended for you to take.

Everyday living is an exercise in decision-making. Today and every day you must make choices: choices about what you will do, what you will worship, and how you will think. When in doubt, make choices that you sincerely believe will bring you to a closer relationship with God. And if you're uncertain of your next step, pray about it. When you do, answers will come—the right answers for you.

God always gives His best to those who leave the choice with Him.

*Jim Elliot*

— A Prayer for Today —

Lord, help me to make decisions that are pleasing to You. Help me to be honest, patient, thoughtful, and obedient. And above all, help me to follow the teachings of Jesus, not just today, but every day. Amen

# Our Faith, His Promises

*Let us hold on to the confession of our hope without wavering, for He who promised is faithful.*

Hebrews 10:23 HCSB

The Christian faith is founded upon promises that are contained in a unique book. That book is the Holy Bible. The Bible is a roadmap for life here on earth and for life eternal. As Christians, we are called upon to study its meaning, to trust its promises, to follow its commandments, and to share its Good News. God's Holy Word is, indeed, a transforming, one-of-a-kind treasure, and must be treated that way.

God has made promises to you, and He intends to keep them. So take God at His word: trust His promises and share them with your family, with your friends, and with the world.

Shake the dust from your past, and move forward in His promises.

*Kay Arthur*

## — A Prayer for Today —

Lord, Your Holy Word contains promises, and I will trust them. I will use the Bible as my guide, and I will trust You, Lord, to speak to me through Your Holy Spirit and through Your Holy Word, this day and forever. Amen

# Trusting His Timing

*He told them, "You don't get to know the time. Timing is the Father's business."*

Acts 1:7 MSG

If you sincerely seek to be a woman of faith, then you must learn to trust God's timing. You will be sorely tempted, however, to do otherwise. Because you are a fallible human being, you are impatient for things to happen. But, God knows better.

God has created a world that unfolds according to His own timetable, not ours . . . thank goodness! We mortals might make a terrible mess of things. God does not.

God's plan does not always happen in the way that we would like or at the time of our own choosing. Our task—as believing Christians who trust in a benevolent, all-knowing Father—is to wait patiently for God to reveal Himself. And reveal Himself He will. Always. But until God's perfect plan is made known, we must walk in faith and never lose hope. And we must continue to trust Him. Always.

— A Prayer for Today —

Lord, my sense of timing is fallible and imperfect; Yours is not. Let me trust in Your timetable for my life, and give me the patience and the wisdom to trust Your plans, not my own. Amen

# How to Treat Others

*Therefore, whatever you want others to do for you, do also the same for them—this is the Law and the Prophets.*

Matthew 7:12 HCSB

Would you like to make the world a better place? If so, you can start by practicing the Golden Rule.

Is the Golden Rule your rule, or is it just another Bible verse that goes in one ear and out the other? Jesus made Himself perfectly clear: He instructed you to treat other people in the same way that you want to be treated. But sometimes, especially when you're feeling the pressures of everyday living, obeying the Golden Rule can seem like an impossible task—but it's not. So if you want to know how to treat other people, ask the person you see every time you look into the mirror. The answer you receive will tell you exactly what to do.

It is one of the most beautiful compensations of life that no one can sincerely try to help another without helping herself.

*Barbara Johnson*

## — A Prayer for Today —

Lord, I thank You for friends and family members who practice the Golden Rule. Because I expect to be treated with kindness, let me be kind. Because I wish to be loved, let me be loving. In all things, Lord, let me live by the Golden Rule, and let me express my gratitude to those who offer kindness to me. Amen

# His Joy . . . and Ours

*Rejoice in the Lord always. I will say it again: Rejoice!*
*Philippians 4:4 HCSB*

Christ made it clear: He intends that His joy should become our joy. Yet sometimes, amid the inevitable hustle and bustle of life-here-on-earth, we can forfeit—albeit temporarily—the joy of Christ as we wrestle with the challenges of daily living.

Corrie ten Boom correctly observed, "Jesus did not promise to change the circumstances around us. He promised great peace and pure joy to those who would learn to believe that God actually controls all things." So here's a prescription for better spiritual health: Learn to trust God, and open the door of your soul to Christ. When you do, He will most certainly give you the peace and pure joy He has promised.

If you're a thinking Christian, you will be a joyful Christian.

*Marie T. Freeman*

## — A Prayer for Today —

Dear Lord, You have created a glorious universe that is far beyond my understanding. You have given me the gift of Your Son and the gift of salvation. Let me be a joyful Christian, Lord, this day and every day. Today is Your gift to me. Let me use it to Your glory as I give all the praise to You. Amen

# Choosing Kindness

*Talk and act like a person expecting to be judged by the Rule that sets us free. For if you refuse to act kindly, you can hardly expect to be treated kindly. Kind mercy wins over harsh judgment every time.*

James 2:12-13 MSG

If we believe the words of Proverbs 11:17—and we should—then we understand that kindness is its own reward. And, if we obey the commandments of our Savior—and we should—we must sow seeds of kindness wherever we go.

Kindness is a choice. Sometimes, when we feel happy or generous, we find it easy to be kind. Other times, when we are discouraged or tired, we can scarcely summon the energy to utter a single kind word. But, God's commandment is clear: He intends that we make the conscious choice to treat others with kindness and respect, no matter our circumstances, no matter our emotions. Kindness, therefore, is a choice that we, as Christians, must make many times each day.

## — A Prayer for Today —

Help me, Lord, to see the needs of those around me. Today, let me spread kind words in honor of Your Son. Today, let forgiveness rule my heart. And every day, Lord, let my love for Christ be demonstrated through deeds of kindness for those who need the healing touch of the Master's hand. Amen

# God's Ally

*Be sober! Be on the alert! Your adversary the Devil is prowling around like a roaring lion, looking for anyone he can devour.*

1 Peter 5:8 HCSB

Nineteenth-century clergyman Edwin Hubbel Chapin warned, "Neutral people are the devil's allies." His words were true then, and they're true now. Neutrality in the face of evil is a sin. Yet all too often, we fail to fight evil, not because we are neutral, but because we are shortsighted: we don't fight the devil because we don't recognize his handiwork.

If we are to recognize evil and fight it, we must pay careful attention. We must pay attention to God's Word, and we must pay attention to the realities of everyday life. When we observe life objectively, and when we do so with eyes and hearts that are attuned to God's Holy Word, we can no longer be neutral believers.

We are in a continual battle with the spiritual forces of evil, but we will triumph when we yield to God's leading and call on His powerful presence in prayer.

*Shirley Dobson*

## — A Prayer for Today —

Protect us, Lord, from the evils and temptations of this difficult age. Help us to trust You, Father, and to obey Your Word, knowing that Your ultimate victory over evil is both inevitable and complete. Amen

# New Beginnings

*I will give you a new heart and put a new spirit within you.*
Ezekiel 36:26 HCSB

If we sincerely want to change ourselves for the better, we must start on the inside and work our way out from there. Lasting change doesn't occur "out there"; it occurs "in here." It occurs not in the shifting sands of our own particular circumstances, but in quiet depths of our own hearts.

Are you in search of a new beginning or, for that matter, a new you? If so, don't expect changing circumstances to miraculously transform you into the person you want to become. Transformation starts with God, and it starts in the silent center of a humble human heart—like yours.

In those desperate times when we feel like we don't have an ounce of strength, He will gently pick up our heads so that our eyes can behold something—something that will keep His hope alive in us.

*Kathy Troccoli*

## — A Prayer for Today —

O Lord, my Creator, conform me to Your image. Create in me a clean heart, a new heart, that reflects the love You lavish upon me. When I need to change, Father, change me, and make me new again. Amen

# Saying Yes to God

*Fear thou not; for I am with thee.*

*Isaiah 41:10 KJV*

Your decision to seek a deeper relationship with God will not remove all problems from your life; to the contrary, it will bring about a series of personal crises as you constantly seek to say "yes" to God although the world encourages you to do otherwise. Each time you are tempted to distance yourself from the Creator, you will face a spiritual crisis. A few of these crises may be monumental in scope, but most will be the small, everyday decisions of life. In fact, life here on earth can be seen as one test after another—and with each crisis comes yet another opportunity to grow closer to God . . . or to distance yourself from His plan for your life.

Today, you will face many opportunities to say "yes" to your Creator—and you will also encounter many opportunities to say "no" to Him. Your answers will determine the quality of your day and the direction of your life, so answer carefully . . . very carefully.

The Christian lifestyle is not one of legalistic do's and don'ts, but one that is positive, attractive, and joyful.

*Vonette Bright*

## — A Prayer for Today —

Dear Lord, when life seems chaotic, remind me of Your love and protection. Difficult times provide opportunities for me to grow closer to You. Thank You for all that this day has to offer. Amen

# Praise Him

*Give thanks to the Lord, for He is good; His faithful love endures forever.*

Psalm 106:1 HCSB

Sometimes, in our rush "to get things done," we simply don't stop long enough to pause and thank our Creator for the countless blessings He has bestowed upon us. But when we slow down and express our gratitude to the One who made us, we enrich our own lives and the lives of those around us.

Thanksgiving should become a habit, a regular part of our daily routines. God has blessed us beyond measure, and we owe Him everything, including our eternal praise. Let us praise Him today, tomorrow, and throughout eternity.

Praise Him! Praise Him! / Tell of His excellent greatness. / Praise Him! Praise Him! / Ever in joyful song!

*Fanny Crosby*

## — A Prayer for Today —

Heavenly Father, today and every day I will praise You. I will praise You with my thoughts, my prayers, my words, and my deeds . . . now and forever. Amen

# Taking Risks

*Is anything too hard for the Lord?*

*Genesis 18:14 NKJV*

As we consider the uncertainties of the future, we are confronted with a powerful temptation: the temptation to "play it safe." Unwilling to move mountains, we fret over molehills. Unwilling to entertain great hopes for the tomorrow, we focus on the unfairness of the today. Unwilling to trust God completely, we take timid half-steps when God intends that we make giant leaps.

Today, ask God for the courage to step beyond the boundaries of your doubts. Ask Him to guide you to a place where you can realize your full potential—a place where you are freed from the fear of failure. Ask Him to do His part, and promise Him that you will do your part. Don't ask Him to lead you to a "safe" place; ask Him to lead you to the "right" place . . . and remember: those two places are seldom the same.

With each new experience of letting God be in control, we gain courage and reinforcement for daring to do it again and again.

*Gloria Gaither*

## — A Prayer for Today —

Dear Lord, I don't want to be reckless, but I want to be totally committed to Your kingdom's work. Sometimes that will involve risk. Help me to know when I need to take sensible risks in service to my family and my service to You. Amen

# During Dark Days

*I have heard your prayer, I have seen your tears; surely I will heal you.*

*2 Kings 20:5 NKJV*

The sadness that accompanies any significant loss is an inevitable fact of life. In time, sadness runs its course and gradually abates. Depression, on the other hand, is a physical and emotional condition that is highly treatable.

If you find yourself feeling "blue," perhaps it's a logical reaction to the ups and downs of daily life. But if you or someone close to you have become dangerously depressed, it's time to seek professional help.

Some days are light and happy, and some days are not. When we face the inevitable dark days of life, we must choose how we will respond. Will we allow ourselves to sink even more deeply into our own sadness, or will we do the difficult work of pulling ourselves out? We bring light to the dark days of life by turning first to God, and then to trusted family members, friends, and medical professionals. When we do, the clouds will eventually part, and the sun will shine once more upon our souls.

## — A Prayer for Today —

Heavenly Father, Your Word promises that You will not give us more than we can bear; You have promised to lift us out of our grief and despair. Today, Lord, I pray for those who mourn, and I thank You for sustaining all of us in our dark days. Amen

# Our Ultimate Savior

*And we have seen and testify that the Father has sent the Son as Savior of the world.*

*1 John 4:14 NKJV*

Hannah Whitall Smith spoke to believers of every generation when she advised, "Keep your face upturned to Christ as the flowers do to the sun. Look, and your soul shall live and grow." How true. When we turn our hearts to Jesus, we receive His blessings, His peace, and His grace.

Christ is the ultimate Savior of mankind and the personal Savior of those who believe in Him. As His servants, we should place Him at the very center of our lives. And, every day that God gives us breath, we should share Christ's love and His message with a world that needs both.

I now know the power of the risen Lord! He lives! The dawn of Easter has broken in my own soul! My night is gone!

*Mrs. Charles E. Cowman*

## — A Prayer for Today —

Dear Lord, keep me mindful of Your priceless gift: my personal Savior, Christ Jesus. I will praise You always, Lord, as I give thanks for Your Son Jesus and for Your everlasting love. Amen

# Contagious Faith

*Whatever you do, do it enthusiastically, as something done for the Lord and not for men.*

*Colossians 3:23 HCSB*

Genuine, heartfelt Christianity is contagious. If you enjoy a life-altering relationship with God, that relationship will have an impact on others—perhaps a profound impact.

Are you genuinely excited about your faith? And do you make your enthusiasm known to those around you? Or are you a "silent ambassador" for Christ? God's preference is clear: He intends that you stand before others and proclaim your faith.

Does Christ reign over your life? Then share your testimony and your excitement. The world needs both.

Enthusiasm, like the flu, is contagious—we get it from one another.

*Barbara Johnson*

## — A Prayer for Today —

Dear Lord, I know that others are watching the way that I live my life. Help me to be an enthusiastic Christian with a faith that is contagious. Amen.

# God's Voice

*For this is commendable, if because of conscience toward God one endures grief, suffering wrongfully.*

*1 Peter 2:19 NKJV*

Billy Graham correctly observed, "Most of us follow our conscience as we follow a wheelbarrow. We push it in front of us in the direction we want to go." To do so, of course, is a profound mistake. Yet all of us, on occasion, have failed to listen to the voice that God planted in our hearts, and all of us have suffered the consequences.

God gave you a conscience for a very good reason: to make your path conform to His will. Wise believers make it a practice to listen carefully to that quiet internal voice. Count yourself among that number. When your conscience speaks, listen and learn. In all likelihood, God is trying to get His message through. And in all likelihood, it is a message that you desperately need to hear.

## — A Prayer for Today —

Dear Lord, You speak to me through the gift of Your Holy Word. And, Father, You speak to me through that still small voice that tells me right from wrong. Let me follow Your way, Lord, and, in these quiet moments, show me Your plan for this day, that I might serve You. Amen

# God Can Handle It

*Fear not, for I have redeemed you; I have called you by your name; You are Mine.*

*Isaiah 43:1 NKJV*

Life-here-on-earth can be difficult and discouraging at times. During our darkest moments, God offers us strength and courage if we turn our hearts and our prayers to Him.

As believing Christians, we have every reason to live courageously. After all, the ultimate battle has already been fought and won on the cross at Calvary. But sometimes, because we are imperfect human beings who possess imperfect faith, we fall prey to fear and doubt. The answer to our fears, of course, is God.

The next time you find your courage tested to the limit, remember that God is as near as your next breath. He is your shield and your strength; He is your protector and your deliverer. Call upon Him in your hour of need and then be comforted. Whatever your challenge, whatever your trouble, God can handle it.

When once we are assured that God is good, then there can be nothing left to fear.

*Hannah Whitall Smith*

## — A Prayer for Today —

Lord, let me turn to You for courage and for strength. You are with me always, Father, and I will face the challenges of this day with trust and assurance in You. Amen

# Limitless Power, Limitless Love

*I pray that the eyes of your heart may be enlightened so you may know what is the hope of His calling, what are the glorious riches of His inheritance among the saints, and what is the immeasurable greatness of His power to us who believe, according to the working of His vast strength.*

Ephesians 1:18-19 HCSB

Because God's power is limitless, it is far beyond the comprehension of mortal minds. Yet even though we cannot fully understand the awesome power of God, we can praise it. When we worship God with faith and assurance, when we place Him at the absolute center of our lives, we invite His love into our hearts. In turn, we grow to love Him more deeply as we sense His love for us. St. Augustine wrote, "I love you, Lord, not doubtingly, but with absolute certainty. Your Word beat upon my heart until I fell in love with you, and now the universe and everything in it tells me to love you."

Let us pray that we, too, will turn our hearts to the Creator, knowing with certainty that His heart has ample room for each of us, and that we, in turn, must make room in our hearts for Him.

## — A Prayer for Today —

Heavenly Father, You are all-knowing and all-powerful. Today, I praise You for Your love, and I marvel at the glory of Your Creation. With You as my protector, Lord, I am secure, today and forever. Amen

# Thy Will Be Done

*"Father, if it is Your will, take this cup away from Me; nevertheless not My will, but Yours, be done."*

Luke 22:42 NKJV

As human beings with limited understanding, we can never fully comprehend the will of God. But as believers in a benevolent God, we must always trust the will of our Heavenly Father.

Before His crucifixion, Jesus went to the Mount of Olives and poured out His heart to God. Jesus knew of the agony that He was destined to endure, but He also knew that God's will must be done. We, like our Savior, face trials that bring fear and trembling to the very depths of our souls, but like Christ, we, too, must ultimately seek God's will, not our own. When we entrust our lives to Him completely and without reservation, He gives us the strength to meet any challenge, the courage to face any trial, and the wisdom to live in His righteousness.

The will of God is the most delicious and delightful thing in the universe.

*Hannah Whitall Smith*

## — A Prayer for Today —

Dear Lord, You are the Creator of the universe, and I know that Your plan for my life is grander than I can imagine. Let Your purposes be my purposes, and let me trust in the assurance of Your promises. Amen

# Happiness and Holiness

*Happy are the people who live at your Temple . . . . Happy are those whose strength comes from you.*

*Psalm 84:4-5 NKJV*

Do you seek happiness, abundance, and contentment? If so, here are some things you should do: Love God and His Son; depend upon God for strength; try, to the best of your abilities, to follow God's will; and strive to obey His Holy Word. When you do these things, you'll discover that happiness goes hand-in-hand with righteousness. The happiest people are not those who rebel against God; the happiest people are those who love God and obey His commandments.

What does life have in store for you? A world full of possibilities (of course it's up to you to seize them), and God's promise of abundance (of course it's up to you to accept it). Your Creator has blessed you beyond measure. Honor Him with your prayers, your words, your deeds, and your joy.

## — A Prayer for Today —

Dear Lord, You are my strength and my joy. I will rejoice in the day that You have made, and I will give thanks for the countless blessings that You have given me. Let me be a joyful Christian, Father, as I share the Good News of Your Son. Amen

# Hope for Today,
# Hope for Tomorrow

*We have this hope—like a sure and firm anchor of the soul—that enters the inner sanctuary behind the curtain.*
*Hebrews 6:19 HCSB*

As every woman knows, hope is a perishable commodity. Despite God's promises, despite Christ's love, and despite our countless blessings, we frail human beings can still lose hope from time to time. When we do, we need the encouragement of Christian friends, the life-changing power of prayer, and the healing truth of God's Holy Word.

If we find ourselves falling into the spiritual traps of worry and discouragement, we should seek the healing touch of Jesus and the encouraging words of fellow Christians. Even though this world can be a place of trials and struggles, God has promised us peace, joy, and eternal life if we give ourselves to Him.

## — A Prayer for Today —

Dear Lord, make me a woman of hope. If I become discouraged, let me turn to You. If I grow weary, let me seek strength in You. When I face disappointments, let me seek Your will and trust Your Word. In every aspect of my life, I will trust You, Father, so that my heart will be filled with faith and hope, this day and forever. Amen

# Knowledge and Wisdom

*A house is built by wisdom, and it is established by understanding; by knowledge the rooms are filled with every precious and beautiful treasure.*

*Proverbs 24:3-4 HCSB*

If we are to grow as Christians and as women, we need both knowledge and wisdom. Knowledge is found in textbooks. Wisdom, on the other hand, is found in God's Holy Word and in the carefully-chosen words of loving parents, family members, and friends. Knowledge is an important building block in a well-lived life, and it pays rich dividends both personally and professionally. But, wisdom is even more important because it refashions not only the mind, but also the heart.

A big difference exists between a head full of knowledge and the words of God literally abiding in us.

*Beth Moore*

## — A Prayer for Today —

Lord, You are my Teacher. Help me to be a student of Your Word and a servant of Your will. Let me live by the truth You reveal, let me trust in the wisdom of Your commandments, and let me teach others the glory of Your ways. Amen

# No Complaints

*Do everything without grumbling and arguing, so that you may be blameless and pure.*

*Philippians 2:14-15 HCSB*

Because we are imperfect human beings, we often lose sight of our blessings. Ironically, most of us have more blessings than we can count, but we may still find reasons to complain about the minor frustrations of everyday life. To do so, of course, is not only wrong; it is also the pinnacle of shortsightedness and a serious roadblock on the path to spiritual abundance.

Are you tempted to complain about the inevitable minor frustrations of everyday living? Don't do it! Today and every day, make it a practice to count your blessings, not your hardships. It's the truly decent way to live.

Thanksgiving or complaining—these words express two contrastive attitudes of the souls of God's children in regard to His dealings with them. The soul that gives thanks can find comfort in everything; the soul that complains can find comfort in nothing.

*Hannah Whitall Smith*

## — A Prayer for Today —

Lord, I know that the choice is mine—I can either count my blessings or recount my disappointments. Today, help me to focus my thoughts upon my blessings, my gifts, and my opportunities. Amen

# The Wisdom to Obey

*And the world with its lust is passing away, but the one who does God's will remains forever.*

*1 John 2:17 HCSB*

Since God created Adam and Eve, we human beings have been rebelling against our Creator. Why? Because we are unwilling to trust God's Word, and we are unwilling to follow His commandments. God has given us a guidebook for righteous living called the Holy Bible. It contains thorough instructions which, if followed, lead to fulfillment, righteousness and salvation. But, if we choose to ignore God's commandments, the results are as predictable as they are tragic.

Talking about God is easy; living by His commandments is considerably harder. But, unless we are willing to abide by God's laws, all of our righteous proclamations ring hollow. How can we best proclaim our love for the Lord? By obeying Him. And, for further instructions, read the manual.

God does not want the forced obedience of slaves. Instead, He covets the voluntary love and obedience of children who love Him for Himself.

*Catherine Marshall*

## — A Prayer for Today —

Dear Heavenly Father, You have blessed me with a love that is infinite and eternal. I will demonstrate my love for You by obeying Your commandments. Amen

# Good Pressures,
# Bad Pressures

*For am I now trying to win the favor of people, or God? Or am I striving to please people? If I were still trying to please people, I would not be a slave of Christ.*

*Galatians 1:10 HCSB*

Our world is filled with pressures: some good, some bad. The pressures that we feel to follow God's will and obey His commandments are positive pressures. God places them on our hearts, and He intends that we act in accordance with His leadings. But we also face different pressures, ones that are definitely not from God. When we feel pressured to do things—or even to think thoughts—that lead us away from God, we must beware.

Society seeks to mold us into more worldly beings; God seeks to mold us into new beings that are most certainly not conformed to this world. If we are to please God, we must resist the pressures that society seeks to impose upon us, and we must conform ourselves, instead, to God's will, to His path, and to His Son.

It wasn't the apple, it was the pair.

*Anonymous*

## — A Prayer for Today —

Thank You Lord, for the people who enrich my life. I pray for them today, and ask Your blessings upon them . . . and upon me. Amen

# When the Answer Is "No"

*For now we see indistinctly, as in a mirror, but then face to face. Now I know in part, but then I will know fully, as I am fully known.*

1 Corinthians 13:12 HCSB

God answers our prayers. What God does not do is this: He does not always answer our prayers as soon as we might like, and He does not always answer our prayers by saying "Yes." God isn't an order-taker, and He's not some sort of cosmic vending machine. Sometimes—even when we want something very badly—our loving Heavenly Father responds to our requests by saying "No," and we must accept His answer, even if we don't understand it.

God answers prayers not only according to our wishes but also according to His master plan. We cannot know that plan, but we can know the Planner . . . and we must trust His wisdom, His righteousness, and His love. Always.

## — A Prayer for Today —

Dear Lord, make me a woman of constant prayer. Your Holy Word commands me to pray without ceasing. In all things great and small, at all times, whether happy or sad, let me seek Your wisdom and Your strength . . . in prayer. Amen

# Seeking and Finding

*Keep asking, and it will be given to you. Keep searching, and you will find. Keep knocking, and the door will be opened to you. For everyone who asks receives, and the one who searches finds, and to the one who knocks, the door will be opened.*

*Matthew 7:7-8 HCSB*

Where is God? He is everywhere you have ever been and everywhere you will ever go. He is with you night and day; He knows your every thought; He hears your every heartbeat.

Sometimes, in the crush of your daily duties, God may seem far away. Or sometimes, when the disappointments and sorrows of life leave you brokenhearted, God may seem distant, but He is not. When you earnestly seek God, you will find Him because He is here, waiting patiently for you to reach out to Him.

Our souls were made to live in an upper atmosphere, and we stifle and choke if we live on any lower level. Our eyes were made to look off from these heavenly heights, and our vision is distorted by any lower gazing.

*Hannah Whitall Smith*

## — A Prayer for Today —

How comforting it is, Dear Lord, to know that if I seek You, I will find You. You are with me, Father, every step that I take. Let me reach out to You, and let me praise You for revealing Your Word, Your way, and Your love. Amen

# Trust the Shepherd

*The Lord is my shepherd; I shall not want. He makes me to lie down in green pastures; He leads me beside the still waters. He restores my soul.*

*Psalm 23:1-3 NKJV*

In the 23rd Psalm, David teaches us that God is like a watchful shepherd caring for His flock. No wonder these verses have provided comfort and hope for generations of believers.

As a busy woman, you know from firsthand experience that life is not always easy. But as a recipient of God's grace, you also know that you are protected by a loving Heavenly Father. On occasion, you will confront circumstances that trouble you to the very core of your soul. When you are afraid, trust in God. When you are worried, turn your concerns over to Him. When you are anxious, be still and listen for the quiet assurance of God's promises. And then, place your life in His hands. He is your Shepherd today and throughout eternity. Trust the Shepherd.

## — A Prayer for Today —

Lord, You are my Shepherd. You care for me; You comfort me; You watch over me; and You have saved me. I will praise you, Father, for Your glorious works, for Your protection, for Your love, and for Your Son. Amen

# Our Rock

*And he said: "The Lord is my rock and my fortress and my deliverer; the God of my strength, in whom I will trust."*
*2 Samuel 22:2-3 NKJV*

Psalm 145 promises, "The Lord is near to all who call on him, to all who call on him in truth. He fulfills the desires of those who fear him; he hears their cry and saves them" (vv. 18-20 NIV). And the words of Jesus offer us comfort: "These things I have spoken to you, that in Me you may have peace. In the world you will have tribulation; but be of good cheer, I have overcome the world" (John 16:33 NKJV).

As believers, we know that God loves us and that He will protect us. In times of hardship, He will comfort us; in times of sorrow, He will dry our tears. When we are troubled or weak or sorrowful, God is always with us. We must build our lives on the rock that cannot be shaken: we must trust in God. And then, we must get on with the hard work of tackling our problems . . . because if we don't, who will? Or should?

## — A Prayer for Today —

Heavenly Father, You are my strength. I can face the difficulties of this day because You are my Rock. As I stand with You, Father, I can overcome adversity just as Jesus overcame this world. Amen

# When Mountains Move

*You do not have because you do not ask.*

*James 4:2 HCSB*

God gives the gifts; we, as believers, should accept them—but oftentimes, we don't. Why? Because we fail to trust our Heavenly Father completely, and because we are, at times, surprisingly stubborn. Luke 11 teaches us that God does not withhold spiritual gifts from those who ask. Our obligation, quite simply, is to ask for them.

Are you a woman who asks God to move mountains in your life, or are you expecting Him to stumble over molehills? Whatever the size of your challenges, God is big enough to handle them. Ask for His help today, with faith and with fervor, and then watch in amazement as your mountains begin to move.

God uses our most stumbling, faltering faith-steps as the open door to His doing for us "more than we ask or think."

*Catherine Marshall*

## — A Prayer for Today —

Dear Lord, the Bible tells me that when I ask for Your help, You will give it. I thank You, Lord, for Your help, for Your love, and for Your Son. Amen

# Believing Makes a Difference

*You love Him, though you have not seen Him. And though not seeing Him now, you believe in Him and rejoice with inexpressible and glorious joy, because you are receiving the goal of your faith, the salvation of your souls.*

*1 Peter 1:8-9 HCSB*

If you'd like to partake in the peace that only God can give, make certain that your actions are guided by His Word. Pay careful attention to the conscience that God, in His infinite wisdom, has placed in your heart. Don't treat your faith as if it were separate from your everyday life. Weave your beliefs into the very fabric of your day. When you do, God will honor your good works, and your good works will honor God.

If you seek to be a responsible believer, you must realize that it is never enough to hear the instructions of God; you must also live by them. And it is never enough to wait idly by while others do God's work here on earth; you, too, must act. Doing God's work is a responsibility that every Christian (including you) should bear. And when you do, your loving Heavenly Father will reward your efforts with a bountiful harvest.

## — A Prayer for Today —

Lord, today I will worry less about pleasing other people and more about pleasing You. I will stand up for my beliefs, and I will honor You with my thoughts, my actions, and my prayers. And I will worship You, Father, with thanksgiving in my heart, this day and forever. Amen

# Blessed Beyond Measure

*The Lord bless you and keep you; The Lord make His face shine upon you, And be gracious to you.*

*Numbers 6:24-25 NKJV*

Have you counted your blessings lately? You should. Of course, God's gifts are too numerous to count, but as a grateful Christian, you should attempt to count them nonetheless. Your blessings include life, family, friends, talents, and possessions, for starters. And your greatest gift—a treasure that was paid for on the cross and is yours for the asking—is God's gift of salvation through Christ Jesus.

As believing Christians, we have all been blessed beyond measure. Thus, thanksgiving should become a habit, a regular part of our daily routines. Today, let us pause and thank our Creator for His blessings. And let us demonstrate our gratitude to the Giver of all things good by using His gifts for the glory of His kingdom.

God is always far more willing to give us good things than we are anxious to have them.

*Catherine Marshall*

## — A Prayer for Today —

Lord, You have given me so much, and I am thankful. I know that every good thing You give me is to be shared with others. I give thanks for Your gifts . . . and I will share them. Amen

# A Pattern of Good Works

*In all things showing yourself to be a pattern of good works;*
*in doctrine showing integrity, reverence, incorruptibility....*
Titus 2:7 NKJV

It has been said that character is what we are when nobody is watching. How true. When we do things that we know aren't right, we try to hide them from our families and friends. But even then, God is watching.

If you sincerely wish to walk with God, you must seek, to the best of your ability, to follow His commandments. When you do, your character will take care of itself . . . and you won't need to look over your shoulder to see who, besides God, is watching.

Often, our character is at greater risk in prosperity than in adversity.

*Beth Moore*

## — A Prayer for Today —

Lord, You are my Father in heaven. You search my heart and know me far better than I know myself. May I be Your worthy servant, and may I live according to Your commandments. Let me be a person of integrity, Lord, and let my words and deeds be a testimony to You, today and always. Amen

# A Relationship that Honors God

*I am always praising you; all day long I honor you.*

*Psalm 71:8 NCV*

As you think about the nature of your relationship with God, remember this: you will always have some type of relationship with Him—it is inevitable that your life must be lived in relationship to God. The question is not if you will have a relationship with Him; the burning question is whether or not that relationship will be one that seeks to honor Him.

Are you willing to place God first in your life? And, are you willing to welcome God's Son into your heart? Unless you can honestly answer these questions with a resounding yes, then your relationship with God isn't what it could be or should be. Thankfully, God is always available, He's always ready to forgive, and He's waiting to hear from you now. The rest, of course, is up to you.

The Holy Spirit testifies of Jesus. So when you are filled with the Holy Spirit, you speak about our Lord and really live to His honor.

*Corrie ten Boom*

## — A Prayer for Today —

Lord. I praise You from the depths of my heart, and I give thanks for Your goodness, for Your mercy, and for Your Son. Let me honor You every day of my life through my words and my deeds. Let me honor You, Father, with all that I have and all that I am. Amen

# A Place of Worship

*For where two or three are gathered together in My name, I am there among them.*

Matthew 18:20 HCSB

In the Book of Acts, Luke reminds us to "feed the church of God" (20:28). As Christians who have been saved by a loving, compassionate Creator, we are compelled not only to worship Him in our hearts but also to worship Him in the presence of fellow believers.

We live in a world that is teeming with temptations and distractions—a world where good and evil struggle in a constant battle to win our hearts and souls. Our challenge, of course, is to ensure that we cast our lot on the side of God. One way to ensure that we do so is by the practice of regular, purposeful worship with our families. When we worship God faithfully and fervently, we are blessed.

Going to church does not make you a Christian anymore than going to McDonalds makes you a hamburger.

*Anonymous*

## — A Prayer for Today —

Dear Lord, today I pray for Your church. Let me help to feed Your flock by helping to build Your church so that others, too, might experience Your enduring love and Your eternal grace. Amen

# The Inner Voice

*Let us draw near with a true heart in full assurance of faith, our hearts sprinkled clean from an evil conscience and our bodies washed in pure water.*

*Hebrews 10:22 HCSB*

American humorist Josh Billings observed, "Reason often makes mistakes, but conscience never does." How true. Even when we deceive our neighbors, and even when we attempt to deceive ourselves, God has given each of us a conscience, a small, quiet voice that tells us right from wrong.

We must listen to that inner voice . . . or else we must accept the consequences that inevitably befall those who choose to rebel against God.

When we learn to listen to Christ's voice for the details of our daily decisions, we begin to know Him personally.

*Catherine Marshall*

## — A Prayer for Today —

Dear Lord, today, I will honor the quiet voice that You have placed in my heart. I will strive to obey Your Word as I follow in the footsteps of Your Son today, tomorrow, and every day of my life. Amen

# Hope for the Journey

*Therefore, we may boldly say: The Lord is my helper; I will not be afraid. What can man do to me?*

*Hebrews 13:6 HCSB*

Because we are saved by a risen Christ, we can have hope for the future, no matter how desperate our circumstances may seem. After all, God has promised that we are His throughout eternity. And, He has told us that we must place our hopes in Him.

Today, summon the courage to follow God. Even if the path seems difficult, even if your heart is fearful, trust your Heavenly Father and follow Him. Trust Him with your day and your life. Do His work, care for His children, and share His Good News. Let Him guide your steps. He will not lead you astray.

With each new experience of letting God be in control, we gain courage and reinforcement for daring to do it again and again.

*Gloria Gaither*

## — A Prayer for Today —

Dear Lord, when I am fearful, I will lean upon You. Keep me ever mindful, Lord, that You are my God, my strength, and my shield. With You by my side, I have nothing to fear. And, with Your Son Jesus as my Savior, I have received the priceless gift of eternal life. Help me to be a grateful and courageous servant this day and every day. Amen

# Dealing with Disappointment

*For we do not want you to be ignorant, brethren, of our trouble which came to us in Asia: that we were burdened beyond measure, above strength, so that we despaired even of life. Yes, we had the sentence of death in ourselves, that we should not trust in ourselves but in God who raises the dead, who delivered us from so great a death, and does deliver us; in whom we trust that He will still deliver us.*

2 Corinthians 1:8-10 NKJV

From time to time, all of us face life-altering disappointments that leave us breathless. Oftentimes, these disappointments come unexpectedly, leaving us with more questions than answers. But even when we don't have all the answers—or, for that matter, even when we don't seem to have any of the answers—God does. Whatever our circumstances, whether we stand atop the highest mountain or wander through the darkest valley, God is ready to protect us, to comfort us, and to heal us. Our task is to let Him.

The difference between winning and losing is how we choose to react to disappointment.

*Barbara Johnson*

## — A Prayer for Today —

Dear Lord, when I face the inevitable disappointments of life, remind me that You are in control. You are the Giver of all good things, Father, and You will bless me today, tomorrow, and forever. Amen

# Beyond Negativity

*Do not be afraid or discouraged, for the LORD is the one who goes before you. He will be with you; he will neither fail you nor forsake you.*

*Deuteronomy 31:8 NLT*

We Christians have many reasons to celebrate. God is in His heaven; Christ has risen, and we are the sheep of His flock. Yet sometimes, even the most devout Christian women can become discouraged. After all, we live in a world where expectations can be high and demands can be even higher.

If you become discouraged with the direction of your day or your life, turn your thoughts and prayers to God. He is a God of possibility, not negativity. He will help you count your blessings instead of your hardships. And then, with a renewed spirit of optimism and hope, you can properly thank your Father in heaven for His blessings, for His love, and for His Son.

Just as courage is faith in good, so discouragement is faith in evil, and, while courage opens the door to good, discouragement opens it to evil.

*Hannah Whitall Smith*

## — A Prayer for Today —

Thank You, Lord, for Your infinite love. Make me an optimistic Christian, Father, as I place my hope and my trust in You. Amen

# Getting It All Done

*Everyone was trying to touch him—so much energy surging from him, so many people healed!*

*Luke 6:19 MSG*

All of us have moments when we feel drained. All of us suffer through difficult days, trying times, and perplexing periods of our lives. During times of hardship, we are tempted to burn the candle at both ends, but we should resist this temptation. Instead, we should strive to place first things first by saying no to the things that we simply don't have the time or the energy to do.

If you're a woman with too many demands and too few hours in which to meet them, don't fret. Instead, focus upon God and upon His love for you. Then, ask Him for the wisdom to prioritize your life and the strength to fulfill your responsibilities. God will give you the energy to do the most important things on today's to-do list . . . if you ask Him. So ask Him.

Worry does not empty tomorrow of its sorrow; it empties today of its strength.

*Corrie ten Boom*

## — A Prayer for Today —

Lord, when this world leaves me exhausted, let me turn to You for strength and for courage. When I follow Your will for my life, You will energize me. Let Your will be my will, Lord, and let me find my strength in You. Amen

# We Are All Role Models

*Therefore, we are ambassadors for Christ; certain that God is appealing through us, we plead on Christ's behalf, "Be reconciled to God."*

2 Corinthians 5:20 HCSB

Whether we like it or not, all of us are role models. Our friends and family members watch our actions and, as followers of Christ, we are obliged to act accordingly.

What kind of example are you? Are you the kind of woman whose life serves as a genuine example of righteousness? Are you a woman whose behavior serves as a positive role model for young people? Are you the kind of woman whose actions, day in and day out, are based upon kindness, faithfulness, and a love for the Lord? If so, you are not only blessed by God; you are also a powerful force for good in a world that desperately needs positive influences such as yours.

Corrie ten Boom advised, "Don't worry about what you do not understand. Worry about what you do understand in the Bible but do not live by." And that's sound advice because our families and friends are watching . . . and so, for that matter, is God.

## — A Prayer for Today —

Dear Lord, let my light shine brightly for You. Let me be a positive example for all to see, and let me share love and kindness with my family and friends, today and every day. Amen

# All in the Family

*Let the message about the Messiah dwell richly among you, teaching and admonishing one another in all wisdom, and singing psalms, hymns, and spiritual songs, with gratitude in your hearts to God.*

*Colossians 3:16 HCSB*

As every woman knows, family life is a mixture of conversations, mediations, irritations, deliberations, commiserations, frustrations, negotiations, and celebrations. In other words, the life of the typical woman is incredibly varied.

Certainly, in the life of every family, there are moments of frustration and disappointment. Lots of them. But, for those who are lucky enough to live in the presence of a close-knit, caring clan, the rewards far outweigh the frustrations. That's why we pray fervently for our family members, and that's why we love them despite their faults.

No family is perfect, and neither is yours. But, despite the inevitable challenges and occasional hurt feelings of family life, your clan is God's gift to you. That little band of men, women, kids, and babies is a priceless treasure on temporary loan from the Father above. Give thanks to the Giver for the gift of family . . . and act accordingly.

## — A Prayer for Today —

Dear Lord, you have given me a wonderful gift: a loving family. Today and every day, let me show my family that I love them by my words and by my deeds. Amen

# The Financial Guide

*The blessing of the Lord makes one rich . . . .*
*Proverbs 10:22 NKJV*

God's Word is not only a roadmap to eternal life; it is also an indispensable guidebook for life here on earth. As such, the Bible has much to say about your life and your finances.

God's Word can be a roadmap to a place of righteousness and abundance. Make it your roadmap. God's wisdom can be a light to guide your steps. Claim it as your light. God's Word can be an invaluable tool for crafting a better day and a better life. Make it your tool. And finally, God's Word can help you organize your financial life in such a way that you have less need to worry and more time to celebrate His glorious creation. If that sounds appealing, open your Bible, read its instructions, and follow them.

Here's a good recipe for managing your money: Never make a big financial decision without first talking it over with God.

*Marie T. Freeman*

## — A Prayer for Today —

Dear Lord, make me a faithful steward of my possessions, my talents, my time, and my testimony. In every aspect of my life, Father, let me be Your humble, obedient servant. And I will obey Your commandment that I give sacrificially to the needs of Your Church. Amen

# Love That Forgiveness

*And whenever you stand praying, if you have anything against anyone, forgive him, so that your Father in heaven may also forgive you your wrongdoing.*

*Mark 11:25 HCSB*

Genuine love is an exercise in forgiveness. If we wish to build lasting relationships, we must learn how to forgive. Why? Because our loved ones are imperfect (as are we). How often must we forgive our family and friends? More times than we can count. Why? Because that's what God wants us to do.

Perhaps granting forgiveness is hard for you. If so, you are not alone. Genuine, lasting forgiveness is often difficult to achieve—difficult but not impossible. Thankfully, with God's help, all things are possible, and that includes forgiveness. But, even though God is willing to help, He expects you to do some of the work. And make no mistake: forgiveness is work, which is okay with God. He knows that the payoffs are worth the effort.

## — A Prayer for Today —

Dear Lord, let forgiveness rule my heart, even when forgiveness is difficult. Let me be Your obedient servant, Lord, and let me be a woman who forgives others just as You have forgiven me. Amen

# In His Hands

*Don't brashly announce what you're going to do tomorrow;*
*you don't know the first thing about tomorrow.*

*Proverbs 27:1 MSG*

The old saying is both familiar and true: "Man proposes and God disposes." Our world unfolds according to God's plans, not our wishes. Thus, boasting about future events is to be avoided by those who acknowledge God's sovereignty over all things.

Are you planning for a better tomorrow for yourself and your family? If so, you are to be congratulated: God rewards forethought in the same way that He often punishes impulsiveness. But as you make your plans, do so with humility, with gratitude, and with trust in your Heavenly Father. His hand directs the future; to think otherwise is both arrogant and naïve.

No matter how heavy the burden, daily strength is given, so I expect we need not give ourselves any concern as to what the outcome will be. We must simply go forward.

*Annie Armstrong*

## — A Prayer for Today —

Dear Lord, as I look to the future, I will place my trust in You. If I become discouraged, I will turn to You. If I am weak, I will seek strength in You. You are my Father, and I will place my hope, my trust, and my faith in You. Amen

# God Is Love

*God is love, and the one who remains in love remains in God, and God remains in him.*

*1 John 4:16 HCSB*

The Bible makes this promise: God is love. It's a sweeping statement, a profoundly important description of what God is and how God works. God's love is perfect. When we open our hearts to His perfect love, we are touched by the Creator's hand, and we are transformed.

Today, even if you can only carve out a few quiet moments, offer sincere prayers of thanksgiving to your Creator. He loves you now and throughout all eternity. Open your heart to His presence and His love.

Let's never forget that some of God's greatest mercies are His refusals. He says no in order that He may, in some way we cannot imagine, say yes. All His ways with us are merciful. His meaning is always love.

*Elisabeth Elliot*

## — A Prayer for Today —

Dear God, You are love. You love me, Father, and I love You. As I love You more, Lord, I am also able to love my family and friends more. I will be Your loving servant, Lord, today and throughout eternity. Amen

# Trust Him to Guide You

*Trust in the Lord with all your heart, and do not rely on your own understanding; think about Him in all your ways, and He will guide you on the right paths.*

Proverbs 3:5-6 HCSB

As Christians whose salvation has been purchased by the blood of Christ, we have every reason to live joyously and courageously. After all, Christ has already fought and won our battle for us—He did so on the cross at Calvary. But despite Christ's sacrifice, and despite God's promises, we may become confused or disoriented by the endless complications and countless distractions of life.

If you're unsure of your next step, lean upon God's promises and lift your prayers to Him. Remember that God is your protector. Open yourself to His heart, and trust Him to guide you. When you do, God will direct your steps, and you will receive His blessings today, tomorrow, and throughout eternity.

It is a joy that God never abandons His children. He guides faithfully all who listen to His directions.

Corrie ten Boom

## — A Prayer for Today —

Dear Lord, today I will trust You more completely. I will lean upon Your understanding, not mine. And I will trust You to guide my steps along a path of Your choosing. Amen

# Seeking God and Finding Happiness

*Happy is the one whose help is the God of Jacob, whose hope is in the Lord his God.*

*Psalm 146:5 HCSB*

Happiness depends less upon our circumstances than upon our thoughts. When we turn our thoughts to God, to His gifts, and to His glorious creation, we experience the joy that God intends for His children. But, when we focus on the negative aspects of life, we suffer needlessly.

Do you sincerely want to be a happy Christian? Then set your mind and your heart upon God's love and His grace. The fullness of life in Christ is available to all who seek it and claim it. Count yourself among that number. Seek first the salvation that is available through a personal relationship with Jesus Christ, and then claim the joy, the peace, and the spiritual abundance that the Shepherd offers His sheep.

We will never be happy until we make God the source of our fulfillment and the answer to our longings.

*Stormie Omartian*

## — A Prayer for Today —

Dear Lord, I am thankful for all the blessings You have given me. Let me be a happy Christian, Father, as I share Your joy with friends, with family, and with the world. Amen

# His Healing Touch

*I am the Lord that healeth thee.*

*Exodus 15:26 KJV*

Are you concerned about your spiritual, physical, or emotional health? If so, there is a timeless source of comfort and assurance that is as near as your bookshelf. That source is the Holy Bible.

God's Word has much to say about every aspect of your life, including your health. And, when you face concerns of any sort—including health-related challenges—God is with you. So trust your medical doctor to do his or her part, but place your ultimate trust in your benevolent Heavenly Father. His healing touch, like His love, endures forever.

Jesus Christ is the One by Whom, for Whom, through Whom everything was made. Therefore, He knows what's wrong in your life and how to fix it.

*Anne Graham Lotz*

## — A Prayer for Today —

Dear Lord, place Your healing hand upon me. Heal my body and my soul. Let me trust Your promises, Father, and let me turn to You for hope, for restoration, for renewal, and for salvation. Amen

# Self-made?

*Respecting the Lord and not being proud will bring you wealth, honor, and life.*

Proverbs 22:4 NCV

We have heard it said on countless occasions: "He's a self-made man," or "She's a self-made woman." In truth, none of us are self-made. We all owe countless debts that we can never repay. Our first debt, of course, is to our Father in heaven—who has given us everything that we are and will ever be—and to His Son who sacrificed His own life so that we might live eternally. We are also indebted to ancestors, parents, teachers, friends, spouses, family members, coworkers, fellow believers . . . and the list, of course, goes on.

Most of us, it seems, are more than willing to stick out our chests and say, "Look at me; I did that!" But in our better moments, in the quiet moments when we search the depths of our own hearts, we know better. Whatever "it" is, God did that. And He deserves the credit.

## — A Prayer for Today —

Heavenly Father, Jesus clothed Himself with humility when He chose to leave heaven and come to earth to live and die for all creation. Christ is my Master and my example. Clothe me with humility, Lord, so that I might be more like Your Son. Amen

# Love Is a Choice

*Dear friends, if God loved us in this way, we also must love one another.*

*1 John 4:11 HCSB*

Love is always a choice. Sometimes, of course, we may "fall in love," but it takes work to stay there. Sometimes, we may be "swept off our feet," but the "sweeping" is only temporary; sooner or later, if love is to endure, one must plant one's feet firmly on the ground. The decision to love another person for a lifetime is much more than the simple process of "falling in" or "being swept up." It requires "reaching out," "holding firm," and "lifting up." Love, then, becomes a decision to honor and care for the other person, come what may.

Charity says, "I grant you your rights. I do not insist on mine. I give myself to you; I do not insist that you give yourself to me."

*Elisabeth Elliot*

## — A Prayer for Today —

Dear Lord, You have given me the gift of love; let me share that gift with others. And, keep me mindful that the essence of love is not to receive it, but to give it, today and forever. Amen

# Beyond Materialism

*For what does it benefit a man to gain the whole world yet lose his life? What can a man give in exchange for his life?*
Mark 8:36-37 HCSB

In our modern society, we need money to live. But as Christians, we must never make the acquisition of money the central focus of our lives. Money is a tool, but it should never overwhelm our sensibilities. The focus of life must be squarely on things spiritual, not things material.

Whenever we place our love for material possessions above our love for God—or when we yield to the countless other temptations of everyday living—we find ourselves engaged in a struggle between good and evil. Let us respond to this struggle by freeing ourselves from that subtle yet powerful temptation: the temptation to love the world more than we love God.

Why is love of gold more potent than love of souls?
*Lottie Moon*

## — A Prayer for Today —

Lord, my greatest possession is my relationship with You through Jesus Christ. You have promised that, when I first seek Your kingdom and Your righteousness, You will give me whatever I need. Let me trust You completely, Lord, for my needs, both material and spiritual, this day and always. Amen

# Blessed Obedience

*When you and your children return to the LORD your God and obey him with all your heart and with all your soul according to everything I command you today, then the LORD your God will restore your fortunes and have compassion on you and gather you again from all the nations where he scattered you.*

*Deuteronomy 30:2-3 NIV*

We live in a world filled with temptations, distractions, and countless opportunities to disobey God. But as women who seek to be godly role models for our families, we must turn our thoughts and our hearts away from the evils of this world. We must turn instead to God.

Talking about God is easy; living by His laws is considerably harder. But unless we are willing to live obediently, all our righteous words ring hollow.

How can we best proclaim our love for the Lord? By obeying Him. We must seek God's counsel and trust the counsel He gives. And, when we invite God into our hearts and live according to His commandments, we are blessed today, tomorrow, and forever.

## — A Prayer for Today —

Dear Lord, when I am tempted to disobey Your commandments, correct my errors and guide my path. Make me a faithful steward of my talents, my opportunities, and my possessions so that Your kingdom may be glorified, now and forever. Amen

# Lost in the Crowd

*The fear of man is a snare, but the one who trusts in the Lord is protected.*

*Proverbs 29:25 HCSB*

Rick Warren observed, "Those who follow the crowd usually get lost in it." We know these words to be true, but oftentimes we fail to live by them. Instead of trusting God for guidance, we imitate our neighbors and suffer the consequences. Instead of seeking to please our Father in heaven, we strive to please our peers, with decidedly mixed results.

Whom will you try to please today: your God or your associates? Your obligation is most certainly not to neighbors, to friends, or even to family members. Your obligation is to an all-knowing, all-powerful God. You must seek to please Him first and always. No exceptions.

It is comfortable to know that we are responsible to God and not to man. It is a small matter to be judged of man's judgement.

*Lottie Moon*

## — A Prayer for Today —

Dear Lord, other people may encourage me to stray from Your path, but I wish to follow in the footsteps of Your Son. Give me the vision to see the right path—and the wisdom to follow it—today and every day of my life. Amen

# Foolish Pride

*Do nothing out of rivalry or conceit, but in humility consider others as more important than yourselves.*

Philippians 2:3 HCSB

Sometimes our faith is tested more by prosperity than by adversity. Why? Because in times of plenty, we are tempted to stick out our chests and say, "I did that." But nothing could be further from the truth. All of our blessings start and end with God, and whatever "it" is, He did it. And He deserves the credit.

Who are the greatest among us? Are they the proud and the powerful? Hardly. The greatest among us are the humble servants who care less for their own glory and more for God's glory. If we seek greatness in God's eyes, we must forever praise God's good works, not our own.

We cannot be filled until we are empty. We have to be poor in spirit ourselves in order to be filled with the Holy Spirit.

Corrie ten Boom

## — A Prayer for Today —

Lord, make me a woman with a humble heart. Keep me mindful, Dear God, that all my gifts come from You. Let me grow beyond my need for earthly praise, Lord, and when I seek approval, let me look only to You. Amen

# Serving Others with Love

*Whoever wants to become great among you must be your servant, and whoever wants to be first among you must be your slave; just as the Son of Man did not come to be served, but to serve, and to give His life—a ransom for many.*

*Matthew 20:26-28 HCSB*

Jesus came to earth as a servant of man and the Savior of mankind. One way that we can demonstrate our love for the Savior is by obeying His commandment to serve one another.

Whom will you choose to serve today? Will you be a woman who cheerfully meets the needs of family and friends? And, will you meet those needs with love in your heart and encouragement on your lips? As you plan for the day ahead, remember that the needs are great and the workers are few. And remember that God is doing His very best to enlist able-bodied believers— like you.

## — A Prayer for Today —

Dear Lord, create in me a servant's heart. And, let be a woman who follows in the footsteps of Your Son Jesus who taught us by example that to be great in Your eyes, Lord, is to serve others humbly, faithfully, and lovingly. Amen

# Setbacks

*And my God shall supply all your need according to His riches in glory by Christ Jesus.*

*Philippians 4:19 NKJV*

All of us experience adversity, disappointments, and hardship. Sometimes we bring these hardships upon ourselves, and sometimes we are victimized by circumstances that we cannot control and cannot fully understand. As human beings with limited insight, we can never completely comprehend the will of our Father in heaven. But as believers in a benevolent God, we must always trust His providence.

Have you been touched by personal tragedy that you did not deserve and cannot understand? If so, it's time to make peace with life. It's time to forgive others, and, if necessary, to forgive yourself. It's time to accept the unchangeable past, to embrace the priceless present, and to have faith in the promise of tomorrow. It's time to trust God completely. And it's time to reclaim the peace—His peace—that can and should be yours.

Measure the size of the obstacles against the size of God.

*Beth Moore*

## — A Prayer for Today —

Lord, give me courage in every circumstance and in every stage of life. Give me the wisdom, Father, to place my hope and my trust in Your perfect plan and Your boundless love. Amen

# Hope Is Contagious

*Finally, all of you be of one mind, having compassion for one another; love as brothers, be tenderhearted, be courteous.*
*1 Peter 3:8 NKJV*

One of the reasons that God placed you here on earth is so that you might become a beacon of encouragement to the world. As a faithful follower of the One from Galilee, you have every reason to be hopeful, and you have every reason to share your hopes with others. When you do, you will discover that hope, like other human emotions, is contagious.

As a follower of Christ, you are instructed to choose your words carefully so as to build others up through wholesome, honest encouragement (Ephesians 4:29). So look for the good in others and celebrate the good that you find. As the old saying goes, "When someone does something good, applaud—you'll make two people happy."

## — A Prayer for Today —

Dear Lord, You have loved me eternally, and cared for me faithfully. Just as You have lifted me up, Lord, let me also lift up others in a spirit of encouragement, optimism, and hope. Today and every day, let me share Your healing message so that I might encourage others. And, Lord, may the glory be Yours. Amen

# A Positive Influence

*Be an example to the believers in word, in conduct, in love, in spirit, in faith, in purity.*

1 Timothy 4:12 NKJV

As followers of Christ, we must each ask ourselves an important question: "What kind of example am I?" The answer to that question determines, in large part, whether or not we are positive influences on our own little corners of the world.

Are you the kind of woman whose life serves as a powerful example of righteousness? Are you a person whose behavior serves as a positive role model for young people? Are you the kind of Christian whose actions, day in and day out, are based upon integrity, fidelity, and a love for the Lord? If so, you are not only blessed by God; you are also a powerful force for good in a world that desperately needs positive influences such as yours.

Among the most joyful people I have known have been some who seem to have had no human reason for joy. The sweet fragrance of Christ has shown through their lives.

*Elisabeth Elliot*

## — A Prayer for Today —

Lord, I am aware that my behavior will influence others. Let my influence be positive. Let me follow in the footsteps of Your Son, and let others see Him through me. Amen

# Caring for Your Family

*Now if anyone does not provide for his own relatives, and especially for his household, he has denied the faith and is worse than an unbeliever.*

1 Timothy 5:8 HCSB

The words of 1 Timothy 5:8 are unambiguous: if God has blessed us with families, then He expects us to care for them. Sometimes, this profound responsibility seems daunting. And sometimes, even for the most dedicated Christian women, family life holds moments of frustration and disappointment. But, for those who are lucky enough to live in the presence of a close-knit, caring clan, the rewards far outweigh the demands.

No family is perfect, and neither is yours. Despite the inevitable challenges of providing for your family, and despite the occasional hurt feelings of family life, your clan is God's gift to you. Give thanks to the Giver for the gift of family . . . and act accordingly.

## — A Prayer for Today —

Dear Lord, I am part of Your family, and I praise You for Your gifts and for Your love. You have also blessed me with my earthly family, and I pray for them, that they might be protected and blessed by You. Let me show love and acceptance for my family, Lord, so that through me, they might come to know and to love You. Amen

# Pass It On

*Do not neglect the gift that is in you.*

*1 Timothy 4:14 HCSB*

God has given you an array of talents, and He has given you unique opportunities to share those talents with the world. Your Creator intends for you to use your talents for the glory of His kingdom in the service of His children. Will you honor Him by sharing His gifts? And, will you share His gifts humbly and lovingly? Hopefully you will.

The old saying is both familiar and true: "What you are is God's gift to you; what you become is your gift to God." As a woman who has been touched by the transforming love of Jesus Christ, your obligation is clear: You must strive to make the most of your own God-given talents, and you must encourage your family and friends to do likewise. So, make this promise to yourself and to God: Promise to use your talents to minister to your family, to your friends, and to the world. And remember: The best way to say "Thank You" for God's gifts is to use them.

## — A Prayer for Today —

Lord, You have given all of us talents, and I am no exception. You have blessed me with a gift—let me discover it, nurture it, and use it for the glory of Your Kingdom. I will share my gifts with the world, and I will praise to You, the Giver of all things good. Amen

# Letting Go

*Blessed are the merciful, because they will be shown mercy.*
Matthew 5:7 HCSB

Even the most mild-mannered women will, on occasion, have reason to become angry with the inevitable shortcomings of family members and friends. But wise women are quick to forgive others, just as God has forgiven them. The commandment to forgive others is clearly a part of God's Word, but oh how difficult a commandment it can be to follow. Because we are imperfect beings, we are quick to anger, quick to blame, slow to forgive, and even slower to forget. No matter. Even when forgiveness is difficult, God's instructions are straightforward: As Christians who have received the gift of forgiveness, we must now share that gift with others.

Bitterness and regret are not part of God's plan for your life. Forgiveness is. And once you've forgiven others, you can then turn your thoughts to a far more pleasant subject: the incredibly bright future that God has promised.

## — A Prayer for Today —

Lord, make me a woman who is slow to anger and quick to forgive. When I am angry, Your Word reminds me that forgiveness is Your commandment. Let me be Your obedient servant, Lord, and let me forgive others just as You have forgiven me. Amen

# Richly Blessed

*Each person should do as he has decided in his heart—not out of regret or out of necessity, for God loves a cheerful giver.*

*2 Corinthians 9:7 HCSB*

God's Word commands us to be generous, compassionate servants to those who need our support. As believers, we have been richly blessed by our Creator. We, in turn, are called to share our gifts, our possessions, our testimonies, and our talents.

The theme of generosity is one of the cornerstones of Christ's teachings. If we are to be disciples of Christ, we, too, must be cheerful, generous, courageous givers. Our Savior expects no less from us. And He deserves no less.

We do not need to beg Him to bless us; He simply cannot help it.

*Hannah Whitall Smith*

## — A Prayer for Today —

Lord, You loved me before I was ever born; You sent Your Son Jesus to redeem me from my sins; You have given me the gift of eternal life. Today, I will share the priceless blessings that I have received: I will share my joy, my possessions, and my faith with others. Amen

# Hearing the Call

*One thing I do, forgetting those things which are behind and reaching forward to those things which are ahead, I press toward the goal for the prize of the upward call of God in Christ Jesus.*

*Philippians 3:13-14 NKJV*

It is vitally important that you heed God's call. In John 15:16, Jesus says, "You did not choose me, but I chose you and appointed you to go and bear fruit—fruit that will last" (NIV). In other words, you have been called by Christ, and now, it is up to you to decide precisely how you will answer.

Have you already found your special calling? If so, you're a very lucky woman. If not, keep searching and keep praying until you discover it. And remember this: God has important work for you to do—work that no one else on earth can accomplish but you.

If God has called you, do not spend time looking over your shoulder to see who is following you.

*Corrie ten Boom*

## — A Prayer for Today —

Heavenly Father, You have called me, and I acknowledge that calling. In these quiet moments before this busy day unfolds, I come to You. I will study Your Word and seek Your guidance. Give me the wisdom to know Your will for my life and the courage to follow wherever You may lead me, today and forever. Amen

# God Is Love

*He who does not love does not know God, for God is love.*
*1 John 4:8 NKJV*

God loves you. He loves you more than you can imagine; His affection is deeper than you can fathom. God made you in His own image and gave you salvation through the person of His Son Jesus Christ. And as a result, you have an important decision to make. You must decide what to do about God's love: you can return it . . . or not.

When you accept the love that flows from the heart of God, you are transformed. When you embrace God's love, you feel differently about yourself, your neighbors, your community, your church, and your world. When you open your heart to God's love, you will feel compelled to share God's message—and His compassion—with others. God's heart is overflowing—accept His love; return His love; and share His love. Today.

Life in God is a great big hug that lasts forever!
*Barbara Johnson*

## — A Prayer for Today —

Lord, the Bible tells me that You are my loving Father. I thank You for Your love and for Your Son. I will praise You, I will worship You, and I will love You, Dear Lord, today, tomorrow, and forever. Amen

# In His Image

*So God created man in his own image, in the image of God he created him; male and female he created them.*

*Genesis 1:27 NIV*

What is your attitude today? Are you fearful or worried? Are you more concerned about pleasing your friends than about pleasing your God? Are you bitter, confused, cynical, or pessimistic? If so, it's time to have a little chat with your Father in heaven.

God intends that your life be filled with spiritual abundance and joy—but God will not force His joy upon you—you must claim it for yourself. So do yourself this favor: accept God's gifts with a smile on your face, a song on your lips, and joy in your heart. Think optimistically about yourself and your future. Give thanks to the One who has given you everything, and trust in your heart that He wants to give you so much more.

The Reference Point for the Christian is the Bible. All values, judgments, and attitudes must be gauged in relationship to this Reference Point.

*Ruth Bell Graham*

## — A Prayer for Today —

Lord, I pray for an attitude that is Christlike. Whatever my situation, whether good or bad, happy or sad, let me respond with an attitude of optimism, faith, and love for You. Amen

# Conquering Our Frustrations

*People with quick tempers cause trouble, but those who control their tempers stop a quarrel.*

Proverbs 15:18 NCV

Life is full of frustrations: some great and some small. On occasion, you, like Jesus, will confront evil, and when you do, you may respond as He did: vigorously and without reservation. But, more often your frustrations will be of the more mundane variety. As long as you live here on earth, you will face countless opportunities to lose your temper over small, relatively insignificant events: a traffic jam, a spilled cup of coffee, an inconsiderate comment, a broken promise.

When you are tempted to lose your temper over the minor inconveniences of life, don't. Turn away from anger, hatred, bitterness, and regret. Turn instead to God. When you do, you'll be following His commandments and giving yourself a priceless gift . . . the gift of peace.

Life is too short to spend it being angry, bored, or dull.

*Barbara Johnson*

## — A Prayer for Today —

Dear Lord, when I am angry, I cannot feel the peace that You intend for my life. When I am bitter, I cannot sense Your love. Let me turn away from anger and instead claim the spiritual abundance that You offer through the priceless gift of Your Son Jesus. Amen

# The Guidebook

*All Scripture is inspired by God and is profitable for teaching, for rebuking, for correcting, for training in righteousness, so that the man of God may be complete, equipped for every good work.*

*2 Timothy 3:16-17 HCSB*

God has given us a guidebook for righteous living called the Holy Bible. It contains thorough instructions which, if followed, lead to fulfillment, righteousness, and salvation. But, if we choose to ignore God's commandments, the results are as predictable as they are tragic.

God has given us the Bible for the purpose of knowing His promises, His power, His commandments, His wisdom, His love, and His Son. As we study God's teachings and apply them to our lives, we live by the Word that shall never pass away. Today, let us follow God's commandments, and let us conduct our lives in such a way that we might be shining examples to our families, and, most importantly, to those who have not yet found Christ.

## — A Prayer for Today —

As I journey through this life, Lord, help me always to consult the true road map: Your Holy Word. I know that when I turn my heart and my thoughts to You, Father, You will lead me along the path that is right for me. Today, let me know Your will and study Your Word so that I might know Your plan for my life. Amen

# Beyond Worry

*Your heart must not be troubled. Believe in God; believe also in Me.*

John 14:1 HCSB

Because we are fallible human beings, we worry. Even though we, as Christians, have the promise of God's love and protection, we find ourselves fretting over the countless details of everyday life.

If you are like most women, you may, on occasion, find yourself worrying about health, about finances, about safety, about relationships, about family, and about countless other challenges of life, some great and some small. Where is the best place to take your worries? Take them to God. Take your troubles to Him and your fears and your sorrows. And remember: God is trustworthy . . . and you are protected.

Worry is a cycle of inefficient thoughts whirling around a center of fear.

Corrie ten Boom

## — A Prayer for Today —

Lord, You understand my worries and my fears, and You forgive me when I am weak. When my faith begins to waver, help me to trust You more. Then, let me live courageously, faithfully, prayerfully, and thankfully today and every day. Amen

# It's Up to You to Ask

*Now if any of you lacks wisdom, he should ask God, who gives to all generously and without criticizing, and it will be given to him.*

*James 1:5 HCSB*

Jesus made it clear to His disciples: they should petition God to meet their needs. So should we. Genuine, heartfelt prayer produces powerful changes in us and in our world. When we lift our hearts to God, we open ourselves to a never-ending source of divine wisdom and infinite love.

Do you have questions about your future that you simply can't answer? Do you have needs that you simply can't meet by yourself? Do you sincerely seek to know God's unfolding plans for your life? If so, ask Him for direction, for protection, and for strength—and then keep asking Him every day that you live. Whatever your need, no matter how great or small, pray about it and never lose hope. God is not just near; He is here, and He's perfectly capable of answering your prayers. Now, it's up to you to ask.

## — A Prayer for Today —

Lord, when I have questions about my purpose in life, I will turn to You. When I am weak, I will seek Your strength. When I am discouraged, Father, I will be mindful of Your love and Your grace. I will ask You for the things I need, Father, and I will trust Your answers, today and forever. Amen

# A Priceless Gift

*Man shall not live by bread alone, but by every word that proceeds from the mouth of God.*

Matthew 4:4 NKJV

The Bible is a priceless gift, a tool for Christians to use as they share the Good News of their Savior, Christ Jesus. Too many Christians, however, keep their spiritual tool kits tightly closed and out of sight.

Jonathan Edwards advised, "Be assiduous in reading the Holy Scriptures. This is the fountain whence all knowledge in divinity must be derived. Therefore let not this treasure lie by you neglected."

God's Holy Word is, indeed, a priceless, one-of-a-kind treasure. Handle it with care, but more importantly, handle it every day . . . starting today.

Either God's Word keeps you from sin, or sin keeps you from God's Word.

*Corrie ten Boom*

## — A Prayer for Today —

Heavenly Father, Your Holy Word is a treasure to me; I will study it, trust it, and share it. In all that I do, help me be a worthy witness for You as I share the Good News of Your perfect Son and Your perfect Word. Amen

# Born Again

*You have been born again—not of perishable seed but of imperishable—through the living and enduring word of God.*
1 Peter 1:23 HCSB

Why did Christ die on the cross? Christ sacrificed His life so that we might be born again. This gift, freely given from God's only begotten Son, is the priceless possession of everyone who accepts Him as Lord and Savior. Let us claim Christ's gift today. Let us walk with the Savior, let us love Him, let us praise Him, and let us share His message of salvation with all those who cross our paths.

The comforting words of Ephesians 2:8 make God's promise clear: "For by grace you have been saved through faith, and that not of yourselves; it is the gift of God" (NKJV). Thus, we are saved not because of our good deeds but because of our faith in Christ. May we, who have been given so much, praise our Savior for the gift of salvation, and may we share the joyous news of our Master's limitless love with our families, with our friends, and with the world.

## — A Prayer for Today —

Lord, when I accepted Jesus as my personal Savior, You changed me forever and made me whole. I was born again. Help me to share Your Son's message with my friends. You are a God of love, redemption, conversion, and salvation. I will praise You today and forever. Amen

# Life's Foundation

*The one who lives with integrity will be helped, but one who distorts right and wrong will suddenly fall.*

*Proverbs 28:18 HCSB*

Wise women understand that character is a crucial building block in the foundation of a well-lived life. Character is built slowly over a lifetime. It is the sum of every right decision, every honest word, every noble thought, and every heartfelt prayer. It is forged on the anvil of honorable work and polished by the twin virtues of generosity and humility. Character is a precious thing—difficult to build, but easy to tear down; godly women value it and protect it at all costs.

Each one of us is God's special work of art. Through us, He teaches and inspires, delights and encourages, informs and uplifts all those who view our lives. God, the master artist, is most concerned about expressing Himself—His thoughts and His intentions—through what He paints in our characters.

*Joni Eareckson Tada*

## — A Prayer for Today —

Dear Lord, You search my heart and know me far better than I know myself. May I be Your worthy servant, and may I live according to Your commandments. Let me be a woman of integrity, Lord, and let my words and deeds be a testimony to You, today and always. Amen

# Enduring Difficult Days

*I have heard your prayer, I have seen your tears; surely I will heal you.*

*2 Kings 20:5 NKJV*

From time to time, all of us must endure discouragement. And, we sometimes experience life-changing personal losses that leave us reeling. When we do, God stands ready to protect us. When we are troubled, we must call upon God, and, in His own time and according to His own plan, He will heal us.

Are you anxious? Take those anxieties to God. Are you troubled? Take your troubles to Him. Does your world seem to be trembling beneath your feet? Seek protection from the One who cannot be moved. The same God who created the universe will protect you if you ask Him . . . so ask Him.

Often, in the midst of great problems, we stop short of the real blessing God has for us, which is a fresh vision of who He is.

*Anne Graham Lotz*

## — A Prayer for Today —

Dear Heavenly Father, You are my strength and my protector. In times of trouble, let me trust Your plan for my life. Your love is infinite, as is Your wisdom. Whatever my circumstances, Dear Lord, let me always give the praise and the thanks and the glory to You. Amen

# Supporting His Church

*For we are God's fellow workers; you are God's field, you are God's building.*

*1 Corinthians 3:9 NKJV*

The church belongs to God; it is His just as certainly as we are His. When we help build God's church, we bear witness to the changes that He has made in our lives.

Today and every day, let us worship God with grateful hearts and helping hands as we support the church that He has created. Let us witness to our friends, to our families, and to the world. When we do so, we bless others—and we are blessed by the One who sent His Son to die so that we might have eternal life.

The church needs the power and the gifts of the Holy Spirit more now than ever before.

*Corrie ten Boom*

## — A Prayer for Today —

Lord, wherever it is that we worship, You are there. Let me support Your church, let me help build Your church, and let me remember that church is not only a place; it is also a state of mind and a state of grace. Amen

# A Clear Conscience

*If then you were raised with Christ, seek those things which are above, where Christ is, sitting at the right hand of God. Set your mind on things above, not on things on the earth.*

*Colossians 3:1-2 NKJV*

Few things in life torment us more than a guilty conscience. And, few things in life provide more contentment than the knowledge that we are obeying God's commandments.

A clear conscience is one of the rewards we earn when we obey God's Word and follow His will. When we follow God's will and accept His gift of salvation, our earthly rewards are never-ceasing, and our heavenly rewards are everlasting.

Whatever weakens your reason, impairs the tenderness of your conscience, obscures your sense of God, or removes your relish for spiritual things—that is sin to you.

*Susanna Wesley*

## — A Prayer for Today —

Lord, You have given me a conscience that tells me right from wrong. Let me listen to that quiet voice so that I might do Your will and follow Your Word today and every day. Amen

# The Morning Watch

*Every morning he wakes me. He teaches me to listen like a student. The Lord God helps me learn . . . .*

Isaiah 50:4-5 NCV

Each new day is a gift from God, and if you are wise, you will spend a few quiet moments each morning thanking the Giver. When you begin each day with your head bowed and your heart lifted, you are reminded of God's love, His protection, and His commandments. Then, you can align your priorities for the coming day with the teachings and commandments that God has placed upon your heart.

So, if you've acquired the unfortunate habit of trying to "squeeze" God into the corners of your life, it's time to reshuffle the items on your to-do list by placing God first. And if you haven't already done so, form the habit of spending quality time with your Father in heaven. He deserves it . . . and so do you.

Think of this—we may live together with Him here and now, a daily walking with Him who loved us and gave Himself for us.

*Elisabeth Elliot*

## — A Prayer for Today —

Lord, help me to hear Your direction for my life in the quiet moments of each day. Let everything that I say and do be in Your perfect will. Amen

# When People Misbehave

*Bad temper is contagious—don't get infected.*

*Proverbs 22:25 MSG*

Face it: sometimes people can be rude . . . very rude. When other people are unkind to you, you may be tempted to strike back, either verbally or in some other way. Don't do it! Instead, remember that God corrects other people's behaviors in His own way, and He doesn't need your help (even if you're totally convinced that He does).

So, when other people behave cruelly, foolishly, or impulsively—as they will from time to time—don't be hotheaded. Instead, speak up for yourself as politely as you can, and walk away. Then, forgive everybody as quickly as you can, and leave the rest up to God.

You can be sure you are abiding in Christ if you are able to have a Christlike love toward the people that irritate you the most.

*Vonette Bright*

## — A Prayer for Today —

Dear Lord, sometimes people behave badly. When other people upset me, help me to calm myself down, and help me to forgive them as quickly as I can. Amen

# Teaching Discipline

*The one who follows instruction is on the path to life, but the one who rejects correction goes astray.*

Proverbs 10:17 HCSB

Wise women understand the importance of discipline. In Proverbs 28:19, God's message is clear: "He who works his land will have abundant food, but the one who chases fantasies will have his fill of poverty" (NIV). When we work diligently and consistently, we can expect a bountiful harvest. But we must never expect the harvest to precede the labor.

Thoughtful Christians understand that God doesn't reward laziness or misbehavior. To the contrary, God expects His children (of all ages) to lead disciplined lives . . . very disciplined lives.

The goal of any discipline is to result in greater freedom. Gal. 5:1

*Anonymous*

## — A Prayer for Today —

Lord, I want to be a disciplined woman. Let me use my time wisely, and let me teach others by the faithfulness of my conduct, today and every day. Amen

# A Helping Hand

*Then a Samaritan traveling down the road came to where the hurt man was. When he saw the man, he felt very sorry for him. The Samaritan went to him, poured olive oil and wine on his wounds, and bandaged them. Then he put the hurt man on his own donkey and took him to an inn where he cared for him.*

*Luke 10:33-34 NCV*

Sometimes we would like to help make the world a better place, but we're not sure how to do it. Jesus told the story of the "Good Samaritan," a man who helped a fellow traveler when no one else would. We, too, should be good Samaritans when we find people who need our help.

When bad things happen in our world, there's always something we can do. So what can you do to make God's world a better place? You can start by making your own corner of the world a little nicer place to live (by sharing kind words and good deeds). And then, you can take your concerns to God in prayer. Whether you've offered a helping hand or a heartfelt prayer, you've done a lot.

## — A Prayer for Today —

Dear Lord, let me help others in every way that I can. Jesus served others; I can too. I will serve other people with my good deeds and with my prayers, today and every day. Amen

# Choices, Choices, Choices

*Therefore, whether we are at home or away, we make it our aim to be pleasing to Him.*

*2 Corinthians 5:9 HCSB*

Your life is a series of choices. From the instant you wake up in the morning until the moment you nod off to sleep at night, you make lots of decisions: decisions about the things you do, decisions about the words you speak, and decisions about the thoughts you choose to think. Simply put, the quality of those decisions determines the quality of your life.

So, if you sincerely want to lead a life that is pleasing to God, you must make choices that are pleasing to Him. He deserves no less . . . and neither, for that matter, do you.

No matter how many books you read, no matter how many schools you attend, you're never really wise until you start making wise choices.

*Marie T. Freeman*

## — A Prayer for Today —

Dear Lord, help me to make choices that are pleasing to You. Help me to be honest, patient, and kind. And above all, help me to follow the teachings of Jesus, not just today, but every day. Amen

# Obedience Now

*And hereby we do know that we know him, if we keep his commandments.*

1 John 2:3 KJV

In order to enjoy a deeper relationship with God, you must strive diligently to live in accordance with His commandments. But there's a problem—you live in a world that seeks to snare your attention and lead you away from God.

Because you are an imperfect mortal being, you cannot be perfectly obedient, nor does God expect you to be. What is required, however, is a sincere desire to be obedient coupled with an awareness of sin and a willingness to distance yourself from it as soon as you encounter it.

Are you willing to conform your behavior to God's rules? Hopefully, you can answer that question with a resounding yes. Otherwise, you'll never experience a full measure of the blessings that the Creator gives to those who obey Him.

## — A Prayer for Today —

Heavenly Father, I want to grow closer to You each day. I know that obedience to Your will strengthens my relationship with You, so help me to follow Your commandments and obey Your Word today . . . and every day of my life. Amen

# Feeding the Church

*The church, you see, is not peripheral to the world; the world is peripheral to the church. The church is Christ's body, in which he speaks and acts, by which he fills everything with his presence.*

*Ephesians 1:23 MSG*

One way that we come to know God is by involving ourselves in His church.

In the Book of Acts, Luke reminds us to "feed the church of God" (20:28). As Christians who have been saved by a loving, compassionate Creator, we are compelled not only to worship Him in our hearts but also to worship Him in the presence of fellow believers.

Do you feed the church of God? Do you attend regularly, and are you an active participant? The answer to these questions will have a profound impact on the quality and direction of your spiritual journey.

So do yourself a favor: become actively involved in your church. Don't just go to church out of habit. Go to church out of a sincere desire to know and worship God. When you do, you'll be blessed by the One who sent His Son to die so that you might have everlasting life.

— A Prayer for Today —

Heavenly Father, I give thanks for my church and for the opportunity to worship there. Guide my steps, Lord, as I worship You in spirit and in truth, today and forever. Amen

# Old You, New You

*Therefore if anyone is in Christ, he is a new creature; the old things passed away; behold, new things have come.*
*2 Corinthians 5:17 HCSB*

Think, for a moment, about the "old" you, the person you were before you invited Christ to reign over your heart. Now, think about the "new" you, the person you have become since then. Is there a difference between the "old" you and the "new and improved" version? There should be! And that difference should be noticeable not only to you but also to others.

The Bible clearly teaches that when we welcome Christ into our hearts, we become new creations through Him. Our challenge, of course, is to behave ourselves like new creations. When we do, God fills our hearts; He blesses our endeavors and transforms our lives . . . forever.

The amazing thing about Jesus is that He doesn't just patch up our lives; He gives us a brand new sheet, a clean slate to start over, all new.

*Gloria Gaither*

## — A Prayer for Today —

Lord, when I accepted Jesus as my personal Savior, You changed me forever and made me whole. Let me share Your Son's message with my friends, with my family, and with the world. You are a God of love, redemption, conversion, and salvation. I will praise You today and forever. Amen

# Life's Mountaintops, Life's Valleys

*I sought the Lord, and He heard me, and delivered me from all my fears.*

*Psalm 34:4 NKJV*

Every life (including yours) is an unfolding series of events: some fabulous, some not-so-fabulous, and some downright disheartening. When you reach the mountaintops of life, praising God is easy. But, when the storm clouds form overhead, your faith will be tested, sometimes to the breaking point. As a believer, you can take comfort in this fact: Wherever you find yourself, whether at the top of the mountain or the depths of the valley, God is there, and because He cares for you, you can live courageously.

The next time you find your courage tested to the limit, remember that God is your shield and your strength; He is your protector and your deliverer. Call upon Him in your hour of need and He will protect you.

Just as courage is faith in good, so discouragement is faith in evil, and, while courage opens the door to good, discouragement opens it to evil.

*Hannah Whitall Smith*

## — A Prayer for Today —
Dear Lord, when I am fearful or worried, give me courage, perspective, and wisdom. In every circumstance, l will trust You to guide me and protect me. Amen

# Expecting the Best

*Set your minds on what is above, not on what is on the earth.*

*Colossians 3:2 HCSB*

What do you expect from the day ahead? Are you expecting God to do wonderful things, or are you living beneath a cloud of apprehension and doubt? The familiar words of Psalm 118:24 remind us of a profound yet simple truth: "This is the day which the LORD hath made; we will rejoice and be glad in it" (KJV). For believers, every day begins and ends with God's Son and God's promises. When we accept Christ into our hearts, God promises us the opportunity for earthly peace and spiritual abundance. But more importantly, God promises us the priceless gift of eternal life.

As we face the inevitable challenges of life-here-on-earth, we must arm ourselves with the promises of God's Holy Word. When we do, we can expect the best, not only for the day ahead, but also for all eternity.

The next time your hear a baby laugh or see an ocean wave, take note. Pause and listen as his Majesty whispers ever so gently, "I'm here."

*Max Lucado*

## — A Prayer for Today —
Dear God, the Bible contains many promises. Let me trust Your promises, and let me live according to Your Holy Word, not just for today, but forever. Amen

# The Remedy for Uncertainty

*But He said to them, "Why are you fearful, you of little faith?" Then He got up and rebuked the winds and the sea. And there was a great calm.*

Matthew 8:26 HCSB

Sometimes, like Jesus' disciples, we feel threatened by the storms of life. During these moments, when our hearts are flooded with uncertainty, we must remember that God is not simply near; He is here.

Have you ever felt your faith in God slipping away? If so, you are in good company. Even the most faithful Christians are, at times, beset by occasional bouts of discouragement and doubt. But even when you feel far removed from God, God never leaves your side. He is always with you, always willing to calm the storms of life. When you sincerely seek His presence—and when you genuinely seek to establish a deeper, more meaningful relationship with His Son—God will calm your fears, answer your prayers, and restore your soul.

## — A Prayer for Today —

Dear God, sometimes this world can be a puzzling place. When I am unsure of my next step, keep me mindful that You are always near and that You can overcome any challenge. With Your love and Your power, Father, I can live courageously and faithfully, today and every day. Amen

# Serenity

*Do not remember the past events, pay no attention to things of old. Look, I am about to do something new; even now it is coming. Do you not see it? Indeed, I will make a way in the wilderness, rivers in the desert.*

*Isaiah 43:18-19 HCSB*

The American theologian Reinhold Niebuhr composed a profoundly simple verse that came to be known as the Serenity Prayer: "God, grant me the serenity to accept the things I cannot change, the courage to change the things I can, and the wisdom to know the difference." Niebuhr's words are far easier to recite than they are to live by. Why? Because most of us want life to unfold in accordance with our own wishes and timetables. But sometimes God has other plans.

If you've encountered unfortunate circumstances that are beyond your power to control, accept those circumstances . . . and trust God. When you do, you can be comforted in the knowledge that your Creator is both loving and wise, and that He understands His plans perfectly, even when you do not.

## — A Prayer for Today —

Dear Lord, the events of this world unfold according to a plan that I cannot fully understand. But You understand. Today, in whatever circumstances I find myself, let me trust Your will and accept Your love . . . completely. Amen

# Thanksgiving Yes . . .
# Envy No!

*Stop your anger! Turn from your rage! Do not envy others—it only leads to harm.*

*Psalm 37:8 NLT*

As the recipient of God's grace, you have every reason to celebrate life. After all, God has promised you the opportunity to receive His abundance and His joy—in fact, you have the opportunity to receive those gifts right now. But if you allow envy to gnaw away at the fabric of your soul, you'll find that joy remains elusive. So do yourself an enormous favor: Rather than succumbing to the sin of envy, focus on the marvelous things that God has done for you—starting with Christ's sacrifice. Thank the Giver of all good gifts, and keep thanking Him for the wonders of His love and the miracles of His creation. Count your own blessings and let your neighbors count theirs. It's the godly way to live.

Discontent dries up the soul.

*Elisabeth Elliot*

## — A Prayer for Today —

Dear Lord, deliver me from the needless pain of envy. You have given me countless blessings. Let me be thankful for the gifts I have received, and let me never be resentful of the gifts You have given others. Amen

# Competence, Yes.
# Excuses, No!

*Do you see people skilled in their work? They will work for kings, not for ordinary people.*

*Proverbs 22:29 NCV*

Excuses are everywhere . . . excellence is not. If you seek excellence (and the rewards that accompany it), you must avoid the bad habit of making excuses.

Whatever your job description, it's up to you, and no one else, to become a master of your craft. It's up to you to do your job right—and to do it right now. When you do, you'll discover that excellence is its own reward . . . but not its only reward.

We need to stop focusing on our lacks and stop giving out excuses and start looking at and listening to Jesus.

*Anne Graham Lotz*

Making up a string of excuses is usually harder than doing the work.

*Marie T. Freeman*

## — A Prayer for Today —

Dear Lord, I will strive to become a woman of dedication and skill. Today, I will do my best, and I will expect the best. Amen

# God's Plan for Your Family

*Unless the Lord builds a house, its builders labor over it in vain; unless the Lord watches over a city, the watchman stays alert in vain.*

*Psalm 127:1 HCSB*

As you consider God's purpose for your own life, you must also consider how your plans will effect the most important people who God has entrusted to your care: your loved ones.

A loving family is a treasure from God. If you happen to be a member of a close knit, supportive clan, offer a word of thanks to your Creator. He has blessed you with one of His most precious earthly possessions. Your obligation, in response to God's gift, is to treat your family in ways that are consistent with His commandments. So, as you prayerfully seek God's direction, remember that He has important plans for your home life as well as your professional life. It's up to you to act—and to plan—accordingly.

The Golden Rule begins at home.

*Marie T. Freeman*

## — A Prayer for Today —

Lord, You have given me a family that cares for me and loves me. Thank You, Father. Let me love all the members of my family despite their imperfections, and let them love me despite mine. Amen

# Our Fear-based World

*They do not fear bad news; they confidently trust the Lord to care for them. They are confident and fearless and can face their foes triumphantly.*

*Psalm 112:7-8 NLT*

We live in a fear-based world, a world where bad news travels at light speed and good news doesn't. These are troubled times, times when we have legitimate fears for the future of our nation, our world, and our families. But as Christians, we have every reason to live courageously. After all, the ultimate battle has already been fought and won on that faraway cross at Calvary.

Perhaps you, like countless other believers, have found your courage tested by the anxieties and fears that are an inevitable part of life. If so, God wants to have a little chat with you. The next time you find your courage tested to the limit, God wants to remind you that He is not just near; He is here. So remember this: your Heavenly Father is your Protector and your Deliverer. Call upon Him in your hour of need, and be comforted. Whatever your challenge, whatever your trouble, God can handle it. And will.

## — A Prayer for Today —

Dear Lord, when I am fearful, keep me mindful that You are my salvation. Because of You, Father, I can live courageously and faithfully this day and every day. Amen

# A Willingness to Forgive

*And be kind and compassionate to one another, forgiving one another, just as God also forgave you in Christ.*

*Ephesians 4:32 HCSB*

To forgive others is difficult. Being frail, fallible, imperfect human beings, we are quick to anger, quick to blame, slow to forgive, and even slower to forget. No matter. Forgiveness, no matter how difficult, is God's way, and it must be our way, too.

God's commandments are not intended to be customized for the particular whims of particular believers. God's Word is not a menu from which each of us may select items à la carte, according to our own desires. Far from it. God's Holy Word is a book that must be taken in its entirety; all of God's commandments are to be taken seriously. And, so it is with forgiveness. So, if you hold bitterness against even a single person, forgive. Then, to the best of your abilities, forget. It's God's way for you to live.

There is nothing, absolutely nothing, that God will not forgive. You cannot "out-sin" His forgiveness. You cannot "out-sin" the love of God.

*Kathy Troccoli*

## — A Prayer for Today —

Heavenly Father, genuine forgiveness is difficult. Help me to forgive those who have injured me, and deliver me from the traps of anger and bitterness. Forgiveness is Your way, Lord; let it be mine. Amen

# Offering Thanks

*In everything give thanks; for this is the will of God in Christ Jesus for you.*

*1 Thessalonians 5:18 NKJV*

Sometimes, life-here-on-earth can be complicated, demanding, and frustrating. When the demands of life leave us rushing from place to place with scarcely a moment to spare, we may fail to pause and thank our Creator for His gifts. But, whenever we neglect to give proper thanks to the Father, we suffer because of our misplaced priorities.

Today, begin making a list of your blessings. You most certainly will not be able to make a complete list, but take a few moments and jot down as many blessings as you can. Then, give thanks to the Giver of all good things: God. His love for you is eternal, as are His gifts. And it's never too soon—or too late—to offer Him thanks.

We prevent God from giving us the great spiritual gifts He has in store for us, because we do not give thanks for daily gifts.

*Dietrich Bonhoeffer*

— A Prayer for Today —

Today, Lord, let me count my blessings with thanksgiving in my heart. You have cared for me, Lord, and I will give You the glory and the praise. Amen

# His Awesome Creation

*Then God saw everything that He had made, and indeed it was very good.*

*Genesis 1:31 NKJV*

When we consider God's glorious universe, we marvel at the miracle of nature. The smallest seedlings and grandest stars are all part of God's infinite creation. God has placed His handiwork on display for all to see, and if we are wise, we will make time each day to celebrate the world that surrounds us.

Today, as you fulfill the demands of everyday life, pause to consider the majesty of heaven and earth. It is as miraculous as it is beautiful, as incomprehensible as it is breathtaking.

The Psalmist reminds us that the heavens are a declaration of God's glory (Psalm 19:1). May we never cease to praise the Father for a universe that stands as an awesome testimony to His presence and His power.

How awesome that the "Word" that was in the beginning, by which and through which God created everything, was—and is—a living Person with a mind, will, emotions, and intellect.

*Anne Graham Lotz*

## — A Prayer for Today —

Dear Lord, You have created a universe that is glorious to behold yet impossible to comprehend. I praise You for Your creation, Father, and for the sense of awe and wonder that You have placed in my heart. Amen

# His Intimate Love

*As the Father loved Me, I also have loved you; abide in My love.*

*John 15:9 NKJV*

St. Augustine observed, "God loves each of us as if there were only one of us." Do you believe those words? Do you seek an intimate, one-on-one relationship with your Heavenly Father, or are you satisfied to keep Him at a "safe" distance?

Sometimes, in the crush of our daily duties, God may seem far away, but He is not. God is everywhere we have ever been and everywhere we will ever go. He is with us night and day; He knows our thoughts and our prayers. And, when we earnestly seek Him, we will find Him because He is here, waiting patiently for us to reach out to Him. May we reach out to Him today and always. And may we praise Him for the glorious gifts that have transformed us today and forever.

Behold, behold the wondrous love, / That ever flows from God above / Through Christ His only Son, Who gave / His precious blood our souls to save.

*Fanny Crosby*

## — A Prayer for Today —

God, You are love. I love You, Lord, and as I love You more, I am able to love my family and friends more. Let me be Your loving servant, Heavenly Father, today and throughout eternity. Amen

# He Reigns

*In all your ways acknowledge Him, and He shall direct your paths.*

*Proverbs 3:6 NKJV*

God is sovereign. He reigns over the entire universe and He reigns over your little corner of that universe. Your challenge is to recognize God's sovereignty and live in accordance with His commandments. Sometimes, of course, this is easier said than done.

Your Heavenly Father may not always reveal Himself as quickly (or as clearly) as you would like. But rest assured: God is in control, God is here, and God intends to use you in wonderful, unexpected ways. He desires to lead you along a path of His choosing. Your challenge is to watch, to listen, to learn . . . and to follow.

As you place yourself under the sovereign lordship of Jesus Christ, each mistake or failure can lead you right back to the throne.

*Barbara Johnson*

## — A Prayer for Today —

Dear Lord, You rule over our world, and I will allow You to rule over my heart. I will obey Your commandments, I will study Your Word, and I will seek Your will for my life, today and every day of my life. Amen

# Sufficient for Your Needs

*And God is able to make all grace abound toward you, that you, always having all sufficiency in all things, may have an abundance for every good work.*

*2 Corinthians 9:8 NKJV*

Of this you can be sure: the love of God is sufficient to meet your needs. Whatever dangers you may face, whatever heartbreaks you must endure, God is with you, and He stands ready to comfort you and to heal you.

The Psalmist writes, "Weeping may endure for a night, but joy comes in the morning" (Psalm 30:5 NKJV). But when we are suffering, the morning may seem very far away. It is not. God promises that He is "near to those who have a broken heart" (Psalm 34:18 NKJV).

If you are experiencing the intense pain of a recent loss, or if you are still mourning a loss from long ago, perhaps you are now ready to begin the next stage of your journey with God. If so, be mindful of this fact: the loving heart of God is sufficient to meet any challenge, including yours.

## — A Prayer for Today —

Dear Lord, whatever "it" is, You can handle it! Let me turn to You when I am fearful or worried. You are my loving Heavenly Father, sufficient in all things and I will always trust You. Amen

# When It's Hard to Be Kind

*Don't be obsessed with getting your own advantage. Forget yourselves long enough to lend a helping hand.*

*Philippians 2:4 MSG*

Sometimes, when we feel happy or generous, we find it easy to be kind. Other times, when we are discouraged or tired, we can scarcely summon the energy to utter a single kind word. But, God's commandment is clear: He intends that we make the conscious choice to treat others with kindness and respect, no matter our circumstances, no matter our emotions.

Today, as you consider all the things that Christ has done in your life, honor Him by following His commandment and obeying the Golden Rule. He expects no less, and He deserves no less.

The Golden Rule starts at home, but it should never stop there.

*Marie T. Freeman*

## — A Prayer for Today —

Dear Lord, because I expect to be treated with kindness, let me be kind. Because I wish to be loved, let me love others. Because I need forgiveness, let me be merciful. In all things, Lord, let me live by the Golden Rule, today and every day. Amen

# Priorities . . .
# Moment by Moment

*You can't go wrong when you love others. When you add up everything in the law code, the sum total is love. But make sure that you don't get so absorbed and exhausted in taking care of all your day-by-day obligations that you lose track of the time and doze off, oblivious to God.*

*Romans 13:10-11 MSG*

Each waking moment holds the potential to think a creative thought or offer a heartfelt prayer. So even if you're a person with too many demands and too few hours in which to meet them, don't panic. Instead, be comforted in the knowledge that when you sincerely seek to discover God's priorities for your life, He will provide answers in marvelous and surprising ways.

Remember: this is the day that God has made and that He has filled it with countless opportunities to love, to serve, and to seek His guidance. Seize those opportunities. And as a gift to yourself, to your family, and to the world, slow down and claim the inner peace that is your spiritual birthright: the peace of Jesus Christ. It is yours for the asking. So ask . . . and be thankful.

## — A Prayer for Today —

Dear Lord, when the demands of the day leave me distracted and discouraged, let me accept the spiritual abundance that is mine through Christ; let me share His message and His love with all who cross my path. Amen

# The Wisdom to Be Humble

*Do nothing out of rivalry or conceit, but in humility consider others as more important than yourselves.*

*Philippians 2:3 HCSB*

God's Word clearly instructs us to be humble. And that's good because, as fallible human beings, we have so very much to be humble about! Yet some of us continue to puff ourselves up, seeming to say, "Look at me!" To do so is wrong.

As Christians, we have been refashioned and saved by Jesus Christ, and that salvation came not because of our own good works but because of God's grace. How, then, can we be prideful? The answer, of course, is that, if we are honest with ourselves and with our God, we simply can't be boastful . . . we must, instead, be eternally grateful and exceedingly humble. The good things in our lives, including our loved ones, come from God. He deserves the credit—and we deserve the glorious experience of giving it to Him.

If you know who you are in Christ, your personal ego is not an issue.

*Beth Moore*

## — A Prayer for Today —

Dear Lord, when I am boastful, keep me mindful that all my gifts come from You. You are the Giver of all things good; let me give all the glory to You. Amen

# Being Patient with Ourselves

*Knowing God leads to self-control. Self-control leads to patient endurance, and patient endurance leads to godliness.*
*2 Peter 1:6 NLT*

Being patient with other people can be difficult. But sometimes, we find it even more difficult to be patient with ourselves. We have high expectations and lofty goals. We want to accomplish things now, not later. And, of course, we want our lives to unfold according to our own timetables, not God's.

Throughout the Bible, we are instructed that patience is the companion of wisdom. God's message, then, is clear: we must be patient with all people, beginning with that particular person who stares back at us each time we gaze into the mirror.

In times of uncertainty, wait. Always, if you have any doubt, wait. Do not force yourself to any action. If you have a restraint in your spirit, wait until all is clear, and do not go against it.

*Mrs. Charles E. Cowman*

## — A Prayer for Today —

Dear Lord, You have been so patient with me, and I praise You for Your forgiveness. Let me be patient with myself, Father, even when I fall short of my own expectations. You have forgiven me, Lord—now I must forgive myself. Amen

# The Love of Money

*For the love of money is a root of all kinds of evil, and by craving it, some have wandered away from the faith and pierced themselves with many pains.*

*1 Timothy 6:10 HCSB*

Our society is in love with money and the things that money can buy. God is not. God cares about people, not possessions, and so must we. We must, to the best of our abilities, love our neighbors as ourselves, and we must, to the best of our abilities, resist the mighty temptation to place possessions ahead of people.

Money, in and of itself, is not evil; worshipping money is. So today, as you prioritize matters of importance for you and yours, remember that God is almighty, but the dollar is not. If we worship God, we are blessed. But if we worship "the almighty dollar," we are inevitably punished because of our misplaced priorities—and our punishment inevitably comes sooner rather than later.

Have you prayed about your resources lately? Find out how God wants you to use your time and your money. No matter what it costs, forsake all that is not of God.

*Kay Arthur*

## — A Prayer for Today —

Dear Lord, I will not worship money. Give me the wisdom and the discipline to be a responsible steward of my financial resources, and let me use those resources for glory of Your kingdom. Amen

# Glorious Opportunities

*Make the most of every opportunity.*

*Colossians 4:5 NIV*

Are you excited about the opportunities of today and thrilled by the possibilities of tomorrow? Do you confidently expect God to lead you to a place of abundance, peace, and joy? And, when your days on earth are over, do you expect to receive the priceless gift of eternal life? If you trust God's promises, and if you have welcomed God's Son into your heart, then you believe that your future is intensely and eternally bright.

Today, as you prepare to meet the duties of everyday life, pause and consider God's promises. And then think for a moment about the wonderful future that awaits all believers, including you. God has promised that your future is secure. Trust that promise, and celebrate the life of abundance and eternal joy that is now yours through Christ.

Worry is the senseless process of cluttering up tomorrow's opportunities with leftover problems from today.

*Barbara Johnson*

## — A Prayer for Today —

Lord, as I take the next steps on my life's journey, let me take them with You. Whatever this day may bring, I thank You for the opportunity to live abundantly. Let me lean upon You, Father—and trust You—this day and forever. Amen

# The Power of Perseverance

*I do not consider myself to have taken hold of it. But one thing I do: forgetting what is behind and reaching forward to what is ahead, I pursue as my goal the prize promised by God's heavenly call in Christ Jesus.*

*Philippians 3:13-14 HCSB*

A well-lived life calls for preparation, determination, and, of course, lots of perseverance. As an example of perfect perseverance, we Christians need look no further than our Savior, Jesus Christ. Jesus finished what He began. Despite His suffering, despite the shame of the cross, Jesus was steadfast in His faithfulness to God. We, too, must remain faithful, especially during times of hardship. Sometimes, God may answer our prayers with silence, and when He does, we must patiently persevere.

Are you facing a tough situation? If so, remember this: whatever your problem, God can handle it. Your job is to keep persevering until He does.

## — A Prayer for Today —

Lord, when life is difficult, I am tempted to abandon hope in the future. But You are my God, and I can draw strength from You. Let me trust You, Father, in good times and in bad times. Let me persevere—even if my soul is troubled—and let me follow Your Son Jesus Christ this day and forever. Amen

# First Things First

*And I pray this: that your love will keep on growing in knowledge and every kind of discernment, so that you can determine what really matters and can be pure and blameless in the day of Christ.*

*Philippians 1:9 HCSB*

"First things first." These words are easy to speak but hard to put into practice. For busy women living in a demanding world, placing first things first can be difficult indeed. Why? Because so many people are expecting so many things from us!

If you're having trouble prioritizing your day, perhaps you've been trying to organize your life according to your own plans, not God's. A better strategy, of course, is to take your daily obligations and place them in the hands of the One who created you. To do so, you must prioritize your day according to God's commandments, and you must seek His will and His wisdom in all matters. Then, you can face the day with the assurance that the same God who created our universe out of nothingness will help you place first things first in your own life. So, turn the concerns of this day over to God—prayerfully, earnestly, and often. Then listen for His answer . . . and trust the answer He gives.

## — A Prayer for Today —

Lord, let Your priorities be my priorities. Let Your will be my will. Let Your Word be my guide, and let me grow in faith and in wisdom this day and every day. Amen

# Being Gentle with Yourself

*You're blessed when you're content with just who you are—no more, no less. That's the moment you find yourselves proud owners of everything that can't be bought.*

Matthew 5:5 MSG

Being patient with other people can be difficult. But sometimes, we find it even more difficult to be patient with ourselves. We have high expectations and lofty goals. We want to receive God's blessings now, not later. And, of course, we want our lives to unfold according to our own wishes and our own timetables—not God's. Yet throughout the Bible, we are instructed that patience is the companion of wisdom. Proverbs 16:32 teaches us that "Patience is better than strength" (NCV). God's message, then, is clear: we must be patient with all people, beginning with that particular woman who stares back at us each time we gaze into the mirror.

The Bible affirms the importance of self-acceptance by exhorting believers to love others as they love themselves (Matthew 22:37-40). Furthermore, the Bible teaches that when we genuinely open our hearts to Him, God accepts us just as we are. And, if He accepts us then who are we to believe otherwise?

## — A Prayer for Today —

Lord, I have so much to learn and so many ways to improve myself, but You love me just as I am. Thank You for Your love and for Your Son. And, help me to become the person that You want me to become. Amen

# Is the Golden Rule Your Rule?

*And let us not grow weary while doing good, for in due season we shall reap if we do not lose heart.*

*Galatians 6:9 NKJV*

Would you like to make the world a better place and feel better about yourself at the same time? If so, you can start by practicing the Golden Rule.

The Bible teaches us to treat other people with respect, kindness, courtesy, and love. When we do, we make other people happy, we make God happy, and we feel better about ourselves.

So if you're wondering how to make the world—and your world—a better place, here's a great place to start: let the Golden Rule be your rule. And if you want to know how to treat other people, ask the woman you see every time you glance in the mirror.

Sometimes one little spark of kindness is all it takes to reignite the light of hope in a heart that's blinded by pain.

*Barbara Johnson*

## — A Prayer for Today —

Dear God, help me remember to treat other people in the same way that I would want to be treated. The Golden Rule is Your rule, Father; I'll make it my rule, too. Amen

# Healthy Choices

*I shall yet praise him, who is the health of my countenance, and my God.*

*Psalm 42:11 KJV*

The journey toward improved health is not only a common-sense exercise in personal discipline; it is also a spiritual journey ordained by our Creator. God does not intend that we abuse our bodies by giving in to excessive appetites or to slothful behavior. To the contrary, God has instructed us to protect our physical bodies to the greatest extent we can. To do otherwise is to disobey Him.

God's plan for you includes provisions for your spiritual, physical, and emotional health. But, He expects you to do your fair share of the work! In a world that is chock-full of tasty temptations, you may find it all too easy to make unhealthy choices. Your challenge, of course, is to resist those unhealthy temptations by every means you can, including prayer. And rest assured: when you ask for God's help, He will give it.

Laughter is the language of the young at heart and the antidote to what ails us.

*Barbara Johnson*

## — A Prayer for Today —

Lord, when I am ill or weak or troubled, You heal me. Renew me, Father, and let me trust Your will for my life. Let me welcome Your unending love and Your healing touch, now and forever. Amen

# The Self-fulfilling Prophecy

*May He grant you according to your heart's desire, and fulfill all your purpose.*

*Psalm 20:4 NKJV*

The self-fulfilling prophecy is alive, well, and living at your house. If you trust God and have faith for the future, your optimistic beliefs will give you direction and motivation. That's one reason that you should never lose hope, but certainly not the only reason. The primary reason that you, as a believer, should never lose hope, is because of God's unfailing promises.

Make no mistake about it: thoughts are powerful things. Your thoughts have the power to lift you up or to hold you down. When you acquire the habit of hopeful thinking, you will have acquired a powerful tool for improving your life. So if you fall into the habit of negative thinking, think again. After all, God's Word teaches us that Christ can overcome every difficulty (John 16:33). And when God makes a promise, He keeps it.

## — A Prayer for Today —

Dear Lord, make me a hope-filled Christian. If I become discouraged, let me turn to You. If I grow weary, let me seek strength in You. In every aspect of my life, I will trust You, Father, today and forever. Amen

# The Voice of God

*Be silent before Me.*

*Isaiah 41:1 HCSB*

Sometimes God speaks loudly and clearly. More often, He speaks in a quiet voice—and if you are wise, you will be listening carefully when He does. To do so, you must carve out quiet moments each day to study His Word and sense His direction.

Can you quiet yourself long enough to listen to your conscience? Are you attuned to the subtle guidance of your intuition? Are you willing to pray sincerely and then to wait quietly for God's response. Hopefully so. Usually God refrains from sending His messages on stone tablets or city billboards. More often, He communicates in subtler ways. If you sincerely desire to hear His voice, you must listen carefully, and you must do so in the silent corners of your quiet, willing heart.

When we come to Jesus stripped of pretensions, with a needy spirit, ready to listen, He meets us at the point of need.

*Catherine Marshall*

## — A Prayer for Today —

Dear Lord, let me listen carefully to You. When I listen, I learn. Let me become a better listener today than I was yesterday, and let me become an even better listener tomorrow. Amen

# Your Spiritual Journey

*I pray that you, being rooted and firmly established in love, may be able to comprehend with all the saints what is the breadth and width, height and depth, and to know the Messiah's love that surpasses knowledge, so you may be filled with all the fullness of God.*

*Ephesians 3:17-19 HCSB*

The journey toward spiritual maturity lasts a lifetime. As Christians, we can and should continue to grow in the love and the knowledge of our Savior as long as we live. When we cease to grow, either emotionally or spiritually, we do ourselves a profound disservice. But, if we study God's Word, if we obey His commandments, and if we live in the center of His will, we will not be "stagnant" believers; we will, instead, be healthy, growing Christians.

Life is a series of decisions. Each day, we make countless decisions that can bring us closer to God . . . or not. When we live according to the principles contained in God's Holy Word, we embark upon a journey of spiritual maturity that results in life abundant and life eternal.

## — A Prayer for Today —

Thank You, Lord, that I am not yet what I am to become. The Holy Scripture tells me that You are at work in my life, continuing to help me grow and to mature in the faith. Show me Your wisdom, Father, and let me live according to Your Word and Your will. Amen

# Love and Commitment

*If you do nothing in a difficult time, your strength is limited.*
Proverbs 24:10 HCSB

In God's program, the words "love" and "commitment" are intertwined. According to God, genuine love is patient, unselfish, and kind, but it's goes beyond that—genuine love is committed love, and that means that genuine love is more than a feeling . . . it is a decision to make love endure, no matter what.

Unfortunately, we live in a world where marriage vows are taken far too lightly. Too many couples are far too quick to push the panic button—or the eject button.

If you're a married woman who has vowed to love your partner "till death do you part," then you must take that vow very seriously. And one more thing: you'd better put God right where He belongs: at the absolute center of your marriage.

## — A Prayer for Today —

Dear Lord, make me a person of unwavering commitment to You and to my husband. Guide me away from the temptations and distractions of this world, so that I might honor You and my husband with my thoughts, my actions, and my prayers. Amen

# The Voice Inside Your Head

*I always do my best to have a clear conscience toward God and men.*

Acts 24:16 HCSB

When you're about to do something that you know is wrong, a little voice inside your head has a way of speaking up. That voice, of course, is your conscience: an early-warning system designed to keep you out of trouble. If you listen to that voice, you'll be okay; if you ignore it, you're asking for headaches or heartbreaks, or both.

Whenever you're about to make an important decision, you should listen carefully to the quiet voice inside. Sometimes, of course, it's tempting to do otherwise. From time to time you'll be tempted to abandon your better judgement by ignoring your conscience. But remember: a conscience is a terrible thing to waste. So instead of ignoring that quiet little voice, pay careful attention to it. If you do, your conscience will lead you in the right direction—in fact, it's trying to lead you right now. So listen . . . and learn.

## — A Prayer for Today —

Dear God, You've given me a conscience that tells me right from wrong. Let me trust my conscience, and let me live according to Your teachings, not just for today, but forever. Amen

## Courtesy Matters

*Out of respect for Christ, be courteously reverent to one another.*

*Ephesians 5:21 MSG*

Did Christ instruct us in matters of etiquette and courtesy? Of course He did. Christ's instructions are clear: "In everything, therefore, treat people the same way you want them to treat you, for this is the Law and the Prophets" (Matthew 7:12 NASB). Jesus did not say, "In some things, treat people as you wish to be treated." And, He did not say, "From time to time, treat others with kindness." Christ said that we should treat others as we wish to be treated in every aspect of our daily lives. This, of course, is a tall order indeed, but as Christians, we are commanded to do our best.

Today, be a little kinder than necessary to family members, friends, and total strangers. And, as you consider all the things that Christ has done in your life, honor Him with your words and with your deeds. He expects no less, and He deserves no less.

Courtesy is contagious.

*Marie T. Freeman*

### — A Prayer for Today —

Guide me, Lord, to treat all those I meet with courtesy and respect. You have created each person in Your own image; let me honor those who cross my path with the dignity that You have bestowed upon them. We are all Your children, Lord; let me show kindness to all. Amen

# Beyond the Difficulties

*When you are in distress and all these things have happened to you, you will return to the Lord your God in later days and obey Him. He will not leave you, destroy you, or forget the covenant with your fathers that He swore to them by oath, because the Lord your God is a compassionate God.*

*Deuteronomy 4:30-31 HCSB*

Sometimes the traffic jams, and sometimes the dog gobbles the homework. But, when we find ourselves overtaken by the minor frustrations of life, we must catch ourselves, take a deep breath, and lift our thoughts upward. Although we are here on earth struggling to rise above the distractions of the day, we need never struggle alone. God is here—eternally and faithfully, with infinite patience and love—and, if we reach out to Him, He will restore perspective and peace to our souls.

If you find yourself enduring difficult circumstances, remember that God remains in His heaven. If you become discouraged with the direction of your day or your life, lift your thoughts and prayers to Him. He will guide you through your difficulties and beyond them.

## — A Prayer for Today —

Lord, on difficult days, I will turn to You for my strength. In times of sadness, I will put my trust in You. In times of frustration, I will find peace in You. And every day, whether I am happy or sad, I will praise You for Your glorious works and for the gift of Your Son. Amen

# Shout for Joy

*Shout triumphantly to the Lord, all the earth. Serve the Lord with gladness; come before Him with joyful songs.*
*Psalm 100:1-2 HCSB*

The 100th Psalm reminds us that the entire earth should "Shout for joy to the Lord." As God's children, we are blessed beyond measure, but sometimes, as busy women living in a demanding world, we are slow to count our gifts and even slower to give thanks to the Giver.

Our blessings include life and health, family and friends, freedom and possessions—for starters. And, the gifts we receive from God are multiplied when we share them. May we always give thanks to God for His blessings, and may we always demonstrate our gratitude by sharing our gifts with others. The 118th Psalm reminds us that, "This is the day which the LORD has made; let us rejoice and be glad in it" (v. 24, NASB). May we celebrate this day and the One who created it.

## — A Prayer for Today —

Dear Lord, today, I will join in the celebration of life. I will be a joyful Christian, and I will share my joy with all those who cross my path. You have given me countless blessings, Lord, and today I will thank You by celebrating my life, my faith, and my Savior. Amen

# Turning Away from Anger

*My dear brothers and sisters, always be willing to listen and slow to speak. Do not become angry easily, because anger will not help you live the right kind of life God wants.*

*James 1:19-20 NCV*

Perhaps God gave each of us one mouth and two ears in order that we might listen twice as much as we speak. Unfortunately, many of us do otherwise, especially when we become angry.

Anger is a natural human emotion that is sometimes necessary and appropriate. Even Jesus Himself became angered when He confronted the moneychangers in the temple. But, more often than not, our frustrations are of the more mundane variety. When you are tempted to lose your temper over the minor inconveniences of life, don't. Turn away from anger, and turn instead to God.

When the winds are cold, and the days are long, / And thy soul from care would hide, / Fly back, fly back, to thy Father then, / And beneath His wings abide.

*Fanny Crosby*

## — A Prayer for Today —

Dear Lord, when I am angry, I cannot feel the peace that You intend for my life. Keep me mindful that forgiveness is Your commandment and Your will for my life. Let me turn away from anger and instead claim the spiritual abundance that You offer through the priceless gift of Your Son Jesus. Amen

# Fearing God

*The fear of the Lord is the beginning of knowledge.*
*Proverbs 1:7 HCSB*

Are you a woman who possesses a healthy, fearful respect for God's power? Hopefully so. After all, God's Word teaches that the fear of the Lord is the beginning of knowledge (Proverbs 1:7).

When we fear the Creator—and when we honor Him by obeying His commandments—we receive God's approval and His blessings. But, when we ignore Him or disobey His commandments, we invite disastrous consequences. God's hand shapes the universe, and it shapes our lives. As believers, we must cultivate a sincere respect for God's awesome power. The fear of the Lord is, indeed, the beginning of knowledge. So today, as you face the realities of everyday life, remember this: until you acquire a healthy, respectful fear of God's power, your education is incomplete, and so is your faith.

Spiritual worship comes from our very core and is fueled by an awesome reverence and desire for God.

*Beth Moore*

## — A Prayer for Today —

Lord, You love me and protect me. I praise You, Father, for Your grace, and I respect You for Your infinite power. Let my greatest fear in life be the fear of displeasing You. Amen

# Nourished by the Word

*You will be a good servant of Christ Jesus, nourished by the words of the faith and of the good teaching that you have followed.*

1 Timothy 4:6 HCSB

Do you read your Bible a lot . . . or not? The answer to this simple question will determine, to a surprising extent, the quality of your life and the direction of your faith.

As you establish priorities for life, you must decide whether God's Word will be a bright spotlight that guides your path every day or a tiny nightlight that occasionally flickers in the dark. The decision to study the Bible—or not—is yours and yours alone. But make no mistake: how you choose to use your Bible will have a profound impact on you and your loved ones.

The Bible is the ultimate guide for life; make it your guidebook as well. When you do, you can be comforted in the knowledge that your steps are guided by a Source of wisdom and truth that never fails.

## — A Prayer for Today —

Lord, You've given me instructions for life here on earth and for life eternal. I will use the Bible as my guide. I will study it and meditate upon it as I trust You, Lord, to speak to me through Your Holy Word. Amen

# Too Busy

*Careful planning puts you ahead in the long run; hurry and scurry puts you further behind.*

Proverbs 21:5 MSG

Are you one of those women who is simply too busy for your own good? Has the hectic pace of life robbed you of the peace that might otherwise be yours through Jesus Christ? If so, you're doing a disservice to yourself and your family.

Through His Son, God offers you a peace that passes our understanding, but He won't force His peace upon you; in order to experience it, you must slow down long enough to sense His presence and His love.

Today, as a gift to yourself, to your family, and to the world, be still and claim the inner peace that is your spiritual birthright—the peace of Jesus Christ. It is offered freely; it has been paid for in full; it is yours for the asking. So ask. And then share.

It's ironic that one of the best remedies for impending burnout is to give yourself away—to pick out one time and place each week where you can stretch out your hands for the pure joy of doing it.

*Liz Curtis Higgs*

## — A Prayer for Today —

Dear Lord, when the quickening pace of life leaves me with little time for worship or for praise, help me to reorder my priorities, and let me turn to Jesus for the peace that only He can give. Amen

# The Gift of Cheerfulness

*Worry is a heavy load, but a kind word cheers you up.*
*Proverbs 12:25 NCV*

Cheerfulness is a gift that we give to others and to ourselves. And, as believers who have been saved by a risen Christ, why shouldn't we be cheerful? The answer, of course, is that we have every reason to honor our Savior with joy in our hearts, smiles on our faces, and words of celebration on our lips.

Christ promises us lives of abundance and joy if we accept His love and His grace. Yet sometimes, even the most righteous among us are beset by fits of ill temper and frustration. During these moments, we may not feel like turning our thoughts and prayers to Christ, but that's precisely what we should do. When we do so, we simply can't stay grumpy for long.

We may run, walk, stumble, drive, or fly, but let us never lose sight of the reason for the journey, or miss a chance to see a rainbow on the way.

*Gloria Gaither*

## — A Prayer for Today —

Dear Lord, You have given me so many reasons to celebrate. Today, let me choose an attitude of cheerfulness. Let me be a joyful Christian, Lord, quick to smile and slow to anger. And, let me share Your goodness with all whom I meet so that Your love might shine in me and through me. Amen

# A Growing Relationship
## with God

*But grow in the grace and knowledge of our Lord and Savior Jesus Christ. To Him be the glory both now and to the day of eternity.*

*2 Peter 3:18 HCSB*

Your relationship with God is ongoing; it unfolds day by day, and it offers countless opportunities to grow closer to Him . . . or not. As each new day unfolds, you are confronted with a wide range of decisions: how you will behave, where you will direct your thoughts, with whom you will associate, and what you will choose to worship. These choices, along with many others like them, are yours and yours alone. How you choose determines how your relationship with God will unfold.

Are you continuing to grow in your love and knowledge of the Lord, or are you "satisfied" with the current state of your spiritual health? Hopefully, you're determined to make yourself a growing Christian. Your Savior deserves no less, and neither, by the way, do you.

### — A Prayer for Today —

Dear Lord, thank You for the opportunity to walk with Your Son. And, thank You for the opportunity to grow closer to You each day. I thank You for the person I am . . . and for the person I can become. Amen

# His Comforting Hand

*But God, who comforts the humble, comforted us . . . .*
*2 Corinthians 7:6 HCSB*

If you have been touched by the transforming hand of Jesus, then you have every reason to live courageously. Still, even if you are a dedicated Christian, you may find yourself discouraged by the inevitable disappointments and tragedies that occur in the lives of believers and non-believers alike.

The next time you find your courage tested to the limit, lean upon God's promises. Trust His Son. Remember that God is always near and that He is your protector and your deliverer. When you are worried, anxious, or afraid, call upon Him and accept the touch of His comforting hand. Remember that God rules both mountaintops and valleys—with limitless wisdom and love—now and forever.

Put your hand into the hand of God. He gives the calmness and serenity of heart and soul.

*Mrs. Charles E. Cowman*

## — A Prayer for Today —

Dear Lord, thank You for Your comfort. You lift me up when I am disappointed. You protect me in times of trouble. Today, I will be mindful of Your love, Your wisdom, and Your grace. Amen

# The Need to Be Disciplined

*Do you not know that the runners in a stadium all race, but only one receives the prize? Run in such a way that you may win. Now everyone who competes exercises self-control in everything. However, they do it to receive a perishable crown, but we an imperishable one.*

1 Corinthians 9:24-25 HCSB

God is clear: we must exercise self-discipline in all matters. Self-discipline is not simply a proven way to get ahead; it's also an integral part of God's plan for our lives. If we genuinely seek to be faithful stewards of our time, our talents, and our resources, we must adopt a disciplined approach to life. Otherwise, our talents are wasted and our resources are squandered.

Our greatest rewards result from hard work and perseverance. May we, as disciplined believers, be willing to work for the rewards we so earnestly desire.

Personal humility is a spiritual discipline and the hallmark of the service of Jesus.

*Franklin Graham*

— A Prayer for Today —

Heavenly Father, make me a woman who understands the need to live a disciplined life. Let me teach others by the faithfulness of my conduct, and let me follow Your will and Your Word, today and every day. Amen

# Strength for Today

*I can do all things through Christ which strengtheneth me.*
*Philippians 4:13 KJV*

Have you made God the cornerstone of your life, or is He relegated to a few hours on Sunday morning? Have you genuinely allowed God to reign over every corner of your heart, or have you attempted to place Him in a spiritual compartment? Your answers will determine the direction of your day and your life.

God loves you. In times of trouble, He will comfort you; in times of sorrow, He will dry your tears. When you are weak or sorrowful, God is as near as your next breath. He stands at the door of your heart and waits. Welcome Him in and allow Him to rule. And then, accept the peace and the strength and the protection and the abundance that only God can give.

In my weakness, I have learned, like Moses, to lean hard on God. The weaker I am, the harder I lean on Him. The harder I lean, the stronger I discover Him to be. The stronger I discover God to be, the more resolute I am in this job He's given me to do.

*Joni Eareckson Tada*

## — A Prayer for Today —

Lord, sometimes life is difficult. Sometimes, I am worried, weary, or discouraged. Life can be a struggle, but when I lift my eyes to You, Father, You strengthen me. Today, I will turn to You, Lord, for strength, for hope, and for salvation. Amen

# Lighting the Path

*Your word is a lamp to my feet and a light to my path.*
*Psalm 119:105 NKJV*

Are you a woman who trusts God's Word without reservation? Hopefully so, because the Bible is unlike any other book—it is a guidebook for life here on earth and for life eternal. The Psalmist describes God's Word as "a light to my path." Is the Bible your lamp? If not, you are depriving yourself of a priceless gift from the Creator.

Vance Havner observed, "It takes calm, thoughtful, prayerful meditation on the Word to extract its deepest nourishment." How true. God's Word can be a light to guide your steps. Claim it as your light today, tomorrow, and every day of your life—and then walk confidently in the footsteps of God's only begotten Son.

Light is stronger than darkness—darkness cannot "comprehend" or "overcome" it.

*Anne Graham Lotz*

## — A Prayer for Today —

Heavenly Father, Your Word is a light unto the world; I will study it and trust it and share it. In all that I do, help me be a worthy witness for You as I share the Good News of Your perfect Son and Your perfect Word. Amen

# Big Dreams

*With God's power working in us, God can do much, much more than anything we can ask or imagine.*

*Ephesians 3:20 NCV*

Are you willing to entertain the possibility that God has big plans in store for you? Hopefully so. Yet sometimes, especially if you've recently experienced a life-altering disappointment, you may find it difficult to envision a brighter future for yourself and your family. If so, it's time to reconsider your own capabilities.

Your Heavenly Father created you with unique gifts and untapped talents; your job is to tap them. When you do, you'll begin to feel an increasing sense of confidence in yourself and in your future. So even if you're experiencing difficult days, don't abandon your dreams. Instead, trust that God is preparing you for greater things.

The future lies all before us. Shall it only be a slight advance upon what we usually do? Ought it not to be a bound, a leap forward to altitudes of endeavor and success undreamed of before?

*Annie Armstrong*

## — A Prayer for Today —

Dear Lord, give me the courage to dream and the faithfulness to trust in Your perfect plan. When I am worried or weary, give me strength for today and hope for tomorrow. Keep me mindful of Your healing power, Your infinite love, and Your eternal salvation. Amen

# Enthusiasm for Christ

*Therefore, get your minds ready for action, being self-disciplined, and set your hope completely on the grace to be brought to you at the revelation of Jesus Christ. As obedient children, do not be conformed to the desires of your former ignorance but, as the One who called you is holy, you also are to be holy in all your conduct.*

1 Peter 1:13-15 HCSB

John Wesley advised, "Catch on fire with enthusiasm and people will come for miles to watch you burn." His words still ring true. When we fan the flames of enthusiasm for Christ, our faith serves as a beacon to others.

Our world desperately needs faithful women who share the Good News of Jesus with joyful exuberance. Be such a woman. The world desperately needs your enthusiasm—and your testimony—now!

We must go out and live among them, manifesting the gentle, loving spirit of our Lord. We need to make friends before we can hope to make converts.

*Lottie Moon*

## — A Prayer for Today —

Dear Lord, let me be an enthusiastic participant in life. And let my enthusiasm bring honor and glory to You. Amen

# A Woman of Prayer

*Rejoice always, pray without ceasing, in everything give thanks; for this is the will of God in Christ Jesus for you.*
*1 Thessalonians 5:16-18 NKJV*

On his second missionary journey, Paul started a small church in Thessalonica. A short time later, he penned a letter that was intended to encourage the new believers at that church. Today, almost 2,000 years later, 1 Thessalonians remains a powerful, practical guide for Christian living.

In his letter, Paul advised members of the new church to "pray without ceasing." His advice applies to Christians of every generation. When we consult God on an hourly basis, we avail ourselves of His wisdom, His strength, and His love. As Corrie ten Boom observed, "Any concern that is too small to be turned into a prayer is too small to be made into a burden."

Today, make yourself a woman of prayer. Instead of turning things over in your mind, turn them over to God in prayer. Instead of worrying about your next decision, ask God to lead the way. Don't limit your prayers to meals or bedtime. Become a woman of constant prayer. God is listening, and He wants to hear from you. Now.

## — A Prayer for Today —

Dear Lord, I will be a woman of prayer. I will pray about matters great and small. I will bring my concerns to You, Father. I will listen for Your voice, and I will follow in the footsteps of Your Son. Amen

# Quality Time, Quantity Time

*Teach us to number our days carefully so that we may develop wisdom in our hearts.*

*Psalm 90:12 HCSB*

Make no mistake: caring for your family requires time—lots of time. You've probably heard about "quality time" and "quantity time." Your family needs both. So, as a responsible Christian, you should willingly invest large quantities of your time and energy in the care and nurturing of your clan.

While caring for your family, you should do your best to ensure that God remains squarely at the center of your household. When you do, God will bless you and yours in ways that you could have scarcely imagined.

There is so much compassion and understanding that is gained when we've experienced God's grace firsthand within our own families.

*Lisa Whelchel*

## — A Prayer for Today —

Father, help me to treasure those moments that I spend with my family—and let me demonstrate, through my words and my actions, how much love I feel in my heart for them. Amen

# Your Body, God's Temple

*Don't you know that you are God's sanctuary and that the Spirit of God lives in you?*

*1 Corinthians 3:16 HCSB*

Are you shaping up or spreading out? Do you eat sensibly and exercise regularly, or do you spend most of your time on the couch with a Twinkie in one hand and a clicker in the other? Are you choosing to treat your body like a temple or a trash heap? How you answer these questions will help determine how long you live and how well you live.

Physical fitness is a choice, a choice that requires discipline—it's as simple as that. So, do yourself this favor: treat your body like a one-of-a-kind gift from God . . . because that's precisely what your body is.

It is important to set goals because if you do not have a plan, a goal, a direction, a purpose, and a focus, you are not going to accomplish anything for the glory of God.

*Bill Bright*

## — A Prayer for Today —

Dear Lord, my body is Your temple—I will treat it with care. Amen

# Finding Fulfillment

*For You, O God, have tested us; You have refined us as silver is refined . . . we went through fire and through water; but You brought us out to rich fulfillment.*

*Psalm 66:10–12 NKJV*

Everywhere we turn, or so it seems, the world promises fulfillment, contentment, and happiness. But the contentment that the world offers is fleeting and incomplete. Thankfully, the fulfillment that God offers is all encompassing and everlasting.

Sometimes, amid the inevitable hustle and bustle of life-here-on-earth, we can forfeit—albeit temporarily—the joy of Christ as we wrestle with the challenges of daily living. Yet God's Word is clear: fulfillment through Christ is available to all who seek it and claim it. Count yourself among that number. Seek first a personal, transforming relationship with Jesus, and then claim the joy, the fulfillment, and the spiritual abundance that the Shepherd offers His sheep.

## — A Prayer for Today —

Dear Lord, when I turn my thoughts and prayers to You, I feel peace and fulfillment. But sometimes, when I am distracted by the busyness of the day, fulfillment seems far away. Today, let me trust Your will, let me follow Your commands, and let me accept Your peace. Amen

# His Generosity . . .
# and Yours

*But God proves His own love for us in that while we were still sinners Christ died for us!*

*Romans 5:8 HCSB*

Christ showed His love for us by willingly sacrificing His own life so that we might have eternal life. We, as Christ's followers, are challenged to share His love. And, when we walk each day with Jesus—and obey the commandments found in God's Holy Word—we are worthy ambassadors for Him.

Just as Christ has been—and will always be—the ultimate friend to His flock, so should we be Christlike in our love and generosity to those in need. When we share the love of Christ, we share a priceless gift. As His servants, we must do no less.

The measure of a life, after all, is not its duration but its donation.

*Corrie ten Boom*

## — A Prayer for Today —

Father, Your gifts are priceless. You gave Your Son Jesus to save us, and Your motivation was love. I pray that the gifts I give to others will come from an overflow of my heart, and that they will echo the great love You have for all of Your children. Amen

# Promises You Can Count On

*God blesses the people who patiently endure testing. Afterward they will receive the crown of life that God has promised to those who love him.*

*James 1:12 NLT*

Throughout the seasons of life, we must all endure life-altering personal losses that leave us breathless. When we do, we may be overwhelmed by fear, by doubt, or by both. Thankfully, God has promised that He will never desert us. And God keeps His promises.

Life is often challenging, but as Christians, we must trust the promises of our Heavenly Father. God loves us, and He will protect us. In times of hardship, He will comfort us; in times of sorrow, He will dry our tears. When we are troubled or weak or sorrowful, God is with us. His love endures, not only for today, but also for all of eternity.

## — A Prayer for Today —

Dear Lord, when I face the inevitable disappointments of life, give me perspective and faith. When I am discouraged, give me the strength to trust Your promises and follow Your will. Then, when I have done my best, Father, let me live with the assurance that You are firmly in control, and that Your love endures forever. Amen

# The Chains of Perfectionism

*Those who wait for perfect weather will never plant seeds;*
*those who look at every cloud will never harvest crops.*

*Ecclesiastes 11:4 NCV*

The media delivers an endless stream of messages that tell you how to look, how to behave, and how to dress. The media's expectations are impossible to meet—God's are not. God doesn't expect perfection . . . and neither should you.

If you find yourself bound up by the chains of perfectionism, it's time to ask yourself who you're trying to impress, and why. If you're trying to impress other people, it's time to reconsider your priorities. Your first responsibility is to the Heavenly Father who created you and to His Son who saved you. Then, you bear a powerful responsibility to your family. But, when it comes to meeting society's unrealistic expectations, forget it! After all, pleasing God is simply a matter of obeying His commandments and accepting His Son. But as for pleasing everybody else? That's impossible!

## — A Prayer for Today —

Lord, this world has so many expectations of me, but today I will not seek to meet the world's expectations; I will do my best to meet Your expectations. I will make You my ultimate priority, Lord, by serving You, by praising You, by loving You, and by obeying You. Amen

# Solving Problems

*People who do what is right may have many problems, but the Lord will solve them all.*

*Psalm 34:19 NCV*

Life is an exercise in problem-solving. The question is not whether we will encounter problems; the real question is how we will choose to address them. When it comes to solving the problems of everyday living, we often know precisely what needs to be done, but we may be slow in doing it—especially if what needs to be done is difficult or uncomfortable for us. So we put off till tomorrow what should be done today.

The words of Psalm 34 remind us that the Lord solves problems for "people who do what is right." And usually, doing "what is right" means doing the uncomfortable work of confronting our problems sooner rather than later. So with no further ado, let the problem-solving begin . . . now.

What a comfort to know that God is present there in your life, available to meet every situation with you, that you are never left to face any problem alone.

*Vonette Bright*

## — A Prayer for Today —

Lord, sometimes my problems are simply too big for me, but they are never too big for You. Let me turn my troubles over to You, Lord, and let me trust in You today and for all eternity. Amen

# The Simple Life

*Whoever becomes simple and elemental again, like this child, will rank high in God's kingdom.*

*Matthew 18:4 MSG*

You live in a world where simplicity is in short supply. Think for a moment about the complexity of your every-day life and compare it to the lives of your ancestors. Certainly, you are the beneficiary of many technological innovations, but those innovations have a price: in all likelihood, your world is highly complex.

Unless you take firm control of your time and your life, you may be overwhelmed by an ever-increasing tidal wave of complexity that threatens your happiness. But your Heavenly Father understands the joy of living simply, and so should you. So do yourself a favor: keep your life as simple as possible. Simplicity is, indeed, genius. By simplifying your life, you are destined to improve it.

Nobody is going to simplify your life for you. You've got to simplify things for yourself.

*Marie T. Freeman*

## — A Prayer for Today —

Lord, help me keep it simple. When I complicate my life, give me the wisdom to simplify. The world values complexity, Father, but You do not. Today, I will strive to keep my thoughts focused intently on Your Word, on Your love, and on Your Son. Amen

# A Helping Hand

*The greatest among you will be your servant. Whoever exalts himself will be humbled, and whoever humbles himself will be exalted.*

Matthew 23:11-12 HCSB

Jesus has much to teach us about generosity. He teaches that the most esteemed men and women are not the self-congratulatory leaders of society but are, instead, the humblest of servants. If you were being graded on generosity, how would you score? Would you earn "A"s in philanthropy and humility? Hopefully so. But if your grades could stand a little improvement, this is the perfect day to begin.

Today, you may feel the urge to hoard your blessings. Don't do it. Instead, give generously to your neighbors, and do so without fanfare. Find a need and fill it . . . humbly. Lend a helping hand and share a word of kindness . . . anonymously. This is God's way.

## — A Prayer for Today —

Dear Lord, make me a sacrificial giver. Let me give of my possessions, my talents, my time, and my testimony. Let me give cheerfully, faithfully, and prayerfully. And make me a humble steward of my talents, Lord, so that the praise might be Yours, not mine. Amen

# with God's Strength

*Come to Me, all you who are weary and burdened, and I will give you rest. Take My yoke upon you and learn from Me, because I am gentle and humble in heart, and you will find rest for your souls. For My yoke is easy and My burden is light.*

Matthew 11:28–30 HCSB

Are you tired? Ask God for strength. Are you discouraged? Believe in His promises. Are you frustrated or fearful? Pray as if everything depended upon God, and work as if everything depended upon you. With God's help, you will find the strength to be the kind of woman who makes your Heavenly Father beam with pride.

Perhaps you are in a hurry for God to reveal His plans for your life. If so, be forewarned: God operates on His own timetable, not yours. Sometimes, God may answer your prayers with silence, and when He does, you must patiently persevere. In times of trouble, you must remain steadfast and trust in the merciful goodness of your Heavenly Father. Whatever your problem, He can handle it. Your job is to keep persevering until He does.

## — A Prayer for Today —

When I'm discouraged—or worse—let me turn to You for strength, for courage, and for love. Amen

# Your Way or God's Way

*A man's heart plans his way, but the Lord determines his steps.*

*Proverbs 16:9 HCSB*

The popular song "My Way" is a perfectly good tune, but it's not a perfect guide for life-here-on-earth. If you're looking for life's perfect prescription, you'd better forget about doing things your way and start doing things God's way. The most important decision of your life is, of course, your commitment to accept Jesus Christ as your personal Lord and Savior. And once your eternal destiny is secured, you will undoubtedly ask yourself the question "What now, Lord?" If you earnestly seek God's will for your life, you will find it . . . in time.

Sometimes, God's plans are crystal clear; sometimes they are not. So be patient, keep searching, and keep praying. If you do, then in time, God will answer your prayers and make His plans known. You'll discover those plans by doing things His way . . . and you'll be eternally grateful that you did.

## — A Prayer for Today —

Lord, today, I will seek Your will for my life. You have a plan for me, Father. Let me discover it and live it, knowing that when I trust in You, I am eternally blessed. Amen

# Trusting Him Completely

*I will be your God throughout your lifetime—until your hair is white with age. I made you, and I will care for you. I will carry you along and save you.*

*Isaiah 46:4 NLT*

God has promised to lift you up and guide your steps if you let Him do so. God has promised that when you entrust your life to Him completely and without reservation, He will give you the strength to meet any challenge, the courage to face any trial, and the wisdom to live in His righteousness.

God's hand uplifts those who turn their hearts and prayers to Him. Will you count yourself among that number? Will you accept God's peace and wear God's armor against the temptations and distractions of our dangerous world? If you do, you can live courageously and optimistically, knowing that you have been forever touched by the loving, unfailing, uplifting hand of God.

Snuggle in God's arms. When you are hurting, when you feel lonely or left out, let Him cradle you, comfort you, reassure you of His all-sufficient power and love.

*Kay Arthur*

## — A Prayer for Today —

Dear Lord, as I face the challenges of this day, You protect me. I thank You, Father, for Your love and for Your strength. I will lean upon You today and forever. Amen

# A Fearless Woman

*Teach me Your way, O Lord; I will walk in Your truth.*
*Psalm 86:11 NKJV*

The Book of Judges (chapters 4 and 5) tells the story of Deborah, the fearless woman who helped lead the army of Israel to victory over the Canaanites. Deborah was a judge and a prophetess, a woman called by God to lead her people. And when she answered God's call, she was rewarded with one of the great victories of Old Testament times. Like Deborah, all of us are called to serve our Creator. And, like Deborah, we may sometimes find ourselves facing trials that can bring trembling to the very depths of our souls. As believers, we must seek God's will and follow it.

As this day unfolds, seek God's will for your own life and obey His Word. He will give you the strength to meet any challenge, the courage to face any trial, and the wisdom to live in His righteousness and in His peace.

We get into trouble when we think we know what to do and we stop asking God if we're doing it.

*Stormie Omartian*

## — A Prayer for Today —

Lord, let Your will be my will. When I am confused, give me maturity and wisdom. When I am worried, give me courage and strength. Let me be Your faithful servant, Father, always seeking Your guidance and Your will for my life. Amen

# Discovering Hope

*These things I have spoken to you, that in Me you may have peace. In the world you will have tribulation; but be of good cheer, I have overcome the world.*

*John 16:33 NKJV*

There are few sadder sights on earth than the sight of a person who has lost all hope. In difficult times, hope can be elusive, but Christians need never lose it. After all, God is good; His love endures; He has promised His children the gift of eternal life.

If you find yourself falling into the spiritual traps of worry and discouragement, consider the words of Jesus. It was Christ who promised, "In the world you will have tribulation; but be of good cheer, I have overcome the world." This world is indeed a place of trials and tribulations, but as believers, we are secure. God has promised us peace, joy, and eternal life. And, of course, God always keeps His promises.

God's Word never said we were not to grieve our losses. It says we are not to grieve as those who have no hope (1 Thessalonians 4:13). Big Difference.

*Beth Moore*

## — A Prayer for Today —

Dear Lord, let my hopes always reside in You. If I become discouraged, let me turn to You. If I grow tired, let me find strength in You. You are my Creator, and I will place my faith, my trust, and my hopes in You. Amen

# When Anger Is Appropriate

*The face of the Lord is against those who do evil.*
*Psalm 34:16 NKJV*

Sometimes, anger can be a good thing. In the 22nd chapter of Matthew, we see how Christ responded when He confronted the evildoings of those who invaded His Father's house of worship: "And Jesus entered the temple and drove out all those who were buying and selling in the temple, and overturned the tables of the moneychangers and the seats of those who were selling doves" (v. 12 NASB). Thus, Jesus proved that righteous indignation is an appropriate response to evil.

When you come face-to-face with the devil's handiwork, don't be satisfied to remain safely on the sidelines. Instead, follow in the footsteps of Jesus. Jesus never compromised with evil, and neither should you.

When something robs you of your peace of mind, ask yourself if it is worth the energy you are expending on it. If not, then put it out of your mind in an act of discipline. Every time the thought of "it" returns, refuse it.

*Kay Arthur*

## — A Prayer for Today —

Lord, give me the wisdom to know when anger is appropriate. Give me the courage to fight injustice, the wisdom to avoid temptation, and the perseverance to follow in the footsteps of Your Son every day of my life. Amen

# Asking and Receiving

*Ask, and it will be given to you; seek, and you will find; knock, and it will be opened to you. For everyone who asks receives, and he who seeks finds, and to him who knocks it will be opened.*

*Matthew 7:7-8 NKJV*

Are you a woman who asks God for guidance and strength? If so, then you're continually inviting your Creator to reveal Himself in a variety of ways. As a follower of Christ, you must do no less.

Jesus made it clear to His disciples: they should petition God to meet their needs. So should we. Genuine, heartfelt prayer produces powerful changes in us and in our world. When we lift our hearts to God, we open ourselves to a never-ending source of divine wisdom and infinite love.

Whatever your need, no matter how great or small, pray about it and never lose hope. God is not just near; He is here, and He's perfectly capable of answering your prayers. Now, it's up to you to ask.

## — A Prayer for Today —

Lord, today I will ask You for the things I need. In every situation, I will come to You in prayer. You know what I want, Lord, and more importantly, You know what I need. Yet even though I know that You know, I still won't be too timid—or too busy—to ask. Amen

# Righteousness Now!

*This is how we are sure that we have come to know Him:*
*by keeping His commands.*

*1 John 2:3 HCSB*

When we seek righteousness in our own lives—and when we seek the companionship of those who do likewise—we reap the spiritual rewards that God intends for us to enjoy. When we behave ourselves as godly women, we honor God. When we live righteously and according to God's commandments, He blesses us in ways that we cannot fully understand.

Today, as you fulfill your responsibilities, hold fast that which is good, and associate yourself with believers who behave themselves in like fashion. When you do, your good works will serve as a powerful example for others and as a worthy offering to your Creator.

## — A Prayer for Today —

Dear Lord, this world has countless temptations, distractions, interruptions, and frustrations. When I allow my focus to drift away from You and Your Word, I suffer. But, when I turn my thoughts and my prayers to You, Heavenly Father, You guide my path. Let me discover the right thing to do—and let me do it—this day and every day that I live. Amen

# Acknowledging Your Blessings

*The Lord bless you and keep you; The Lord make His face shine upon you, And be gracious to you.*

*Numbers 6:24-25 NKJV*

When the demands of life leave us rushing from place to place with scarcely a moment to spare, we may fail to pause and thank our Creator for His gifts. But, whenever we neglect to give proper thanks to the Father, we suffer because of our misplaced priorities.

Today, begin making a list of your blessings. You most certainly will not be able to make a complete list, but take a few moments and jot down as many blessings as you can. Then, give thanks to the Giver of all good things: God. His love for you is eternal, as are His gifts. And it's never too soon—or too late—to offer Him thanks.

Get rich quick! Count your blessings!

*Anonymous*

— A Prayer for Today —

Lord, I have more blessings than I can count, and I praise You for Your gifts. Let me use my talents and my possessions for Your glory . . . and for Your Son. Amen

# Cheerful Christianity

*Be cheerful. Keep things in good repair. Keep your spirits up. Think in harmony. Be agreeable. Do all that, and the God of love and peace will be with you for sure.*

2 Corinthians 13:11 MSG

Mrs. Charles E. Cowman, the author of the classic devotional text, *Streams in the Desert*, wrote, "Two wings are necessary to lift our souls toward God: prayer and praise. Prayer asks. Praise accepts the answer." That's why we should find the time to lift our concerns to God in prayer, and to praise Him for all that He has done. John Wesley correctly observed, "Sour godliness is the devil's religion." His words remind us that pessimism and doubt are some of the most important tools that Satan uses to achieve his objectives. Our challenge, of course, is to ensure that Satan cannot use these tools on us.

Are you a cheerful Christian? You should be! And what is the best way to attain the joy that is rightfully yours? By giving Christ what is rightfully His: your heart, your soul, and your life.

## — A Prayer for Today —

Dear Lord, Your Word reminds me that this is the day that You have created; let me rejoice in it. Today, let me choose an attitude of cheerfulness and celebration. Let me be a joyful Christian, Lord, quick to smile and slow to anger. And, let me share Your goodness with all whom I meet so that Your love might shine in me and through me. Amen

# A Series of Choices

*But seek first the kingdom of God and His righteousness, and all these things will be provided for you.*

*Matthew 6:33 HCSB*

Your life is a series of choices. From the instant you wake up in the morning until the moment you nod off to sleep at night, you make countless decisions—decisions about the things you do, decisions about the words you speak, and decisions about the way that you choose to direct your thoughts.

As a woman who has been transformed by the love of Jesus, you have every reason to make wise choices. But sometimes, when the daily grind threatens to grind you up and spit you out, you may make choices that are displeasing to God. When you do, you'll pay a price because you'll forfeit the happiness and the peace that might otherwise have been yours.

So, as you pause to consider the kind of Christian you are—and the kind of Christian you want to become—ask yourself whether you're sitting on the fence or standing in the light. The choice is yours . . . and so are the consequences.

— A Prayer for Today —

Heavenly Father, I have many choices to make. Help me choose wisely as I follow in the footsteps of Your only begotten Son. Amen

# Compassionate Servants

*Finally, all of you be of one mind, having compassion for one another; love as brothers, be tenderhearted, be courteous.*
*1 Peter 3:8 NKJV*

God's Word commands us to be compassionate, generous servants to those who need our support. As believers, we have been richly blessed by our Creator. We, in turn, are called to share our gifts, our possessions, our testimonies, and our talents.

Concentration camp survivor Corrie ten Boom correctly observed, "The measure of a life is not its duration but its donation." These words remind us that the quality of our lives is determined not by what are able to take from others, but instead by what we are able to share with others.

The thread of compassion is woven into the very fabric of Christ's teachings. If we are to be disciples of Christ, we, too, must be zealous in caring for others. Our Savior expects no less from us. And He deserves no less.

Before you can dry another's tears, you too must weep.
*Barbara Johnson*

## — A Prayer for Today —

Lord, make me a loving, encouraging, compassionate woman. And, let my love for Christ be reflected through the kindness that I show to my family, to my friends, and to all who need the healing touch of the Master's hand. Amen

# Confident Christianity

*You are my hope; O Lord GOD, You are my confidence.*
*Psalm 71:5 NASB*

We Christians have many reasons to be confident. God is in His heaven; Christ has risen, and we are the sheep of His flock. Yet sometimes, even the most devout Christians can become discouraged. Discouragement, however, is not God's way; He is a God of possibility not negativity.

Are you a confident Christian? You should be. God's grace is eternal and His promises are unambiguous. So count your blessings, not your hardships. And live courageously. God is the Giver of all things good, and He watches over you today and forever.

The Creator has made us each one of a kind. There is nobody else exactly like us, and there never will be. Each of us is his special creation and is alive for a distinctive purpose.

*Luci Swindoll*

## — A Prayer for Today —

Lord, when I place my confidence in the things of this earth, I will be disappointed. But, when I put my confidence in You, I am secure. In every aspect of my life, Father, let me place my hope and my trust in Your infinite wisdom and Your boundless grace. Amen

# Neighbors in Need

*Each one of us needs to look after the good of the people around us, asking ourselves, "How can I help?" That's exactly what Jesus did.*

Romans 15:2-3 MSG

Neighbors. We know that we are instructed to love them, and yet there's so little time . . . and we're so busy. No matter. As Christians, we are commanded by our Lord and Savior Jesus Christ to love our neighbors just as we love ourselves. Period.

This very day, you will encounter someone who needs a word of encouragement or a pat on the back or a helping hand or a heartfelt prayer. And, if you don't reach out to your friend, who will? If you don't take the time to understand the needs of your neighbors, who will? If you don't love your brothers and sisters, who will? So, today, look for a neighbor in need . . . and then do something to help. Father's orders.

No matter how crazy or nutty your life has seemed, God can make something strong and good out of it. He can help you grow wide branches for others to use as shelter.

*Barbara Johnson*

— A Prayer for Today —

Heavenly Father, help me be a Good Samaritan to the people You place along my path, today and every day. Amen

# A Life of Integrity

*The godly walk with integrity; blessed are their children after them.*

*Proverbs 20:7 NLT*

Wise women understand that integrity is a crucial building block in the foundation of a well-lived life. Integrity is built slowly over a lifetime. It is the sum of every right decision, every honest word, every noble thought, and every heartfelt prayer. It is forged on the anvil of honorable work and polished by the twin virtues of generosity and humility. Integrity is a precious thing—difficult to build, but easy to tear down; godly women value it and protect it at all costs.

As believers in Christ, we must seek to live each day with discipline, honesty, and faith. When we do, at least two things happen: integrity becomes a habit, and God blesses us because of our obedience to Him.

God never called us to naïveté. He called us to integrity . . . . The biblical concept of integrity emphasizes mature innocence not childlike ignorance.

*Beth Moore*

## — A Prayer for Today —

Heavenly Father, help me live a life of integrity. Let my words be true, and let my actions lead others to You. Amen

# God's Lessons

*Listen to counsel and receive instruction so that you may be wise in later life.*

*Proverbs 19:20 HCSB*

When it comes to learning life's lessons, we can either do things the easy way or the hard way. The easy way can be summed up as follows: when God teaches us a lesson, we learn it . . . the first time! Unfortunately, too many of us learn much more slowly than that.

When we resist God's instruction, He continues to teach, whether we like it or not. Our challenge, then, is to discern God's lessons from the experiences of everyday life. Hopefully, we learn those lessons sooner rather than later because the sooner we do, the sooner He can move on to the next lesson and the next and the next . . .

While chastening is always difficult, if we look to God for the lesson we should learn, we will see spiritual fruit.

*Vonette Bright*

## — A Prayer for Today —

Dear Lord, I have so much to learn. Help me to watch, to listen, to think, and to learn every day of my life. Amen

# The Wisdom of Moderation

*Patience is better than power, and controlling one's temper, than capturing a city.*

Proverbs 16:32 HCSB

Moderation and wisdom are traveling companions. If we are wise, we must learn to temper our appetites, our desires, and our impulses. When we do, we are blessed, in part, because God has created a world in which temperance is rewarded and intemperance is inevitably punished.

Would you like to improve your life? Then harness your appetites and restrain your impulses. Moderation is difficult, of course; it is especially difficult in a prosperous society such as ours. But the rewards of moderation are numerous and long-lasting. Claim those rewards today. No one can force you to moderate your appetites. The decision to live temperately (and wisely) is yours and yours alone. And so are the consequences.

To many, total abstinence is easier than perfect moderation.

St. Augustine

## — A Prayer for Today —

Dear Lord, give me the wisdom to be moderate and self-disciplined. Let me strive to do Your will here on earth, and as I do, let me find contentment and balance. Let me be a disciplined woman, today and every day. Amen

# Optimism 101

*I am able to do all things through Him who strengthens me.*
*Philippians 4:13 HCSB*

Pessimism and Christianity don't mix. Why? Because Christians have every reason to be optimistic about life here on earth and life eternal. Mrs. Charles E. Cowman advised, "Never yield to gloomy anticipation. Place your hope and confidence in God. He has no record of failure."

Sometimes, despite our trust in God, we may fall into the spiritual traps of worry, frustration, anxiety, or sheer exhaustion, and our hearts become heavy. What's needed is plenty of rest, a large dose of perspective, and God's healing touch, but not necessarily in that order. So, make this promise to yourself and keep it: vow to be a hope-filled Christian. Think optimistically about your life, your profession, and your future. Trust your hopes, not your fears. Take time to celebrate God's glorious creation. And then, when you've filled your heart with hope and gladness, share your optimism with others. They'll be better for it, and so will you. But not necessarily in that order.

## — A Prayer for Today —

Lord, let me be an expectant Christian. Let me expect the best from You, and let me look for the best in others. If I become discouraged, Father, turn my thoughts and my prayers to You. And, let me share my faith and optimism with others, today and every day that I live. Amen

# His Calling

*But as God has distributed to each one, as the Lord has called each one, so let him walk.*

*1 Corinthians 7:17 NKJV*

It is terribly important that you heed God's calling by discovering and developing your talents and your spiritual gifts. If you seek to make a difference—and if you seek to bear eternal fruit—you must discover your gifts and begin using them for the glory of God.

Every believer has at least one gift. In John 15:16, Jesus says, "You did not choose Me, but I chose you and appointed you that you should go and bear fruit, and that your fruit should remain, that whatever you ask the Father in My name He may give you." Have you found your special calling? If not, keep searching and keep praying until you find it. God has important work for you to do, and the time to begin that work is now.

God has given you special talents—now it's your turn to give them back to God.

*Marie T. Freeman*

## — A Prayer for Today —

Dear Lord, You created me, and You have called me to do Your work here on earth. Today, I choose to seek Your will and to live it, knowing that when I trust in You, I am eternally blessed. Amen

# Now, Not Later

*We can't afford to waste a minute, must not squander these precious daylight hours in frivolity and indulgence . . . . Don't loiter and linger, waiting until the very last minute. Dress yourselves in Christ, and be up and about!*

*Romans 13:13-14 MSG*

The habit of procrastination takes a two-fold toll on its victims. First, important work goes unfinished; second, valuable energy is wasted in the process of putting off the things that remain undone. Procrastination results from an individual's short-sighted attempt to postpone temporary discomfort. What results is a senseless cycle of 1. delay, followed by 2. worry followed by 3. a panicky and often futile attempt to "catch up." Procrastination is, at its core, a struggle against oneself; the only antidote is action.

Once you acquire the habit of doing what needs to be done when it needs to be done, you will avoid untold trouble, worry, and stress. So learn to defeat procrastination by paying less attention to your fears and more attention to your responsibilities. God has created a world that punishes procrastinators and rewards women who "do it now." Life doesn't procrastinate—neither should you.

## — A Prayer for Today —

Dear Lord, today is a new day. Help me finish the important tasks first, even if those tasks are unpleasant. Don't let me put off until tomorrow what I should do today. Amen

# The Power of Words

*The wise store up knowledge, but the mouth of the fool hastens destruction.*

*Proverbs 10:14 HCSB*

All too often, in the rush to have ourselves heard, we speak first and think next . . . with unfortunate results. God's Word reminds us that, "Reckless words pierce like a sword, but the tongue of the wise brings healing" (Proverbs 12:18 NIV). If we seek to be a source of encouragement to friends and family, then we must measure our words carefully. Words are important: they can hurt or heal. Words can uplift us or discourage us, and reckless words, spoken in haste, cannot be erased.

Today, measure your words carefully. Use words of kindness and praise, not words of anger or derision. Remember that you have the power to heal others or to injure them, to lift others up or to hold them back. When you lift them up, your wisdom will bring healing and comfort to a world that needs both.

## — A Prayer for Today —

Dear Lord, You have commanded me to choose my words carefully so that I might be a source of encouragement and hope to all whom I meet. Keep me mindful, Lord, that I have influence on many people. Let the words that I speak today be worthy of the One who has saved me forever. Amen

# An Intensely Bright Future: Yours

*My purpose is to give life in all its fullness.*

*John 10:10 HCSB*

Are you excited about the opportunities of today and thrilled by the possibilities of tomorrow? Do you confidently expect God to lead you to a place of abundance, peace, and joy? And, when your days on earth are over, do you expect to receive the priceless gift of eternal life? If you trust God's promises, and if you have welcomed God's Son into your heart, then you believe that your future is intensely and eternally bright.

It takes courage to dream big dreams. You will discover that courage when you do three things: accept the past, trust God to handle the future, and make the most of the time He has given you today. No dreams are too big for God—not even yours. So start living—and dreaming—accordingly.

Allow your dreams a place in your prayers and plans. God-given dreams can help you move into the future He is preparing for you.

*Barbara Johnson*

## — A Prayer for Today —

Dear Lord, my hope is in You. Give me the courage to face the future with certainty, and give me the wisdom to follow in the footsteps of Your Son, today and forever. Amen

# What Kind of Example?

*Set an example of good works yourself, with integrity and dignity in your teaching.*

*Titus 2:7 HCSB*

What kind of example are you? Are you the kind of woman whose life serves as a powerful example of decency and morality? Are you a woman whose behavior serves as a positive role model for others? Are you the kind of person whose actions, day in and day out, are based upon integrity, fidelity, and a love for the Lord? If so, you are not only blessed by God; you are also a powerful force for good in a world that desperately needs positive influences such as yours. And that's good because your family and friends are watching . . . and so, for that matter, is God.

In serving we uncover the greatest fulfillment within and become a stellar example of a woman who knows and loves Jesus.

*Vonette Bright*

— A Prayer for Today —

Lord, make me a worthy example to my family and friends. And, let my words and my actions show people how my life has been changed by You. I will praise You, Father, by following in the footsteps of Your Son. Let others see Him through me. Amen

# Temporary Setbacks

*A time to weep, and a time to laugh; a time to mourn, and a time to dance . . . .*

*Ecclesiastes 3:4 KJV*

The occasional disappointments and failures of life are inevitable. Such setbacks are simply the price that we must occasionally pay for our willingness to take risks as we follow our dreams. But even when we encounter bitter disappointments, we must never lose faith.

When we encounter the inevitable difficulties of life-here-on-earth, God stands ready to protect us. Our responsibility, of course, is to ask Him for protection. When we call upon Him in heartfelt prayer, He will answer—in His own time and according to His own plan—and He will heal us. And, while we are waiting for God's plans to unfold and for His healing touch to restore us, we can be comforted in the knowledge that God can overcome any obstacle, even if we cannot.

Every misfortune, every failure, every loss may be transformed. God has the power to transform all misfortunes into "God-sends."

*Mrs. Charles E. Cowman*

## — A Prayer for Today —

Dear Lord, even when I'm afraid of failure, give me the courage to try. Remind me that with You by my side, I really have nothing to fear. So today, Father, I will live courageously as I place my faith in You. Amen

# Financial Security

*Honor the Lord with your wealth and the firstfruits from all your crops. Then your barns will be full . . . .*

*Proverbs 3:9-10 NCV*

The quest for financial security is a journey that leads us across many peaks and through a few unexpected valleys. When we reach the mountaintops, we find it easy to praise God and to give thanks. But, when we face disappointment or financial hardship, it seems so much more difficult to trust God's perfect plan. But, trust Him we must.

As you strive to achieve financial security for your family, remember this: The next time you find your courage tested to the limit (and it will be), lean upon God's promises. Trust His Son. Remember that God is always near and that He is your protector and your deliverer. Always.

If the Living Logos of God has the power to create and sustain the universe . . . He is more than able to sustain your marriage and your ministry, your faith and your finances, your hope and your health.

*Anne Graham Lotz*

## — A Prayer for Today —

Dear Lord, I will be a faithful steward of my resources. But keep me mindful that my greatest possession has nothing to do with my checkbook—my greatest possession is my relationship with You through Jesus Christ. Amen

# Now Is the Time

*So, my son, throw yourself into this work for Christ.*
2 Timothy 1:1 MSG

God's love for you is deeper and more profound than you can imagine. God's love for you is so great that He sent His only Son to this earth to die for your sins and to offer you the priceless gift of eternal life. Now, you must decide whether or not to accept God's gift. Will you ignore it or embrace it? Will you return it or neglect it? Will you accept Christ's love and build a lifelong relationship with Him, or will you turn away from Him and take a different path?

Your decision to allow Christ to reign over your heart is the pivotal decision of your life. It is a decision that you cannot ignore. It is a decision that is yours and yours alone. Accept God's gift now: allow His Son to preside over your heart, your thoughts, and your life, starting this very instant.

I can tell you, from personal experience of walking with God for over fifty years, that He is the Lover of my soul.
*Vonette Bright*

## — A Prayer for Today —

Dear Lord, You are my Teacher—I will study Your Word, and I will seek Your will. Today, I will stand upon the truth that You reveal, and I will share Your wisdom with my family, with my friends, and with the world. Amen

# Forgiving and Forgetting

*But the wisdom from above is first pure, then peace-loving, gentle, compliant, full of mercy and good fruits, without favoritism and hypocrisy.*

*James 3:17 HCSB*

Do you have a tough time forgiving and forgetting? If so, welcome to the club. Most of us find it difficult to forgive the people who have hurt us. And that's too bad because life would be much simpler if we could forgive people "once and for all" and be done with it. Yet forgiveness is seldom that easy. Usually, the decision to forgive is straightforward, but the process of forgiving is more difficult. Forgiveness is a journey that requires time, perseverance, and prayer.

If you sincerely wish to forgive someone, pray for that person. And then pray for yourself by asking God to heal your heart. Don't expect forgiveness to be easy or quick, but rest assured: with God as your partner, you can forgive . . . and you will.

Forgiveness is not an emotion. Forgiveness is an act of the will, and the will can function regardless of the temperature of the heart.

*Corrie ten Boom*

## — A Prayer for Today —

Dear Lord, today, I ask You to help me move beyond feelings of bitterness and anger. Jesus forgave those who hurt Him; let me walk in His footsteps by forgiving those who have injured me. Amen

# Far Beyond Envy

*Therefore, laying aside all malice, all deceit, hypocrisy, envy, and all evil speaking, as newborn babes, desire the pure milk of the word, that you may grow thereby.*

1 Peter 2:1-2 NKJV

Because we are frail, imperfect human beings, we are sometimes envious of others. But God's Word warns us that envy is sin. Thus, we must guard ourselves against the natural tendency to feel resentment and jealousy when other people experience good fortune. As believers, we have absolutely no reason to be envious of any people on earth. After all, as Christians we are already recipients of the greatest gift in all creation: God's grace. We have been promised the gift of eternal life through God's only begotten Son, and we must count that gift as our most precious possession.

So here's a simple suggestion that is guaranteed to bring you happiness: fill your heart with God's love, God's promises, and God's Son . . . and when you do so, leave no room for envy, hatred, bitterness, or regret.

What God asks, does, or requires of others is not my business; it is His.

*Kay Arthur*

## — A Prayer for Today —

Dear Lord, when I am envious of others, redirect my thoughts to the blessings I have received from You. Make me a thankful Christian, Father, and deliver me from envy. Amen

# Faith That Works

*In the same way faith, if it doesn't have works, is dead by itself.*

James 2:17 HCSB

Corrie ten Boom advised, "Be filled with the Holy Spirit; join a church where the members believe the Bible and know the Lord; seek the fellowship of other Christians; learn and be nourished by God's Word and His many promises. Conversion is not the end of your journey—it is only the beginning."

The work of nourishing your faith can and should be joyful work. The hours that you invest in Bible study, prayer, meditation, and worship should be times of enrichment and celebration. And, as you continue to build your life upon a foundation of faith, you will discover that the journey toward spiritual maturity lasts a lifetime. As a child of God, you are never fully "grown"; instead, you can continue "growing up" every day of your life. And that's exactly what God wants you to do.

## — A Prayer for Today —

Lord, sometimes this world is a terrifying place. When I am filled with uncertainty and doubt, give me faith. In life's dark moments, help me remember that You are always near and that You can overcome any challenge. Today, Lord, and forever, I will place my trust in You. Amen

# Faith Versus Fear

*Do not fear, for I am with you; do not be afraid, for I am your God. I will strengthen you; I will help you; I will hold on to you with My righteous right hand.*

*Isaiah 41:10 HCSB*

A terrible storm rose quickly on the Sea of Galilee, and the disciples were afraid. Although they had witnessed many miracles, the disciples feared for their lives, so they turned to Jesus, and He calmed the waters and the wind.

The next time you find yourself facing a fear-provoking situation, remember that the One who calmed the wind and the waves is also your personal Savior. Then ask yourself which is stronger: your faith or your fear? The answer should be obvious. So, when the storm clouds form overhead and you find yourself being tossed on the stormy seas of life, remember this: Wherever you are, God is there, too. And, because He cares for you, you are protected.

Only believe, don't fear. Our Master, Jesus, always watches over us, and no matter what the persecution, Jesus will surely overcome it.

*Lottie Moon*

## — A Prayer for Today —

Heavenly Father, when I am fearful, keep me mindful that You are my protector and my salvation. Give me strength, Lord, to face the challenges of this day as I gain my courage from You. Amen

# In Focus

*Look straight ahead, and fix your eyes on what lies before you. Mark out a straight path for your feet; then stick to the path and stay safe. Don't get sidetracked; keep your feet from following evil.*

*Proverbs 4:25-27 NLT*

What is your focus today? Are you willing to focus your thoughts and energies on God's blessings and upon His will for your life? Or will you turn your thoughts to other things? This day—and every day hereafter—is a chance to celebrate the life that God has given you. It's also a chance to give thanks to the One who has offered you more blessings than you can possibly count.

Today, why not focus your thoughts on the joy that is rightfully yours in Christ? Why not take time to celebrate God's glorious creation? Why not trust your hopes instead of your fears? When you do, you will think optimistically about yourself and your world . . . and you can then share your optimism with others. They'll be better for it, and so will you. But not necessarily in that order.

Jesus challenges you and me to keep our focus daily on the cross of His will if we want to be His disciples.

*Anne Graham Lotz*

## — A Prayer for Today —

Dear Lord, help me to face this day with a spirit of optimism and thanksgiving. And let me focus my thoughts on You and Your incomparable gifts. Amen

# A Terrific Tomorrow

*"For I know the plans I have for you"*—[this is] the Lord's declaration—*"plans for [your] welfare, not for disaster, to give you a future and a hope."*

Jeremiah 29:11 HCSB

How bright do you believe your future to be? Well, if you're a faithful believer, God has plans for you that are so bright that you'd better pack several pairs of sunglasses and a lifetime supply of sunblock!

The way that you think about your future will play a powerful role in determining how things turn out (it's called the "self-fulfilling prophecy," and it applies to everybody, including you). So here's another question: Are you expecting a terrific tomorrow, or are you dreading a terrible one? The answer to that question will have a powerful impact on the way tomorrow unfolds.

Today, as you live in the present and look to the future, remember that God has an amazing plan for you. Act—and believe—accordingly. And one more thing: don't forget the sunblock.

## — A Prayer for Today —

Dear Lord, sometimes when I think about the future, I worry. Today, I will do a better job of trusting You. You are my Father, and I will place my hope and my faith in You. Amen

# The Thread of Generosity

*The one who has two shirts must share with someone who has none, and the one who has food must do the same.*

Luke 3:11 HCSB

The thread of generosity is woven—completely and inextricably—into the very fabric of Christ's teachings. As He sent His disciples out to heal the sick and spread God's message of salvation, Jesus offered this guiding principle: "Freely you have received, freely give" (Matthew 10:8 NIV). The principle still applies.

Lisa Whelchel spoke for Christian women everywhere when she observed, "The Lord has abundantly blessed me all of my life. I'm not trying to pay Him back for all of His wonderful gifts; I just realize that He gave them to me to give away." All of us have been blessed, and all of us are called to share those blessings without reservation. So, make this pledge and keep it: Be a cheerful, generous, courageous giver. The world needs your help, and you need the spiritual rewards that will be yours when you share your possessions, your talents, and your time.

## — A Prayer for Today —

Lord, You have been so generous with me; let me be generous with others. Help me to give generously of my time and my possessions as I care for those in need. And, make me a humble giver, Lord, so that all the glory and the praise might be Yours. Amen

# Obey and Be Blessed

*If you obey my commands, you will remain in my love, just as I have obeyed my Father's commands and remain in his love.*

*John 15:10 NIV*

God gave us His commandments for a reason: so that we might obey them and be blessed. Elisabeth Elliot advised, "Obedience to God is our job. The results of that obedience are God's." These words should serve to remind us that obedience is imperative. But, we live in a world that presents us with countless temptations to disobey God's laws.

When we stray from God's path, we suffer. So, whenever we are confronted with sin, we have clear instructions: we must walk—or better yet run—in the opposite direction.

Don't worry about what you do not understand. Worry about what you do understand in the Bible but do not live by.

*Corrie ten Boom*

## — A Prayer for Today —

Lord, let me live by Your commandments and let me help others do the same. Give me the wisdom to walk righteously in the footsteps of Your Son, Dear Father. And let me place my trust in You, today and forever. Amen

# Additional Responsibilities

*So he who had received five talents came and brought five other talents, saying, "Lord, you delivered to me five talents; look, I have gained five more talents besides them." His lord said to him, "Well done, good and faithful servant; you were faithful over a few things, I will make you ruler over many things. Enter into the joy of your lord."*

Matthew 25:20-21 NKJV

God has promised us this: when we do our duties in small matters, He will give us additional responsibilities. Sometimes, those responsibilities come when God changes the course of our lives so that we may better serve Him. Sometimes, our rewards come in the form of temporary setbacks that lead, in turn, to greater victories. Sometimes, God rewards us by answering "no" to our prayers so that He can say "yes" to a far grander request that we, with our limited understanding, would never have thought to ask for.

If you seek to be God's servant in great matters, be faithful, be patient, and be dutiful in smaller matters. Then step back and watch as God surprises you with the spectacular creativity of His infinite wisdom and His perfect plan.

— A Prayer for Today —

Lord, You have a plan for my life. Let me discover it and live it. Today, I will seek Your will, knowing that when I trust in You, dear Father, I am eternally blessed. Amen

# Safe in God's Hands

*When you pass through the waters, I will be with you; and through the rivers, they shall not overflow you. When you walk through the fire, you shall not be burned, nor shall the flame scorch you. For I am the Lord your God, The Holy One of Israel, your Savior.*

*Isaiah 43:2-3 NKJV*

As a busy woman, you know from firsthand experience that life is not always easy. But as a recipient of God's grace, you also know that you are protected by a loving Heavenly Father.

In times of trouble, God will comfort you; in times of sorrow, He will dry your tears. When you are troubled or weak or sorrowful, God is neither distant nor disinterested. To the contrary, God is always present and always vitally engaged in the events of your life. Reach out to Him, and build your future on the rock that cannot be shaken . . . trust in God and rely upon His provisions. He can provide everything you really need . . . and far, far more.

## — A Prayer for Today —

Lord, sometimes life is difficult. Sometimes, I am worried, weary, or heartbroken. And sometimes, I encounter powerful temptations to disobey Your commandments. But, when I lift my eyes to You, Father, You strengthen me. When I am weak, You lift me up. Today, I will turn to You for strength, for hope, for direction, and for deliverance. Amen

# An Attitude of Gratitude

*And let the peace of God rule in your hearts . . . and be ye thankful.*

*Colossians 3:15 KJV*

For most of us, life is busy and complicated. We have countless responsibilities, some of which begin before sunrise and many of which end long after sunset. Amid the rush and crush of the daily grind, it is easy to lose sight of God and His blessings. But, when we forget to slow down and say "Thank You" to our Maker, we rob ourselves of His presence, His peace, and His joy.

Our task, as believing Christians, is to praise God many times each day. Then, with gratitude in our hearts, we can face our daily duties with the perspective and power that only He can provide.

Let's thank God for allowing us to experience troubles that drive us closer to Him.

*Shirley Dobson*

## — A Prayer for Today —

Lord, make me a woman with a grateful heart. You have given me much; when I think of Your grace and goodness, I am humbled and thankful. Today, I will praise You with my words my deeds . . . and may all the glory be Yours. Amen

# Doers of the Word

*But be doers of the word and not hearers only.*

*James 1:22 HCSB*

The old saying is both familiar and true: actions speak louder than words. And as believers, we must beware: our actions should always give credence to the changes that Christ can make in the lives of those who walk with Him.

God calls upon each of us to act in accordance with His will and with respect for His commandments. If we are to be responsible believers, we must realize that it is never enough simply to hear the instructions of God; we must also live by them. And it is never enough to wait idly by while others do God's work here on earth; we, too, must act. Doing God's work is a responsibility that each of us must bear, and when we do, our loving Heavenly Father rewards our efforts with a bountiful harvest.

We spend our lives dreaming of the future, not realizing that a little of it slips away every day.

*Barbara Johnson*

## — A Prayer for Today —

Dear Lord, I have heard Your Word, and I have felt Your presence in my heart; let me act accordingly. Let my words and deeds serve as a testimony to the changes You have made in my life. Let me praise You, Father, by following in the footsteps of Your Son, and let others see Him through me. Amen

# Considering the Cross

*But God forbid that I should boast except in the cross of our Lord Jesus Christ, by whom the world has been crucified to me, and I to the world.*

*Galatians 6:14 NKJV*

As we consider Christ's sacrifice on the cross, we should be profoundly humbled and profoundly grateful. And today, as we come to Christ in prayer, we should do so in a spirit of quiet, heartfelt devotion to the One who gave His life so that we might have life eternal.

He was the Son of God, but He wore a crown of thorns. He was the Savior of mankind, yet He was put to death on a roughhewn cross made of wood. He offered His healing touch to an unsaved world, and yet the same hands that had healed the sick and raised the dead were pierced with nails.

Christ humbled Himself on a cross—for you. As you approach Him today in prayer, think about His love and His sacrifice. And be grateful.

## — A Prayer for Today —

Dear Jesus, You are my Savior and my protector. You suffered on the cross for me, and I will give You honor and praise every day of my life. I will honor You with my words, my thoughts, and my prayers. And I will live according to Your commandments, so that through me, others might come to know Your perfect love. Amen

# A Worthy Disciple

*He has told you men what is good and what it is the Lord requires of you: Only to act justly, to love faithfulness, and to walk humbly with your God.*

Micah 6:8 HCSB

When Jesus addressed His disciples, He warned that each one must, "take up his cross and follow me." The disciples must have known exactly what the Master meant. In Jesus' day, prisoners were forced to carry their own crosses to the location where they would be put to death. Thus, Christ's message was clear: in order to follow Him, Christ's disciples must deny themselves and, instead, trust Him completely. Nothing has changed since then.

If we are to be disciples of Christ, we must trust Him and place Him at the very center of our beings. Jesus never comes "next." He is always first.

Do you seek to be a worthy disciple of Christ? Then pick up His cross today and every day that you live. When you do, He will bless you now and forever.

## — A Prayer for Today —

Dear Lord, thank You for the gift of Your Son Jesus, my personal Savior. Let me be a worthy disciple of Christ, and let me be ever grateful for His love. I will praise You always, Father, as I give thanks for Your Son and for Your everlasting love. Amen

# Filled with the Spirit

*And don't get drunk with wine, which leads to reckless actions, but be filled with the Spirit.*

*Ephesians 5:18 HCSB*

When you are filled with the Holy Spirit, your words and deeds will reflect a love and devotion to Christ. When you are filled with the Holy Spirit, the steps of your life's journey are guided by the Lord. When you allow God's Spirit to work in you and through you, you will be energized and transformed.

Today, allow yourself to be filled with the Spirit of God. And then stand back in amazement as God begins to work miracles in your own life and in the lives of those you love.

The Holy Spirit is like a living and continually flowing fountain in believers. We have the boundless privilege of tapping into that fountain every time we pray.

*Shirley Dobson*

## — A Prayer for Today —

Dear Lord, You are my sovereign God. Your Son defeated death; Your Holy Spirit comforts and guides me. Let me celebrate all Your gifts, Father, and let me be a hope-filled Christian today and every day. Amen

# The World's Best Friend

*No one has greater love than this, that someone would lay down his life for his friends.*

*John 15:13 HCSB*

Who's the best friend this world has ever had? Jesus, of course. When you invite Him into your heart, Jesus will be your friend, too . . . your friend forever. Jesus has offered to share the gifts of everlasting life and everlasting love with the world . . . and with you. If you make mistakes, He'll still be your friend. If you behave badly, He'll still love you. If you feel sorry or sad, He will help you feel better about your world and yourself.

Jesus wants you to have a happy, meaningful life. He wants you to be generous and kind, and He wants you to follow Him. The rest, of course, is up to you. You can do it! And with a friend like Jesus, you most certainly will.

When we are in a situation where Jesus is all we have, we soon discover He is all we really need.

*Gigi Graham Tchividjian*

## — A Prayer for Today —

Dear Jesus, You are my Savior and my protector. Give me the courage to trust You completely. Today, I will praise You, I will honor You, and I will live according to Your commandments. Amen

# Too Many Possessions

*Do not love the world or the things that belong to the world.*
*If anyone loves the world, love for the Father is not in him.*
*1 John 2:15 HCSB*

On the grand stage of a well-lived life, material possessions should play a rather small role. Of course, we all need the basic necessities of life, but once we meet those needs for ourselves and for our families, the piling up of possessions creates more problems than it solves. Our real riches, of course, are not of this world. We are never really rich until we are rich in spirit.

How much stuff is too much stuff? Well, if your desire for stuff is getting in the way of your desire to know God, then you've got too much stuff—it's as simple as that. So, if you find yourself wrapped up in the concerns of the material world, it's time to reorder your priorities. And, it's time to begin storing up riches that will endure throughout eternity—the spiritual kind.

We own too many things that aren't worth owning.

*Marie T. Freeman*

## — A Prayer for Today —

Dear Lord, keep me mindful that material possessions cannot bring me joy—my joy comes from You. I will share that joy with family, with friends, and with neighbors, this day and every day. Amen

# On a Mission

*But you are a chosen race, a royal priesthood, a holy nation, a people for His possession, so that you may proclaim the praises of the One who called you out of darkness into His marvelous light.*

*1 Peter 2:9 HCSB*

Whether you realize it or not, you are on a personal mission for God. As a Christian, that mission is straightforward: Honor God, accept Christ as your personal Savior, and serve God's children.

Of course, you will encounter impediments as you attempt to discover the exact nature of God's purpose for your life, but you must never lose sight of the overriding purposes that God has established for all believers. You will encounter these overriding purposes again and again as you worship your Creator and study His Word.

Every day offers countless opportunities to serve God and to worship Him. When you do so, He will bless you in miraculous ways. May you continue to seek God's will, may you trust His Word, and may you place Him where He belongs: at the very center of your life.

## — A Prayer for Today —

Dear Lord, I know that You have a purpose for my life, and I will seek that purpose today and every day that I live. Let my actions be pleasing to You, and let me share Your Good News with a world that so desperately needs Your healing hand and the salvation of Your Son. Amen

# God's Guidance and Your Path

*Trust in the LORD with all your heart; do not depend on your own understanding. Seek his will in all you do, and he will direct your paths.*

*Proverbs 3:5-6 NLT*

Proverbs 3:5-6 makes this promise: if you acknowledge God's sovereignty over every aspect of your life, He will guide your path. And, as you prayerfully consider the path that God intends for you to take, here are things you should do: You should study His Word and be ever-watchful for His signs. You should associate with fellow believers who will encourage your spiritual growth. You should listen carefully to that inner voice that speaks to you in the quiet moments of your daily devotionals. And you should be patient. Your Heavenly Father may not always reveal Himself as quickly as you would like, but rest assured that God intends to use you in wonderful, unexpected ways. Your challenge is to watch, to listen, to learn . . . and to follow.

## — A Prayer for Today —

Dear Lord, let my plans and hopes be pleasing to You. Let me live according to Your commandments. Direct my path far from the temptations and distractions of this world. And, let me discover Your will and follow it, Father, this day and always. Amen

# The Power Of Prayer

*The intense prayer of the righteous is very powerful.*
                                                James 5:16 HCSB

"The power of prayer": these words are so familiar, yet sometimes we forget what they mean. Prayer is a powerful tool for communicating with our Creator; it is an opportunity to commune with the Giver of all things good. Prayer helps us find strength for today and hope for the future. Prayer is not a thing to be taken lightly or to be used infrequently.

The quality of your spiritual life will be in direct proportion to the quality of your prayer life. Prayer changes things, and it changes you. Today, instead of turning things over in your mind, turn them over to God in prayer. Instead of worrying about your next decision, ask God to lead the way. Pray constantly about things great and small. God is listening, and He wants to hear from you now.

## — A Prayer for Today —

Dear Lord, let me raise my hopes and my dreams, my worries and my fears to You. Let me be a worthy example to family and friends, showing them the importance and the power of prayer. Let me take everything to You in prayer, Lord, and when I do, let me trust in Your answers. Amen

# A Quiet Place

*Now in the morning, having risen a long while before daylight, He went out and departed to a solitary place; and there He prayed.*

*Mark 1:35 NKJV*

In the first chapter of Mark, we read that in the darkness of the early morning hours, Jesus went to a solitary place and prayed. So, too, should we. But sometimes, finding quiet moments of solitude is difficult indeed. We live in a noisy world, a world filled with distractions, frustrations, and complications. But if we allow the distractions of a clamorous world to separate us from God's peace, we do ourselves a profound disservice.

Are you one of those busy women who rush through the day with scarcely a single moment for quiet contemplation and prayer? If so, it's time to reorder your priorities. Nothing is more important than the time you spend with your Savior. So be still and claim the inner peace that is your spiritual birthright: the peace of Jesus Christ.

## — A Prayer for Today —

Lord, Your Holy Word is a light unto the world; let me study it, trust it, and share it with all who cross my path. Let me discover You, Father, in the quiet moments of the day. And, in all that I say and do, help me to be a worthy witness as I share the Good News of Your perfect Son and Your perfect Word. Amen

# So Many Temptations

*No temptation has overtaken you except what is common to humanity. God is faithful and He will not allow you to be tempted beyond what you are able, but with the temptation He will also provide a way of escape, so that you are able to bear it.*

*1 Corinthians 10:13 HCSB*

This world is filled to the brim with temptations. Some of these temptations are small; eating a second scoop of ice cream, for example, is tempting but not very dangerous. Other temptations, however, are not nearly so harmless. The devil is working 24/7, and he's causing pain and heartache in more ways than ever before. Thankfully, in the battle against Satan, we are never alone. God is always with us, and He gives us the power to resist temptation whenever we ask Him for the strength to do so.

In a letter to believers, Peter offered a stern warning: "Your adversary, the devil, prowls around like a roaring lion, seeking someone to devour" (1 Peter 5:8 NASB). As Christians, we must take that warning seriously, and we must behave accordingly.

## — A Prayer for Today —

Dear Lord, this world is filled with temptations, distractions, and frustrations. When I turn my thoughts away from You and Your Word, I suffer bitter consequences. But, when I trust in Your commandments, I am safe. Direct my path far from the temptations of the world, Father, this day and always. Amen

# The Power of Our Words

*No rotten talk should come from your mouth, but only what is good for the building up of someone in need, in order to give grace to those who hear.*

*Ephesians 4:29 HCSB*

The words that we speak have the power to do great good or great harm. If we speak words of encouragement and hope, we can lift others up. And that's exactly what God commands us to do!

Sometimes, when we feel uplifted and secure, it is easy to speak kind words. Other times, when we are discouraged or tired, we can scarcely summon the energy to uplift ourselves, much less anyone else. God intends that we speak words of kindness, wisdom, and truth, no matter our circumstances, no matter our emotions. When we do, we share a priceless gift with the world, and we give glory to the One who gave His life for us. As believers, we must do no less.

Encouragement is the oxygen of the soul.

*John Maxwell*

— A Prayer for Today —

Lord, make me mindful of my words. Make me a powerful source of encouragement to those in need, and let my words and deeds be worthy of Your Son, the One who gives me courage and strength for this day and for all eternity. Amen

# Forgiveness Starts at Home

*Let all bitterness, wrath, anger, clamor, and evil speaking be put away from you, with all malice. And be kind to one another, tenderhearted, forgiving one another, just as God in Christ forgave you.*

*Ephesians 4:31-32 NKJV*

Sometimes, it's easy to become angry with the people we love most, and sometimes it's hard to forgive them. After all, we know that our family will still love us no matter how angry we become. But while it's easy to become angry at home, it's usually wrong.

The next time you're tempted to lose your temper or to remain angry at a close family member, ask God to help you find the wisdom to forgive. And while you're at it, do your best to calm down sooner rather than later because peace is always beautiful, especially when it's peace at your house.

Anger unresolved will only bring you woe.

*Kay Arthur*

— A Prayer for Today —

Lord, sometimes, I am quick to anger and slow to forgive. But, I know that You seek abundance and peace for my life. You command us to forgive; let me obey You as I follow the example of Your Son Jesus who forgave His persecutors. As I turn away from anger, Father, let me claim the peace that You intend for my life. Amen

# Facing Fears, Living Boldly

*For God has not given us a spirit of fearfulness, but one of power, love, and sound judgment.*

*2 Timothy 1:7 HCSB*

Do you prefer to face your fears rather than run from them? If so, you will be blessed because of your willingness to live courageously.

When Paul wrote Timothy, he reminded his young protégé that the God they served was a bold God, and God's spirit empowered His children with boldness also. Like Timothy, we face times of uncertainty and fear. God's message is the same to us, today, as it was to Timothy: We can live boldly because the spirit of God resides in us.

So today, as you face the challenges of everyday living, remember that God is with you . . . and you are protected.

The pathway of obedience can sometimes be difficult, but it always leads to a strengthening of our inner woman.

*Vonette Bright*

## — A Prayer for Today —

Lord, I'm only human, and sometimes I am afraid. But You are always with me, and when I turn to You, You give me courage. Let me be a faith-filled Christian, God, and keep me mindful that, with You as my protector, I am secure today . . . and throughout eternity. Amen

# The Pursuit of God's Truth

*But grow in the grace and knowledge of our Lord and Savior Jesus Christ. To Him be the glory both now and forever. Amen.*

2 Peter 3:18 NKJV

Have you established a passionate relationship with God's Holy Word? Hopefully so. After all, the Bible is a roadmap for life here on earth and for life eternal. And, as a believer who has been touched by God's grace, you are called upon to study God's Holy Word, to trust His Word, to follow its commandments, and to share its Good News with the world.

The words of Matthew 4:4 remind us that, "Man shall not live by bread alone but by every word that proceedeth out of the mouth of God" (KJV). As believers, we must study the Bible and meditate upon its meaning for our lives. Otherwise, we deprive ourselves of a priceless gift from our Creator. God's Holy Word is, indeed, a transforming gift from the Father in heaven. That's why passionate believers must never live by bread alone . . .

## — A Prayer for Today —

Dear Lord, the Bible is Your gift to me; let me use it. When I place Your Word at the very center of my life, I am blessed. Make me a faithful student of Your Word so that I might be a faithful servant in Your world this day and every day. Amen

# Celebration with a Smile

*Jacob said, "For what a relief it is to see your friendly smile. It is like seeing the smile of God!"*

*Genesis 33:10 NLT*

Life should never be taken for granted. Each day is a priceless gift from God and should be treated as such.

Hannah Whitall Smith observed, "How changed our lives would be if we could only fly through the days on wings of surrender and trust!" How true!

Today, let us celebrate life with smiles on our faces and kind words on our lips. After all, this is God's day, and He has given us clear instructions for its use. We are commanded to rejoice and be glad. So, with no further ado, let the celebration begin . . .

A smile is the light in the window of your face that tells people you're at home.

*Barbara Johnson*

## — A Prayer for Today —

Lord, Your desire is that I be complete in Your joy. Joy begets celebration. Today, I celebrate the life and work You have given me, and I celebrate the lives of my friends and family. Thank You, Father, for Your love, for Your blessings, and for Your joy. Let me treasure Your gifts and share them this day and forever. Amen

# Unbending Truth

*And put on the new self, which in the likeness of God has been created in righteousness and holiness of the truth. Therefore, laying aside falsehood, speak truth, each one of you, with his neighbor, for we are members of one another.*
*Ephesians 4:24-25 NASB*

We live in a world that presents us with countless temptations to wander far from God's path. These temptations have the potential to destroy us, in part, because they cause us to be dishonest with ourselves and with others. Dishonesty is a habit. Once we start bending the truth, we're likely to keep bending it. A far better strategy, of course, is to acquire the habit of being completely forthright with God, with other people, and with ourselves.

Honesty is also a habit, a habit that pays powerful dividends for those who place character above convenience. So, the next time you're tempted to bend the truth—or to break it—ask yourself this simple question: "What does God want me to do?" Then listen carefully to your conscience. When you do, your actions will be honorable, and your character will take care of itself.

## — A Prayer for Today —

Lord, help me see the truth, help me speak the truth, and help me live the truth—today and every day of my life. Amen

# Calmness In Chaos

*Thou wilt keep him in perfect peace, whose mind is stayed on thee.*

*Isaiah 26:3 KJV*

The words of John 14:27 give us hope: "Peace I leave with you, my peace I give unto you . . . ." Jesus offers us peace, not as the world gives, but as He alone gives.

When we accept the peace of Jesus Christ into our hearts, our lives are transformed. And then, because we possess the gift of peace, we can share that gift with fellow Christians, family members, friends, and associates. If, on the other hand, we choose to ignore the gift of peace—for whatever reason—we cannot share what we do not possess.

As every woman knows, peace can be a scarce commodity in a demanding world. How, then, can we find the peace that we so desperately desire? By turning our days and our lives over to God. Elisabeth Elliot writes, "If my life is surrendered to God, all is well. Let me not grab it back, as though it were in peril in His hand but would be safer in mine!" May we give our lives, our hopes, and our prayers to the Lord, and, by doing so, accept His will and His peace.

## — A Prayer for Today —

Dear Lord, sometimes, I am distracted by the busyness of the day or the demands of the moment. When I am worried or anxious, Father, turn my thoughts back to You and to Your peace, today and forever. Amen

# Comforting Others

*Carry one another's burdens; in this way you will fulfill the law of Christ.*

*Galatians 6:2 HCSB*

We live in a world that is, on occasion, a frightening place. Sometimes, we sustain life-altering losses that are so profound and so tragic that it seems we could never recover. But, with God's help and with the help of encouraging family members and friends, we can recover.

In times of need, God's Word is clear: as believers, we must offer comfort to those in need by sharing not only our courage but also our faith. As the revivalist Vance Havner observed, "No journey is complete that does not lead through some dark valleys. We can properly comfort others only with the comfort wherewith we ourselves have been comforted of God."

So often we think that to be encouragers we have to produce great words of wisdom when, in fact, a few simple syllables of sympathy and an arm around the shoulder can often provide much needed comfort.

*Florence Littauer*

## — A Prayer for Today —

Dear Lord, this world can be a difficult place, a place full of suffering and tears. Let me give comfort to those in need, and let me share Your love with those who grieve. And when I, too, become discouraged, keep me mindful of Your infinite love. Amen

# Contentment That Lasts

*But godliness with contentment is a great gain. For we brought nothing into the world, and we can take nothing out. But if we have food and clothing, we will be content with these. But those who want to be rich fall into temptation, a trap, and many foolish and harmful desires, which plunge people into ruin and destruction.*

*1 Timothy 6:6-9 HCSB*

The preoccupation with happiness and contentment is an ever-present theme in the modern world. We are bombarded with messages that tell us where to find peace and pleasure in a world that worships materialism and wealth. But, lasting contentment is not found in material possessions; genuine contentment is a spiritual gift from God to those who trust in Him and follow His commandments. When God dwells at the center of our lives, peace and contentment will belong to us just as surely as we belong to God.

The key to contentment is to consider. Consider who you are and be satisfied with that. Consider what you have and be satisfied with that. Consider what God's doing and be satisfied with that.

*Luci Swindoll*

## — A Prayer for Today —

Lord, I find protection when I seek Your healing hand; I discover joy when I welcome Your healing Spirit. Let me look to You for the peace and contentment that You have offered me through the gift of Your Son. Amen

# Good Thinking

*Guard your heart above all else, for it is the source of life.*
*Proverbs 4:23 HCSB*

Are you an upbeat believer? Are you a woman whose hopes and dreams are alive and well? Do you regularly put a smile on your face? And then, do you share that smile with family and friends? Hopefully so. After all, when you decided to allow Christ to rule over your heart, you entitled yourself to share in His promise of spiritual abundance and eternal joy. But sometimes, when pessimism and doubt invade your thoughts, you won't feel like celebrating. Why? Because thoughts are intensely powerful things.

Are you fearful, angry, bored, or worried? Are you so preoccupied with the concerns of this day that you fail to thank God for the promise of eternity? Are you confused, bitter, or pessimistic? If so, spend more time thinking about your blessings, and less time fretting about your hardships. Then, take time to thank the Giver of all things good for gifts that are, in truth, far too numerous to count.

## — A Prayer for Today —

Dear Lord, You teach me that my thoughts are important to You. Help me to think good thoughts and to do good deeds, today and every day. Amen

# The Lessons of Tough Times

*I waited patiently for the Lord, and He turned to me and heard my cry for help. He brought me up from a desolate pit, out of the muddy clay, and set my feet on a rock, making my steps secure. He put a new song in my mouth, a hymn of praise to our God.*

*Psalm 40:1-3 HCSB*

Have you experienced a recent setback? If so, look for the lesson that God is trying to teach you. Instead of complaining about life's sad state of affairs, learn what needs to be learned, change what needs to be changed, and move on. View failure as an opportunity to reassess God's will for your life. View life's inevitable disappointments as opportunities to learn more about yourself and your world.

Life can be difficult at times. And everybody makes mistakes. Your job is to make them only once.

God is able to take mistakes, when they are committed to Him, and make of them something for our good and for His glory.

*Ruth Bell Graham*

## — A Prayer for Today —

Lord, I know that I am imperfect and that I fail You in many ways. Thank You for Your forgiveness and for Your unconditional love. Show me the error of my ways, Lord, that I might confess my wrongdoing and correct my mistakes. And, let me grow each day in wisdom, in faith, and in my love for You. Amen

# God's Forgiveness

*If we confess our sins, He is faithful and righteous to forgive us our sins and to cleanse us from all unrighteousness.*

1 John 1:9 HCSB

The Bible promises you this: When you ask God for forgiveness, He will give it. No questions asked; no explanations required. God's power to forgive, like His love, is infinite. Despite your sins, God offers immediate forgiveness. And it's time to take Him up on His offer.

When it comes to forgiveness, God doesn't play favorites and neither should you. You should forgive all the people who have harmed you (not just the people who have asked for forgiveness or the ones who have made restitution). Complete forgiveness is God's way, and it should be your way, too. Anything less is not enough.

Forgiveness is actually the best revenge because it not only sets us free from the person we forgive, but it frees us to move into all that God has in store for us.

*Stormie Omartian*

## — A Prayer for Today —

Lord, when it is difficult to forgive those who have hurt me, I will draw strength from You. When forgiveness is hard work, I will persevere. You have given me the gift of forgiveness, Father; I will share that gift today, tomorrow, and forever. Amen

# His Rightful Place

*You shall have no other gods before Me.*

*Exodus 20:3 NKJV*

When Jesus was tempted by Satan, the Master's response was unambiguous. Jesus chose to worship the Lord and serve Him only. We, as followers of Christ, must follow in His footsteps by placing God first.

When we place God in a position of secondary importance, we do ourselves great harm. When we allow temptations or distractions to come between us and our Creator, we suffer. But, when we imitate Jesus and place the Lord in His rightful place—at the center of our lives—then we claim spiritual treasures that will endure forever.

To God be the glory, great things He has done; / So loved He the world that He gave us His Son.

*Fanny Crosby*

## — A Prayer for Today —

Lord, You have commanded that I have no gods before You. Let me place You first in my heart, Father, and let me accept the salvation of Your Son Jesus. Then, let me encourage others to accept Your love and Your grace. Amen

# The Source of Our Comfort

*When I am filled with cares, Your comfort brings me joy.*
*Psalm 94:19 HCSB*

In times of adversity, we are wise to remember the words of Jesus, who, when He walked on the waters, reassured His disciples, saying, "Take courage! It is I. Don't be afraid" (Matthew 14:27 NIV). Then, with Christ on His throne—and with trusted friends and loving family members at our sides—we can face our fears with courage and with faith.

Are you facing a difficult challenge? If so, remember that no problem is too big for God . . . not even yours.

In Jesus, the service of God and the service of the least of the brethren were one.

*Dietrich Bonhoeffer*

— A Prayer for Today —

Dear Lord, when I am troubled, You comfort me. When I am discouraged, You lift me up. Whatever my circumstances, Lord, I will trust Your plan for my life. And, when my family and friends are troubled, I will remind them of Your love, Your wisdom, and Your grace. Amen

# Moving On

*"You have heard that it was said, 'You shall love your neighbor and hate your enemy.' But I say to you, love your enemies, bless those who curse you, do good to those who hate you, and pray for those who spitefully use you and persecute you, that you may be sons of your Father in heaven."*

*Matthew 5:43-45 NKJV*

Sometimes, people can be discourteous and cruel. Sometimes people can be unfair, unkind, and unappreciative. Sometimes people get angry and frustrated. So what's a Christian to do? God's answer is straightforward: forgive, forget, and move on. In Luke 6:37, Jesus instructs, "Do not judge, and you will not be judged. Do not condemn, and you will not be condemned. Forgive, and you will be forgiven" (HCSB).

Today and every day, make sure that you're quick to forgive others for their shortcomings. And when other people misbehave (as they most certainly will from time to time), don't pay too much attention. Just forgive those people as quickly as you can, and try to move on . . . as quickly as you can.

## — A Prayer for Today —

Heavenly Father, make me a kind person even to those who don't treat me kindly. Let me forgive others, just as You have forgiven me. Amen

# Relying Upon Him

*Be humble under God's powerful hand so he will lift you up when the right time comes. Give all your worries to him, because he cares about you.*

*1 Peter 5:6-7 NCV*

God is a never-ending source of support and courage for those of us who call upon Him. When we are weary, He gives us strength. When we see no hope, God reminds us of His promises. When we grieve, God wipes away our tears.

Do the demands of this day threaten to overwhelm you? If so, you must rely not only upon your own resources but also upon the promises of your Father in heaven. God will hold your hand and walk with you every day of your life if you let Him. So even if your circumstances are difficult, trust the Father. His love is eternal and His goodness endures forever.

We had plenty of challenges, some of which were tremendously serious, yet God has enabled us to walk, crawl, limp, or leap—whatever way we could progress—toward wholeness.

*Beth Moore*

## — A Prayer for Today —

Heavenly Father, You never leave or forsake me. You are always with me, protecting me and encouraging me. Whatever this day may bring, I thank You for Your love and Your strength. Amen

# Growing in Christ

*When I was a child, I spoke like a child, I thought like a child, I reasoned like a child. When I became a man, I put aside childish things.*

*1 Corinthians 13:11 HCSB*

The journey toward spiritual maturity lasts a lifetime. As Christians, we can and should continue to grow in the love and the knowledge of our Savior as long as we live. Norman Vincent Peale had the following advice for believers of all ages: "Ask the God who made you to keep remaking you." That advice, of course, is perfectly sound, but often ignored.

When we cease to grow, either emotionally or spiritually, we do ourselves a profound disservice. But, if we study God's Word, if we obey His commandments, and if we live in the center of His will, we will not be "stagnant" believers; we will, instead, be growing Christians . . . and that's exactly what God wants for our lives.

No matter what we are going through, no matter how long the waiting for answers, of one thing we may be sure. God is faithful. He keeps His promises. What He starts, He finishes . . . including His perfect work in us.

*Gloria Gaither*

## — A Prayer for Today —

Lord, I know that I still have so many things to learn. I won't stop learning, I won't give up, and I won't stop growing. Every day, I will do my best to become a little bit more like the person You intend for me to be. Amen

# Relationships Built Upon Honesty

*The one who lives with integrity lives securely, but whoever perverts his ways will be found out.*

Proverbs 10:9 HCSB

Lasting relationships are built upon a foundation of honesty and trust. It has been said on many occasions that honesty is the best policy. For believers, it is far more important to note that honesty is God's policy. And if we are to be servants worthy of our Savior, Jesus Christ, we must be honest and forthright in all our communications with others.

Sometimes, honesty is difficult; sometimes, honesty is painful; sometimes, honesty makes us feel uncomfortable. Despite these temporary feelings of discomfort, we must make honesty the hallmark of all our relationships; otherwise, we invite needless suffering into our own lives and into the lives of those we love.

The single most important element in any human relationship is honesty—with oneself, with God, and with others.

*Catherine Marshall*

## — A Prayer for Today —

Lord, You instruct Your children to seek truth and to live righteously. Help me always to live according to Your commandments. Sometimes, Lord, speaking the truth is difficult, but let me always speak truthfully and forthrightly. Amen

# To God Be the Glory

*Clothe yourselves with humility toward one another, because God resists the proud, but gives grace to the humble.*

*1 Peter 5:5 HCSB*

As Christians, we have a profound reason to be humble: We have been refashioned and saved by Jesus Christ, and that salvation came not because of our own good works but because of God's grace. Thus, we are not "self-made"; we are "God-made" and "Christ-saved." How, then, can we be boastful?

Dietrich Bonhoeffer observed, "It is very easy to overestimate the importance of our own achievements in comparison with what we owe others." In other words, reality breeds humility. So, instead of puffing out your chest and saying, "Look at me!", give credit where credit is due, starting with God. And, rest assured: There is no such thing as a self-made woman. All of us are made by God . . . and He deserves the glory, not us.

Our God is so wonderfully good, and lovely, and blessed in every way that the mere fact of belonging to Him is enough for an untellable fullness of joy!

*Hannah Whitall Smith*

## — A Prayer for Today —

Lord, keep me mindful that all my gifts come from You. Let me grow beyond my need for earthly praise, God, and let me look only to You for approval. Amen

# Mistakes Happen

*Have mercy on me, O God, according to your unfailing love; according to your great compassion blot out my transgressions. Wash away all my iniquity and cleanse me from my sin.*

Psalm 51:1-2 NIV

We are imperfect women living in an imperfect world; mistakes are simply part of the price we pay for being here. But, even though mistakes are an inevitable part of life's journey, repeated mistakes should not be. When we commit the inevitable blunders of life, we must correct them, learn from them, and pray to God for the wisdom not to repeat them. And then, if we are successful, our mistakes become lessons, and our lives become adventures in growth, not stagnation.

Mistakes offer the possibility for redemption and a new start in God's kingdom. No matter what you're guilty of, God can restore your innocence.

*Barbara Johnson*

## — A Prayer for Today —

Lord, sometimes I make mistakes and fall short of your commandments. When I do, forgive me, Father. And help me learn from my mistakes so that I can be a better servant to You and a better example to my friends and family. Amen

# Enough Hours in the Day?

*It is good to give thanks to the Lord, to sing praises to the Most High. It is good to proclaim your unfailing love in the morning, your faithfulness in the evening.*

*Psalm 92:1-2 NLT*

Each day has 1,440 minutes—do you value your relationship with God enough to spend a few of those minutes with Him? He deserves that much of your time and more—is He receiving it from you? Hopefully so. But if you find that you're simply "too busy" for a daily chat with your Father in heaven, it's time to take a long, hard look at your priorities and your values.

As you consider your plans for the day ahead, here's a tip: organize your life around this simple principle: "God first." When you place your Creator where He belongs—at the very center of your day and your life—the rest of your priorities will fall into place.

## — A Prayer for Today —

Dear Lord, every day of my life is a journey with You. I will take time today to think, to pray, and to study Your Word. Guide my steps, Father, and keep me mindful that today offers yet another opportunity to celebrate Your blessings, Your love, and Your Son. Amen

# Doubt and Belief

*Immediately the father of the child cried out and said with tears, "Lord, I believe; help my unbelief!"*

Mark 9:24 NKJV

Even the most faithful Christians are overcome by occasional bouts of fear and doubt. You are no different. When you feel that your faith is being tested to its limits, seek the comfort and assurance of the One who sent His Son as a sacrifice for you.

Have you ever felt your faith in God slipping away? If so, you are not alone. Every life—including yours—is a series of successes and failures, celebrations and disappointments, joys and sorrows, hopes and doubts. But even when you feel very distant from God, God is never distant from you. When you sincerely seek His presence, He will touch your heart, calm your fears, and restore your faith in the future . . . and your faith in Him.

Resisting His will for your life will cause you to doubt.

*Anne Graham Lotz*

## — A Prayer for Today —

Dear Lord, when I am filled with uncertainty and doubt, give me faith. In the dark moments of life, keep me mindful of Your healing power and Your infinite love, so that I may live courageously and faithfully today and every day. Amen

# The Best Policy

*The righteousness of the blameless clears his path, but the wicked person will fall because of his wickedness.*

Proverbs 11:5 HCSB

From the time we are children, we are taught that honesty is the best policy, but sometimes, being honest is hard. So, we convince ourselves that it's alright to tell "little white lies." But there's a problem: Little white lies tend to grow up, and when they do, they cause havoc and pain in our lives.

For Christians, the issue of honesty is not a topic for debate. Honesty is not just the best policy; it is God's policy, pure and simple. And if we are to be servants worthy of our Savior, Jesus Christ, we must avoid all lies, white or otherwise. So, if you're tempted to sow the seeds of deception (perhaps in the form of a "harmless" white lie), resist that temptation. Truth is God's way, and a lie—of whatever color—is not.

Much guilt arises in the life of the believer from practicing the chameleon life of environmental adaptation.

*Beth Moore*

## — A Prayer for Today —

Dear Lord, give me the courage to speak honestly, and let me walk righteously with You so that others might see Your eternal truth reflected in my words and my deeds. Amen

# Imperfect Beings, Imperfect Faith

*The one who trusts in the Lord will be happy.*

Proverbs 16:20 HCSB

Why are we humans plagued by worry? Because we are imperfect beings with imperfect faith. Even though we are Christians who have been given the assurance of salvation—even though we are Christians who have received the promise of God's love and protection—we find ourselves fretting over the countless details of everyday life. Jesus understood our concerns when He spoke the reassuring words found in Matthew 6: "Therefore I tell you, do not worry about your life . . ."

As you consider the promises of Jesus, remember that God still sits in His heaven and you are His beloved child. Then, perhaps, you will worry a little less and trust God a little more, and that's as it should be because God is trustworthy . . . and you are protected.

Remember always that there are two things which are more utterly incompatible even than oil and water, and these two are trust and worry.

*Hannah Whitall Smith*

## — A Prayer for Today —

Forgive me, Lord, when I worry. Worry reflects a lack of trust in You. Help me to work, Lord, and not to worry. And, keep me mindful, Father, that nothing, absolutely nothing, will happen this day that You and I cannot handle together. Amen

# So Laugh!

*A joyful heart makes a face cheerful.*

*Proverbs 15:13 HCSB*

Laughter is God's gift, and He intends that we enjoy it. Yet sometimes, because of the inevitable stresses of everyday life, laughter seems only a distant memory. As Christians we have every reason to be cheerful and to be thankful. Our blessings from God are beyond measure, starting, of course, with a gift that is ours for the asking, God's gift of salvation through Christ Jesus.

Few things in life are more absurd than the sight of a grumpy Christian. So today, as you go about your daily activities, approach life with a grin and a chuckle. After all, God created laughter for a reason . . . to use it. So laugh!

Laughter dulls the sharpest pain and flattens out the greatest stress. To share it is to give a gift of health.

*Barbara Johnson*

## — A Prayer for Today —

Lord, when I begin to take myself or my life too seriously, let me laugh. When I rush from place to place, slow me down, Lord, and let me laugh. Put a smile on my face, Dear Lord, and let me share that smile with all who cross my path . . . and let me laugh. Amen

# Sharing the Good News

*As you go, announce this: "The kingdom of heaven has come near."*

*Matthew 10:7 HCSB*

The Good News of Jesus Christ should be shouted from the rooftops by believers the world over. But all too often, it is not. For a variety of reasons, many Christians keep their beliefs to themselves, and when they do, the world suffers because of their failure to speak up.

As believers, we are called to share the transforming message of Jesus with our families, with our neighbors, and with the world. Jesus commands us to become fishers of men. And, the time to go fishing is now. We must share the Good News of Jesus Christ today— tomorrow may indeed be too late.

There is no thrill quite as wonderful as seeing someone else come to trust Christ because I have been faithful in sharing the story of my own faith.

*Vonette Bright*

## — A Prayer for Today —

Lord, even if I never leave home, make me a missionary for You. Let me share the Good News of Your Son, and let me tell of Your love and of Your grace. Make me a faithful servant for You, Father, now and forever. Amen

# Wisdom in a Donut Shop

*My cup runs over. Surely goodness and mercy shall follow me all the days of my life; and I will dwell in the house of the Lord Forever.*

*Psalm 23:5-6 NKJV*

Many years ago, this rhyme was posted on the wall of a small donut shop:

As you travel through life brother,
Whatever be your goal,
Keep your eye upon the donut,
And not upon the hole.

These simple words remind us of a profound truth: we should spend more time looking at the things we have, not worrying about the things we don't have.

When you think about it, you've got more blessings than you can count. So make it a habit to thank God for the gifts He's given you, not the gifts you wish He'd given you.

Don't miss the beautiful colors of the rainbow while you're looking for the pot of gold at the end of it!

*Barbara Johnson*

## — A Prayer for Today —

Dear Lord, I will look for the best in other people, I will expect the best from You, and I will try my best to do my best—today and every day. Amen

# Pleasing God

*Therefore, whether we are at home or away, we make it our aim to be pleasing to Him.*

*2 Corinthians 5:9 HCSB*

When God made you, He equipped you with an array of talents and abilities that are uniquely yours. It's up to you to discover those talents and to use them, but sometimes the world will encourage you to do otherwise. At times, society will attempt to cubbyhole you, to standardize you, and to make you fit into particular, preformed mold. Perhaps God has other plans.

Sometimes, because you're an imperfect being, you may become so wrapped up in meeting society's expectations that you fail to focus on God's expectations. To do so is a mistake of major proportions—don't make it. Instead, seek God's guidance as you focus your energies on becoming the best "you" that you can possibly be. And, when it comes to matters of conscience, seek approval not from your peers, but from your Creator.

## — A Prayer for Today —

Dear Lord, today I will honor You with my thoughts, my actions, and my prayers. I will seek to please You, and I will strive to serve You. Your blessings are as limitless as Your love. And because I have been so richly blessed, I will worship You, Father, with thanksgiving in my heart and praise on my lips, this day and forever. Amen

# Community Life

*Regarding life together and getting along with each other, you don't need me to tell you what to do. You're God-taught in these matters. Just love one another!*

*1 Thessalonians 4:9 MSG*

As we travel along life's road, we build lifelong relationships with a small, dear circle of family and friends. And how best do we build and maintain these relationships? By following the Word of God. Healthy relationships are built upon honesty, compassion, responsible behavior, trust, and optimism. Healthy relationships are built upon the Golden Rule. Healthy relationships are built upon sharing and caring. All of these principles are found time and time again in God's Holy Word. When we read God's Word and follow His commandments, we enrich our own lives and the lives of those who are closest to us.

Line by line, moment by moment, special times are etched into our memories in the permanent ink of everlasting love in our relationships.

*Gloria Gaither*

## — A Prayer for Today —

Dear Lord, You have brought family members and friends into my life. Let me love them, let me help them, let me treasure them, and let me lead them to You. Amen

# Sharing the Good News

*Christ did not send me to baptize people but to preach the Good News. And he sent me to preach the Good News without using words of human wisdom so that the cross of Christ would not lose its power.*

*1 Corinthians 1:17 NCV*

In his second letter to Timothy, Paul offers a message to believers of every generation when he writes, "God has not given us a spirit of timidity" (1:7 NASB). Paul's meaning is crystal clear: When sharing our testimonies, we, as Christians, must be courageous, forthright, and unashamed.

We live in a world that desperately needs the healing message of Christ Jesus. Every believer, each in his or her own way, bears a personal responsibility for sharing that message.

You know how Christ has touched your heart and changed your life. Now it's your turn to share the Good News with others. And remember: today is the perfect time to share your testimony because tomorrow may quite simply be too late.

## — A Prayer for Today —

Lord, the life that I live and the words that I speak will tell the world how I feel about You. Today and every day, let my testimony be worthy of You. Let my words be sure and true, and let my actions point others to You. Amen

# Standing Up for Our Faith

*Be alert, stand firm in the faith, be brave and strong.*
*1 Corinthians 16:13 HCSB*

Are you a woman whose faith is obvious to your family and to the world, or are you a spiritual shrinking violet? God needs more women who are willing to stand up and be counted for Him.

Genuine faith is never meant to be locked up in the heart of a believer; to the contrary, it is meant to be shared. And a woman who wishes to share God's Good News with the world should begin by sharing that message with her own family.

Through every triumph and tragedy, God will stand by your side and strengthen you . . . if you have faith in Him. Jesus taught His disciples that if they had faith, they could move mountains. You can too, and so can your family . . . if you have faith.

If God chooses to remain silent, faith is content.

*Ruth Bell Graham*

## — A Prayer for Today —

Dear Lord, make me Your obedient, faithful servant. You are with me always. Give me faith and let me remember that with Your love and Your power, I can live courageously and faithfully today and every day. Amen

# The Gift of the Shepherd

*My cup runs over. Surely goodness and mercy shall follow me all the days of my life; and I will dwell in the house of the Lord forever.*

*Psalm 23:5-6 NKJV*

The Word of God is clear: Christ came in order that we might have life abundant and life eternal. Eternal life is the priceless possession of all who invite Christ into their hearts, but God's abundance is optional: He does not force it upon us.

Do you sincerely seek the riches that our Savior offers to those who give themselves to Him? Then follow Him completely and obey Him without reservation. When you do, you will receive the love and the abundance that He has promised. Seek first the salvation that is available through a personal relationship with Jesus Christ, and then claim His joy, His peace, and His abundance.

## — A Prayer for Today —

Good Shepherd, thank You for the abundant life that is mine through Christ Jesus. Guide me according to Your will, and help me to be a worthy servant in all that I say and do. Give me courage, Lord, to claim the rewards You have promised, and when I do, let the glory be Yours. Amen

# Why Do Bad Things Happen?

*They won't be afraid of bad news; their hearts are steady because they trust the Lord.*

*Psalm 112:7 NCV*

If God is good, and if He made the world, why do bad things happen? Part of that question is easy to answer, and part of it isn't. Let's get to the easy part first: Sometimes, bad things happen because people disobey God's commandments and invite sadness and heartache into God's beautiful world.

But on other occasions, bad things happen, and it's nobody's fault. So who is to blame? Sometimes, nobody is to blame. Sometimes, things just happen and we simply cannot know why. Thankfully, all our questions will be answered . . . some day. The Bible promises that in heaven we will understand all the reasons behind God's plans. But until then, we must simply trust that God is good, and that, in the end, He will make things right.

On the darkest day of your life, God is still in charge. Take comfort in that.

*Marie T. Freeman*

## — A Prayer for Today —

Lord, give me courage in every circumstance and in every stage of life. Give me the wisdom, Father, to place my hope and my trust in Your perfect plan and Your boundless love. Amen

# Practicing What We Preach

*If the way you live isn't consistent with what you believe, then it's wrong.*

*Romans 14:23 MSG*

In describing our beliefs, our actions are far better descriptors than our words. Yet far too many of us spend more energy talking about our beliefs than living by them—with predictably poor results.

As believers, we must beware: Our actions should always give credence to the changes that Christ can make in the lives of those who walk with Him.

Your beliefs shape your values, and your values shape your life. Is your life a clearly-crafted picture book of your creed? Are your actions always consistent with your beliefs? Are you willing to practice the philosophies that you preach? Hopefully so; otherwise, you'll be tormented by inconsistencies between your beliefs and your behaviors.

Faith sees the invisible, believes the unbelievable, and receives the impossible.

*Corrie ten Boom*

## — A Prayer for Today —

Lord, it is so much easier to speak of the righteous life than it is to live it. Let me live righteously, and let my actions be consistent with my beliefs. Let every step that I take reflect Your truth, and let me live a life that is worthy of Your Son. Amen

# Always with Us

*For unto us a Child is born, Unto us a Son is given; And the government will be upon His shoulder. And His name will be called Wonderful, Counselor, Mighty God, Everlasting Father, Prince of Peace.*

*Isaiah 9:6 NKJV*

Are you facing difficult circumstances or unwelcome changes? If so, please remember that God is far bigger than any problem you may face. So, instead of worrying about life's inevitable challenges, put your faith in the Father and His only begotten Son: "Jesus Christ is the same yesterday, today, and forever" (Hebrews 13:8 NKJV). And remember: it is precisely because your Savior does not change that you can face your challenges with courage for today and hope for tomorrow.

Life is often challenging, but as Christians, we should not be afraid. God loves us, and He will protect us. In times of hardship, He will comfort us; in times of change, He will guide our steps. When we are troubled or weak or sorrowful, God is always with us. We must build our lives on the rock that cannot be moved . . . we must trust in God. Always.

## — A Prayer for Today —

Dear Lord, our world is constantly changing. When I face the inevitable transitions of life, I will turn to You for strength and assurance. Thank You, Father, for love that is unchanging and everlasting. Amen

# Critics Beware

*Don't pick on people, jump on their failures, criticize their faults—unless, of course, you want the same treatment. Don't condemn those who are down; that hardness can boomerang. Be easy on people; you'll find life a lot easier.*
*Luke 6:37 MSG*

From experience, we know that it is easier to criticize than to correct. And we know that it is easier to find faults than solutions. Yet the urge to criticize others remains a powerful temptation for most of us. Our task, as obedient believers, is to break the twin habits of negative thinking and critical speech.

Negativity is highly contagious: we give it to others who, in turn, give it back to us. This cycle can be broken by positive thoughts, heartfelt prayers, and encouraging words. As thoughtful servants of a loving God, we can use the transforming power of Christ's love to break the chains of negativity. And we should.

Never be afraid of the world's censure; it's praise is much more to be dreaded.
*C. H. Spurgeon*

## — A Prayer for Today —

Help me, Lord, rise above the need to criticize others. May my own shortcomings humble me, and may I always be a source of genuine encouragement to my family and friends. Amen

# A Sacrificial Love

*I am the good shepherd. The good shepherd lays down his life for the sheep.*

John 10:11 HCSB

How much does Christ love us? More than we, as mere mortals, can comprehend. His love is perfect and steadfast. Even though we are fallible and wayward, the Shepherd cares for us still. Even though we have fallen far short of the Father's commandments, Christ loves us with a power and depth that is beyond our understanding. The sacrifice that Jesus made upon the cross was made for each of us, and His love endures to the edge of eternity and beyond.

Christ's love changes everything. When you accept His gift of grace, you are transformed, not only for today, but also for all eternity. If you haven't already done so, accept Jesus Christ as your Savior. He's waiting patiently for you to invite Him into your heart. Please don't make Him wait a single minute longer.

God is my Heavenly Father. He loves me with an everlasting love. The proof of that is the Cross.

*Elisabeth Elliot*

## — A Prayer for Today —

Dear Jesus, I am humbled by Your love and mercy. You went to Calvary so that I might have eternal life. Thank You, Jesus, for Your priceless gift, and for Your love. You loved me first, Lord, and I will return Your love today and forever. Amen

# God's Guidance

*Those who are blessed by Him will inherit the land.*
Psalm 37:22 HCSB

God is intensely interested in each of us, and He will guide our steps if we serve Him obediently.

When we sincerely offer heartfelt prayers to our Heavenly Father, He will give direction and meaning to our lives—but He won't force us to follow Him. To the contrary, God has given us the free will to follow His commandments . . . or not.

When we stray from God's commandments, we invite bitter consequences. But, when we follow His commandments, and when we genuinely and humbly seek His will, He touches our hearts and leads us on the path of His choosing.

Will you trust God to guide your steps? You should. When you entrust your life to Him completely and without reservation, God will give you the strength to meet any challenge, the courage to face any trial, and the wisdom to live in His righteousness and in His peace. So trust Him today and seek His guidance. When you do, your next step will be the right one.

## — A Prayer for Today —

Dear Lord, You always stand ready to guide me. Let me accept Your guidance, today and every day of my life. Lead me, Father, so that my life can be a tribute to Your grace, to Your mercy, to Your love, and to Your Son. Amen

# Contentment Through Christ

*The LORD will give strength to His people; The LORD will bless His people with peace.*

Psalm 29:11 NKJV

Everywhere we turn, or so it seems, the world promises us contentment and happiness. But the contentment that the world offers is fleeting and incomplete. Thankfully, the contentment that God offers is all encompassing and everlasting. Happiness, of course, depends less upon our circumstances than upon our thoughts. When we turn our thoughts to God, to His gifts, and to His glorious creation, we experience the joy that God intends for His children. But, when we focus on the negative aspects of life—or when we disobey God's commandments—we cause ourselves needless suffering.

Do you sincerely want to be a contented Christian? Then set your mind and your heart upon God's love and His grace. Seek first the salvation that is available through a personal relationship with Jesus Christ, and then claim the joy, the contentment, and the spiritual abundance that the Shepherd offers His sheep.

## — A Prayer for Today —

Dear Lord, You offer me contentment and peace; let me accept Your peace. Help me to trust Your Word, to follow Your commandments, and to welcome the peace of Jesus into my heart, today and forever. Amen

# For All Eternity

*"I assure you: Anyone who hears My word and believes Him who sent Me has eternal life and will not come under judgment, but has passed from death to life."*

*John 5:24–25 HCSB*

As mere mortals, our vision for the future, like our lives here on earth, is limited. God's vision is not burdened by such limitations: His plans extend throughout all eternity. Thus, God's plans for you are not limited to the ups and downs of everyday life. Your Heavenly Father has bigger things in mind . . . much bigger things.

Let us praise the Creator for His priceless gift, and let us share the Good News with all who cross our paths. We return our Father's love by accepting His grace and by sharing His message and His love. When we do, we are blessed here on earth and throughout all eternity.

Your choice to either receive or reject the Lord Jesus Christ will determine where you spend eternity.

*Anne Graham Lotz*

## — A Prayer for Today —

Lord, I am only here on this earth for a brief while. But, You have offered me the gift of eternal life through Your Son Jesus. I accept Your gift, Lord, with thanksgiving and praise. Let me share the good news of my salvation with those who need Your healing touch. Amen

# Faith That Moves Mountains

*I assure you: If anyone says to this mountain, "Be lifted up and thrown into the sea," and does not doubt in his heart, but believes that what he says will happen, it will be done for him.*

*Mark 11:23 HCSB*

Because we live in a demanding world, all of us have mountains to climb and mountains to move. Moving those mountains requires faith.

Are you a mountain mover whose faith is evident for all to see? Hopefully so. God needs more women who are willing to move mountains for His glory and for His kingdom.

God walks with you, ready and willing to strengthen you. Accept His strength today. And remember—Jesus taught His disciples that if they had faith, they could move mountains. You can too . . . so with no further ado, let the mountain-moving begin.

Let me encourage you to continue to wait with faith. God may not perform a miracle, but He is trustworthy to touch you and make you whole where there used to be a hole.

*Lisa Whelchel*

## — A Prayer for Today —

Dear Lord, I want faith that moves mountains. You have big plans for this world and big plans for me. Help me fulfill those plans, Father, as I follow in the footsteps of Your Son. Amen

# Plans: Yours and God's

*People may make plans in their minds, but the Lord decides what they will do.*

Proverbs 16:9 NCV

If you're like most people, you want things to happen according to your wishes and according to your timetable. But sometimes, God has other plans . . . and He always has the final word.

Are you embittered by a personal tragedy that you did not deserve and cannot understand? If so, it's time to make peace with life. It's time to forgive others, and, if necessary, to forgive yourself. It's time to accept the unchangeable past, to embrace the priceless present, and to have faith in the promise of tomorrow. It's time to trust God completely. And it's time to reclaim the peace—His peace—that can and should be yours. So, if you've encountered unfortunate circumstances that are beyond your power to control, accept those circumstances . . . and trust God. When you do, you can be comforted in the knowledge that your Creator is both loving and wise, and that He understands His plans perfectly, even when you do not.

## — A Prayer for Today —

Lord, when I am discouraged, give me hope. When I am impatient, give me peace. When I face circumstances that I cannot change, give me a spirit of acceptance. In all things great and small, let me trust in Your plans, Dear Lord, today and forever. Amen

# The Search for Significance

*For everything, absolutely everything, above and below, visible and invisible, rank after rank after rank of angels— everything got started in him and finds its purpose in him.*
Colossians 1:16 MSG

"What on earth does God intend for me to do with my life?" It's an easy question to ask but, for many of us, a difficult question to answer. Why? Because God's purposes aren't always clear to us. Sometimes we wander aimlessly in a wilderness of our own making. And sometimes, we struggle mightily against God in an unsuccessful attempt to find success and happiness through our own means, not His.

If you're a woman who sincerely seeks God's guidance, He will give it. But, He will make His revelations known to you in a way and in a time of His choosing, not yours, so be patient. Even on those difficult days when you are unsure which way to turn, you must never lose sight of these overriding facts: God created you for a reason; He has important work for you to do; and He's waiting patiently for you to do it. The next step is up to you.

## — A Prayer for Today —

Dear Lord, I seek to live a meaningful life; I will turn to You to find that meaning. I will study Your Word, I will obey Your commandments, I will trust Your providence, and I will honor Your Son. Give me Your blessings, Father, and lead me along a path that is pleasing to You, today, tomorrow, and forever. Amen

# The Joys of Friendship

*I give thanks to my God for every remembrance of you.*
*Philippians 1:3 HCSB*

What is a friend? The dictionary defines the word *friend* as "a person who is attached to another by feelings of affection or personal regard." This definition is accurate, as far as it goes, but when we examine the deeper meaning of friendship, so many more descriptors come to mind: trustworthiness, loyalty, helpfulness, kindness, encouragement, humor, and cheerfulness, to mention but a few.

Today, as you consider the many blessings that God has given you, remember to thank Him for the friends He has chosen to place along your path. May you be a blessing to them, and may they richly bless you today, tomorrow, and every day that you live.

Don't bypass the potential for meaningful friendships just because of differences. Explore them. Embrace them. Love them.

*Luci Swindoll*

## — A Prayer for Today —

Dear Lord, I thank You for my friends. You have brought wonderful Christian friends into my life. Let our friendships honor You as we walk in the footsteps of Your Son. Amen

# Ready. Set. Go!

*Do not neglect the gift that is in you.*

1 Timothy 4:14 HCSB

God has given you talents and opportunities that are uniquely yours. Are you willing to use your gifts in the way that God intends? And are you willing to summon the discipline that is required to develop your talents and to hone your skills? That's precisely what God wants you to do, and that's precisely what you should desire for yourself.

As you seek to expand your talents, you will undoubtedly encounter stumbling blocks along the way, such as the fear of rejection or the fear of failure. When you do, don't stumble! Just continue to refine your skills, and offer your services to God. And when the time is right, He will use you—but it's up to you to be thoroughly prepared when He does.

Great relief and satisfaction can come from seeking God's priorities for us in each season, discerning what is "best" in the midst of many noble opportunities, and pouring our most excellent energies into those things.

*Beth Moore*

## — A Prayer for Today —

Lord, I praise You for Your priceless gifts. I give thanks for Your creation, for Your Son, and for the unique talents and opportunities that You have given me. Let me use my gifts for the glory of Your kingdom, this day and every day. Amen

# Great Is Thy Faithfulness

*God is faithful, by whom you were called into the fellowship of His Son, Jesus Christ our Lord.*

*1 Corinthians 1:9 NKJV*

God is faithful to us even when we are not faithful to Him. God keeps His promises to us even when we stray far from His will. He continues to love us even when we disobey His commandments. But God does not force His blessings upon us. If we are to experience His love and His grace, we must claim them for ourselves.

Are you tired, discouraged, or fearful? Be comforted: God is with you. Are you confused? Listen to the quiet voice of your Heavenly Father. Are you bitter? Talk with God and seek His guidance. Are you celebrating a great victory? Thank God and praise Him. He is the Giver of all things good. In whatever condition you find yourself, trust God and be comforted. The Father is with you now and forever.

God is always sufficient in perfect proportion to our need.

*Beth Moore*

## — A Prayer for Today —

Your faithfulness, Lord, is everlasting. You are faithful to me even when I am not faithful to You. Today, let me serve You with my heart, my soul, and my mind. And, then, let me rest in the knowledge of Your constant love for me. Amen

# Infinite Possibilities

*Is anything too hard for the LORD?*

*Genesis 18:14 KJV*

Ours is a God of infinite possibilities. But sometimes, because of limited faith and limited understanding, we wrongly assume that God cannot or will not intervene in the affairs of mankind. Such assumptions are simply wrong.

Are you afraid to ask God to do big things in your life? Is your faith threadbare and worn? If so, it's time to abandon your doubts and reclaim your faith in God's promises. God's Holy Word makes it clear: absolutely nothing is impossible for the Lord. And since the Bible means what it says, you can be comforted in the knowledge that the Creator of the universe can do miraculous things in your own life and in the lives of your loved ones. Your challenge, as a believer, is to take God at His word, and to expect the miraculous.

We will see more and more that we are chosen not because of our ability, but because of the Lord's power, which will be demonstrated in our not being able.

*Corrie ten Boom*

## — A Prayer for Today —

Dear God, nothing is impossible for You—keep me always mindful of Your strength. When I lose hope, give me faith; when others lose hope, let me tell them of Your glory and Your works. Today, Lord, let me expect the miraculous, and let me trust in You. Amen

# God's Timetable

*Humble yourselves therefore under the mighty hand of God, so that He may exalt you in due time, casting all your care upon Him, because He cares about you.*

*1 Peter 5:6-7 HCSB*

Sometimes, the hardest thing to do is to wait. This is especially true when we're in a hurry and when we want things to happen now, if not sooner! But God's plan does not always happen in the way that we would like or at the time of our own choosing. Our task—as believing Christians—is to wait patiently for God to reveal Himself.

We human beings are, by nature, impatient. We know what we want, and we know exactly when we want it: RIGHT NOW! But, God knows better. He has created a world that unfolds according to His own timetable, not ours . . . thank goodness!

When we read of the great Biblical leaders, we see that it was not uncommon for God to ask them to wait, not just a day or two, but for years, until God was ready for them to act.

*Gloria Gaither*

## — A Prayer for Today —
Dear Lord, Your timing is always right for me. You have a plan for my life that is grander than I can imagine. When I am impatient, remind me that You are never early or late. You are always on time, Father, so let me trust in You . . . always. Amen

# Beyond Guilt

*There is therefore now no condemnation to those who are in Christ Jesus, who do not walk according to the flesh, but according to the Spirit.*

*Romans 8:1 NKJV*

All of us have sinned. Sometimes our sins result from our own stubborn rebellion against God's commandments. And sometimes, we are swept up in events that are beyond our abilities to control. Under either set of circumstances, we may experience intense feelings of guilt. But God has an answer for the guilt that we feel. That answer, of course, is His forgiveness. When we confess our wrongdoings and repent from them, we are forgiven by the One who created us.

Are you troubled by feelings of guilt or regret? If so, you must repent from your misdeeds, and you must ask your Heavenly Father for His forgiveness. When you do so, He will forgive you completely and without reservation. Then, you must forgive yourself just as God has forgiven you: thoroughly and unconditionally.

If God has forgiven you, why can't you forgive yourself?

*Marie T. Freeman*

## — A Prayer for Today —

Dear Lord, thank You for the guilt that I feel when I disobey You. Help me confess my wrongdoings, help me accept Your forgiveness, and help me renew my passion to serve You. Amen

# Accepting God's Gifts

*For God loved the world in this way: He gave His only Son, so that everyone who believes in Him will not perish but have eternal life.*

John 3:16 HCSB

God loves you—His love for you is deeper and more profound than you can imagine. God's love for you is so great that He sent His only Son to this earth to die for your sins and to offer you the priceless gift of eternal life.

You must decide whether or not to accept God's gift. Will you ignore it or embrace it? Will you return it or neglect it? Will you invite Christ to dwell in the center of your heart, or will you relegate Him to a position of lesser importance? The decision is yours, and so are the consequences. So choose wisely . . . and choose today.

## — A Prayer for Today —

Dear Lord, You sent Your Son to this earth that we might have the gift of eternal life. Thank You, Father, for that priceless gift. Help me to share the wondrous message of Jesus with others so that they, too, might accept Him as their Savior. And, let me praise You always for the new life You have given me, a life that is both abundant and eternal. Amen

# Above and Beyond Our Circumstances

*Should we accept only good from God and not adversity?*
*Job 2:10 HCSB*

All of us face difficult days. Sometimes even the most devout Christian women can become discouraged, and you are no exception. After all, you live in a world where expectations can be high and demands can be even higher.

If you find yourself enduring difficult circumstances, remember that God remains in His heaven. If you become discouraged with the direction of your day or your life, turn your thoughts and prayers to Him. He is a God of possibility, not negativity. He will guide you through your difficulties and beyond them . . . far beyond.

Worry is the senseless process of cluttering up tomorrow's opportunities with leftover problems from today.
*Barbara Johnson*

## — A Prayer for Today —

Dear Heavenly Father, when I am troubled, You heal me. When I am afraid, You protect me. When I am discouraged, You lift me up. During the difficult days of my life, I will me trust You. And whatever my circumstances, Lord, I thank You for Your blessings, for Your love, and for Your Son. Amen

# Taking Up the Cross

*Then He said to them all, "If anyone wants to come with Me, he must deny himself, take up his cross daily, and follow Me."*

Luke 9:23 HCSB

When we have been saved by Christ, we can, if we choose, become passive Christians. We can sit back, secure in our own salvation, and let other believers spread the healing message of Jesus. But to do so is wrong. Instead, we are commanded to become disciples of the One who has saved us, and to do otherwise is a sin of omission with terrible consequences. When Jesus addressed His disciples, He warned them that each one must, "take up his cross daily and follow me" (Luke 9:23 NIV). Christ's message was clear: in order to follow Him, Christ's disciples must deny themselves and, instead, trust Him completely. Nothing has changed since then.

Do you seek to fulfill God's purpose for your life? Then follow Christ. Follow Him by picking up His cross today and every day that you live. Then, you will quickly discover that Christ's love has the power to change everything, including you.

## — A Prayer for Today —

Help me, Lord, to understand what cross I am to bear this day. Give me the strength and the courage to carry that cross along the path of Your choosing so that I may be a worthy disciple of Your Son. Amen

# Encouragement Now!

*Bright eyes cheer the heart; good news strengthens the bones.*
*Proverbs 15:30 HCSB*

Barnabas, a man whose name meant "Son of Encouragement," was a leader in the early Christian church. He was known for his kindness and for his ability to encourage others. Because of Barnabas, many people were introduced to Christ. And today, as believers living in a difficult world, we must seek to imitate the "Son of Encouragement."

We imitate Barnabas when we speak kind words to our families and to our friends. We imitate Barnabas when our actions give credence to our beliefs. We imitate Barnabas when we are generous with our possessions and with our praise. We imitate Barnabas when we give hope to the hopeless and encouragement to the downtrodden.

Today, be like Barnabas: become a source of encouragement to those who cross your path. When you do so, you will quite literally change the world, one person—and one moment—at a time.

## — A Prayer for Today —

Make me sensitive, O Lord, to the many gifts of encouragement I receive each day. And, let me be a source of encouragement to all who cross my path. The Bible tells of Your servant Barnabas. Like Barnabas, I, too, want to be an encourager to my family and friends so that I might do Your work and share Your love. Amen

# A Passion for Life

*But those who trust in the Lord will renew their strength; they will soar on wings like eagles; they will run and not grow weary; they will walk and not faint.*

Isaiah 40:31 HCSB

Are you enthusiastic about your life and your faith? Hopefully so. But if your zest for life has waned, it is now time to redirect your efforts and recharge your spiritual batteries. And that means refocusing your priorities (by putting God first) and counting your blessings (instead of your troubles).

Nothing is more important than your wholehearted commitment to your Creator and to His only begotten Son. Your faith must never be an afterthought; it must be your ultimate priority, your ultimate possession, and your ultimate passion. When you become passionate about your faith, you'll become passionate about your life, too. And God will smile.

If your heart has grown cold, it is because you have moved away from the fire of His presence.

Beth Moore

## — A Prayer for Today —

Dear Lord, if the obligations of the day leave me exhausted or discouraged, I will turn to You for strength and for renewal. When I follow Your will for my life, You will renew my enthusiasm. Let Your will be my will, Lord, and let me find strength and courage in You. Amen

# The Greatest of These

*Now these three remain: faith, hope, and love. But the greatest of these is love.*

1 Corinthians 13:13 HCSB

The beautiful words of 1st Corinthians 13 remind us that love is God's commandment: Faith is important, of course. So, too, is hope. But, love is more important still. We are commanded (not advised, not encouraged . . . commanded!) to love one another just as Christ loved us (John 13:34). That's a tall order, but as Christians, we are obligated to follow it.

Christ showed His love for us on the cross, and we are called upon to return Christ's love by sharing it. Today, let us spread Christ's love to families, friends, and even strangers, so that through us, others might come to know Him.

Prayer is the ultimate love language. It communicates in ways we can't.

*Stormie Omartian*

## — A Prayer for Today —

Lord, love is Your commandment. Help me always to remember that the gift of love is a precious gift indeed. Let me nurture love and treasure it, today and forever. Amen

# The Cornerstone

*Let us fix our eyes on Jesus, the author and perfecter of
our faith, who for the joy set before him endured the cross,
scorning its shame, and sat down at the right hand of the
throne of God.*

*Hebrews 12:2 NIV*

Is Christ the focus of your life? Are you fired with
enthusiasm for Him? Are you an energized Christian
who allows God's Son to reign over every aspect of your
day? Make no mistake: that's exactly what God intends
for you to do.

God has given you the gift of eternal life through
His Son. In response to God's priceless gift, you are
instructed to focus your thoughts, your prayers, and your
energies upon God and His only begotten Son. To do
so, you must resist the subtle yet powerful temptation
to become a "spiritual dabbler." A person who dabbles
in the Christian faith is unwilling to place God above
all other things. Resist that temptation; make God the
cornerstone and the touchstone of your life. When you
do, He will give you all the strength and wisdom you
need to live victoriously for Him.

## — A Prayer for Today —

Lord, You have told me to give thanks always and to
rejoice in Your marvelous creation. Let me be a joyful
Christian, Lord, and let me focus my thoughts upon
Your blessings and Your love. Amen

# In a Hurry?

*I wait for the Lord; I wait, and put my hope in His word.*
*Psalm 130:5 HCSB*

Are you a woman in a hurry? If so, you may be in for a few disappointments. Why? Because life has a way of unfolding according to God's timetable, not yours. That's why life requires patience . . . and lots of it!

Lamentations 3:25-26 reminds us that, "The Lord is wonderfully good to those who wait for him and seek him. So it is good to wait quietly for salvation from the Lord" (NIV). But, for most of us, waiting quietly for God is difficult because we're in such a hurry for things to happen!

The next time you find your patience tested to the limit, slow down and trust God. Sometimes, we must wait patiently for Him, and that's as it should be. After all, think how patient God has been with us.

Let me encourage you to continue to wait with faith. God may not perform a miracle, but He is trustworthy to touch you and make you whole where there used to be a hole.

*Lisa Whelchel*

## — A Prayer for Today —

Dear Lord, give me wisdom and patience. When I am hurried, give me peace. When I am frustrated, give me perspective. When I am angry, keep me mindful of Your presence. Today, let me be a patient Christian, Lord, as I trust in You and in Your master plan for my life. Amen

# Keeping Possessions in Perspective

*And He told them, "Watch out and be on guard against all greed, because one's life is not in the abundance of his possessions."*

*Luke 12:15 HCSB*

All too often, we focus our thoughts and energies on the accumulation of earthly treasures, leaving precious little time to accumulate the only treasures that really matter: the spiritual kind. Our material possessions have the potential to do great good or terrible harm, depending upon how we choose to use them. As believers, our instructions are clear: we must use our possessions in accordance with God's commandments, and we must be faithful stewards of the gifts He has seen fit to bestow upon us.

Today, let us honor God by placing no other gods before Him. God comes first; everything else comes next—and "everything else" most certainly includes all of our earthly possessions.

## — A Prayer for Today —

Dear Lord, Your Word teaches me to seek first Your kingdom and Your righteousness. Today, I will trust You completely for my needs, both spiritual and material. Thank You, Father, for Your protection, for Your love, and for Your Son. Amen

# Spiritual Renewal

*Therefore if anyone is in Christ, he is a new creature; the old things passed away; behold, new things have come.*

*2 Corinthians 5:17 HCSB*

Even the most inspired Christian women can, from time to time, find themselves running on empty. The demands of daily life can drain us of our strength and rob us of the joy that is rightfully ours in Christ.

Are you tired or troubled? Turn your heart toward God in prayer. Are you weak or worried? Take the time—or, more accurately, make the time—to delve deeply into God's Holy Word. Are you spiritually depleted? Call upon fellow believers to support you, and call upon Christ to renew your spirit and your life. When you do, you'll discover that the Creator of the universe stands always ready and always able to create a new sense of wonderment and joy in you.

He is the God of wholeness and restoration.

*Stormie Omartian*

## — A Prayer for Today —

Lord, I am an imperfect woman. Because my faith is limited, I may become overwhelmed by the demands of the day. When I feel tired or discouraged, renew my strength. When I am worried, let me turn my thoughts and my prayers to You. Let me trust Your promises, Dear Lord, and let me accept Your unending love, now and forever. Amen

# His Transforming Power

*Your old sinful self has died, and your new life is kept with Christ in God.*

*Colossians 3:3 NCV*

God's hand has the power to transform your day and your life. Your task is to accept Christ's grace with a humble, thankful heart as you receive the "new life" that can be yours through Him. Righteous believers who fashion their days around Jesus see the world differently; they act differently, and they feel differently about themselves and their neighbors. Hopefully, you, too, will be such a believer.

Do you desire to improve some aspect of your life? If so, don't expect changing circumstances to miraculously transform you into the person you want to become. Transformation starts with God, and it starts in the quiet corners of a willing human heart—like yours.

God's work is not in buildings, but in transformed lives.

*Ruth Bell Graham*

## — A Prayer for Today —

Dear Lord, let my thoughts and my actions demonstrate the difference that Your Son has made in my life. Let me live righteously, and let my actions be consistent with my beliefs. Let every step that I take reflect Your truth, and let me live a life that is worthy of Your Son. Amen

# Sharing Words of Hope

*And let us be concerned about one another in order to promote love and good works.*

*Hebrews 10:24 HCSB*

Hope, like other human emotions, is contagious. When we associate with hope-filled Christians, we are encouraged by their faith and optimism. But, if we spend too much time in the company of naysayers and pessimists, our attitudes, like theirs, tend to be cynical and negative.

Are you a hopeful, optimistic, encouraging believer? And do you associate with like-minded people? Hopefully so. As a faithful follower of the One from Galilee, you have every reason to be hopeful, and you have every reason to share your hopes with others. So today, look for reasons to celebrate God's endless blessings. And while you're at it, look for people who will join you in the celebration. You'll be better for their company, and they'll be better for yours.

## — A Prayer for Today —

Dear Lord, make me a source of genuine, lasting encouragement to my family and friends. Today, I will celebrate Your blessings, and I will share Your Good News with those who cross my path. Let my words and deeds be worthy of Your Son, the One who gives me strength and salvation. Amen

# Facing Life's Trials

*So because of Christ, I am pleased in weaknesses, in insults, in catastrophes, in persecutions, and in pressures. For when I am weak, then I am strong.*

*2 Corinthians 12:10 HCSB*

Life is a tapestry of good days and difficult days, with good days predominating. During the good days, we are tempted to take our blessings for granted (a temptation that we must resist with all our might). But, during life's difficult days, we discover precisely what we're made of. And more importantly, we discover what our faith is made of.

Has your faith been put to the test yet? If so, then you know that with God's help, you can endure life's darker days. But if you have not yet faced the inevitable trials and tragedies of life-here-on-earth, don't worry: you will. And when your faith is put to the test, rest assured that God is perfectly willing—and always ready—to give you strength for the struggle.

God knows exactly how much you can take, and He will never permit you to reach a breaking point.

*Barbara Johnson*

## — A Prayer for Today —

Dear Lord, in the dark moments of my life, help me to remember that You, my Savior, are always near and that You can overcome any challenge. Keep me mindful of Your love and Your power, so that I may live courageously and faithfully today and every day. Amen

# Practical Christianity

*Therefore, get your minds ready for action, being self-disciplined, and set your hope completely on the grace to be brought to you at the revelation of Jesus Christ.*

1 Peter 1:13 HCSB

As Christians, we must do our best to ensure that our actions are accurate reflections of our beliefs. Our theology must be demonstrated, not only by our words but, more importantly, by our actions. In short, we should be practical believers, quick to act whenever we see an opportunity to serve God.

Are you the kind of practical Christian woman who is willing to dig in and do what needs to be done when it needs to be done? If so, congratulations: God acknowledges your service and blesses it. But if you find yourself more interested in the fine points of theology than in the needs of your neighbors, it's time to rearrange your priorities. God needs believers who are willing to roll up their sleeves and go to work for Him. Count yourself among that number. Theology is a good thing unless it interferes with God's work. And it's up to you to make certain that your theology doesn't.

## — A Prayer for Today —

Heavenly Father, I believe in You, and I believe in Your Word. Help me to live in such a way that my actions validate my beliefs—and let the glory be Yours forever. Amen

# Beyond Bitterness

*Don't insist on getting even; that's not for you to do. "I'll do the judging," says God. "I'll take care of it."*

Romans 12:19 MSG

Bitterness is a spiritual sickness. It will consume your soul; it is dangerous to your emotional health. It can destroy you if you let it . . . so don't let it! If you are caught up in intense feelings of anger or resentment, you know all too well the destructive power of these emotions. How can you rid yourself of these feelings? First, you must prayerfully ask God to cleanse your heart. Then, you must learn to catch yourself whenever thoughts of bitterness or hatred begin to attack you. Your challenge is this: You must learn to resist negative thoughts before they hijack your emotions.

Matthew 5:22 teaches us that if we judge our brothers and sisters, we, too, will be subject to judgement. Let us refrain, then, from judging our neighbors. Instead, let us forgive them and love them, while leaving their judgement to a far more capable authority: the One who sits on His throne in heaven.

## — A Prayer for Today —

Dear Lord, free me from the poison of bitterness and the futility of blame. Let me turn away from destructive emotions so that I may know the perfect peace and spiritual abundance that can be mine through Your Son, and when I discover His peace, let me share it with praise on my lips and love in my heart. Amen

# Mid-Course Corrections

*The sensible see danger and take cover; the foolish keep going and are punished.*

*Proverbs 27:12 HCSB*

In our fast-paced world, everyday life has become an exercise in managing change. Our circumstances change; our relationships change; our bodies change. We grow older every day, as does our world. Thankfully, God does not change. He is eternal, as are the truths that are found in His Holy Word.

Are you facing one of life's inevitable "mid-course corrections"? If so, you must place your faith, your trust, and your life in the hands of the One who does not change: your Heavenly Father. He is the unmoving rock upon which you must construct this day and every day. When you do, you are secure.

Mistakes offer the possibility for redemption and a new start in God's kingdom. No matter what you're guilty of, God can restore your innocence.

*Barbara Johnson*

## — A Prayer for Today —

Heavenly Father, when the world seems to be spinning out of control, I will turn to You. I will trust Your wisdom, I will trust Your plans for my life, and I will trust Your Son, this day and every day. Amen

# Our Children, Our Hope

*Let the little children come to Me; don't stop them, for the kingdom of God belongs to such as these.*

Mark 10:14 HCSB

Every child is different, but every child is similar in this respect: he or she is a priceless gift from the Father above. And, with the Father's gift comes immense responsibilities.

Our children are our most precious resource. And, as responsible adults, we must create homes in which the future generation can grow and flourish.

Today, let us pray for our children . . . all of them. Let us pray for children here at home and for children around the world. Every child is God's child. May we, as concerned adults, behave—and pray—accordingly.


Children are not so different from kites. Children were created to fly. But, they need wind, the undergirding, and strength that comes from unconditional love, encouragement, and prayer.

*Gigi Graham Tchividjian*


## — A Prayer for Today —

Today, Dear Lord, I pray for all Your children. This world holds countless dangers and temptations. I pray that our children may be protected from harm, and that they may discover Your will, Your love, and Your Son. Amen

# Living in Christ's Love

*So now, little children, remain in Him, so that when He appears we may have boldness and not be ashamed before Him at His coming.*

1 John 2:28-29 HCSB

Even though we are imperfect, fallible human beings, even though we have fallen far short of God's commandments, Christ loves us still. His love is perfect and steadfast; it does not waver—it does not change. Our task, as believers, is to accept Christ's love and to encourage others to do likewise.

In today's troubled world, we all need the love and the peace that is found through the Son of God. Thankfully, Christ's love has no limits; it can encircle all of us. And it's up to each of us to ensure that it does.

It has been the faith of the Son of God who loves me and gave Himself for me that has held me in the darkest valley and the hottest fires and the deepest waters.

*Elisabeth Elliot*

## — A Prayer for Today —

Dear Jesus, I know that You love me today and that You will love me forever. And I thank You for Your love . . . today and forever. Amen

# His Power and Yours

*When we were baptized, we were buried with Christ and shared his death. So, just as Christ was raised from the dead by the wonderful power of the Father, we also can live a new life.*

*Romans 6:4 NCV*

When you invite Christ to rule over your heart, you avail yourself of His power. And make no mistake about it: You and Christ, working together, can do miraculous things. In fact, miraculous things are exactly what Christ intends for you to do, but He won't force you to do great things on His behalf. The decision to become a full-fledged participant in His power is a decision that you must make for yourself.

In John 14:12, Christ make this promise: "I tell you the truth, whoever believes in me will do the same things that I do" (NCV). So trust the Savior's promise, and expect a miracle in His name.

The amount of power you experience to live a victorious, triumphant Christian life is directly proportional to the freedom you give the Spirit to be Lord of your life!

*Anne Graham Lotz*

## — A Prayer for Today —

Dear Lord, Your Son died for the salvation of all mankind, and He died for me. Through the power of Christ, I can be compassionate, courageous, and strong. Help me use that power, Father, for the glory of Your kingdom, today and forever. Amen

# Finding Contentment

*I am able to do all things through Him who strengthens me.*
*Philippians 4:13 HCSB*

Where can we find contentment? Is it a result of wealth or power or beauty or fame? Hardly. Genuine contentment is a gift from God to those who trust Him and follow His commandments.

Our modern world seems preoccupied with the search for happiness. We are bombarded with messages telling us that happiness depends upon the acquisition of material possessions. These messages are false. Enduring peace is not the result of our acquisitions; it is a spiritual gift from God to those who obey Him and accept His will.

If we don't find contentment in God, we will never find it anywhere else. But, if we seek Him and obey Him, we will be blessed with an inner peace that is beyond human understanding. When God dwells at the center of our lives, peace and contentment will belong to us just as surely as we belong to God.

We will never be happy until we make God the source of our fulfillment and the answer to our longings.

*Stormie Omartian*

## — A Prayer for Today —

Dear Lord, let me find contentment and balance. Let Your priorities be my priorities. And when I have done my best, give me the wisdom to place my faith and my trust in You. Amen

# Beyond Anxiety

*In the multitude of my anxieties within me, Your comforts delight my soul.*

*Psalm 94:19 NKJV*

God calls us to live above and beyond anxiety. God calls us to live by faith, not by fear. He instructs us to trust Him completely, this day and forever. But sometimes, trusting God is difficult, especially when we become caught up in the incessant demands of an anxious world.

When you feel anxious—and you will—return your thoughts to God's love. Then, take your concerns to Him in prayer, and to the best of your ability, leave them there. Whatever "it" is, God is big enough to handle it. Let Him. Now.

The moment anxious thoughts invade your mind, go to the Lord in prayer. Look first to God. Then, you will see the cause of your anxiety in a whole new light.

*Kay Arthur*

## — A Prayer for Today —

Lord, sometimes this world is a difficult place, and, as a frail human being, I am fearful. When I am worried, restore my faith. When I am anxious, turn my thoughts to You. Amen

# Keeping Up Appearances

*We justify our actions by appearances; God examines our motives.*

*Proverbs 21:2 MSG*

The world sees you as you appear to be; God sees you as you really are . . . He sees your heart, and He understands your intentions. The opinions of others should be relatively unimportant to you; however, God's view of you—His understanding of your actions, your thoughts, and your motivations—should be vitally important.

Few things in life are more futile than "keeping up appearances" for the sake of neighbors. What is important, of course, is pleasing your Father in heaven. You please Him when your intentions are pure and your actions are just.

Outside appearances, things like the clothes you wear or the car you drive, are important to other people but totally unimportant to God. Trust God.

*Marie T. Freeman*

## — A Prayer for Today —

Heavenly Father, examine my heart and show me ways that I can become a better woman. Let my motives be pure, Lord, and let my actions please You, today and every day of my life. Amen

# The Direction of Your Thoughts

*My cup runs over. Surely goodness and mercy shall follow me all the days of my life; and I will dwell in the house of the Lord Forever.*

*Psalm 23:5-6 NKJV*

God has given you free will, including the ability to influence the direction and the tone of your thoughts. And, here's how God wants you to direct those thoughts: "Finally brothers, whatever is true, whatever is honorable, whatever is just, whatever is pure, whatever is lovely, whatever is commendable—if there is any moral excellence and if there is any praise—dwell on these things" (Philippians 4:8 HCSB).

The quality of your attitude will help determine the quality of your life, so you must guard your thoughts accordingly. If you make up your mind to approach life with a healthy mixture of realism and optimism, you'll be rewarded. But, if you allow yourself to fall into the unfortunate habit of negative thinking, you will doom yourself to unhappiness or mediocrity, or worse. So, the next time you find yourself dwelling upon the negative aspects of your life, refocus your attention on things positive. That's the wise way to direct your thoughts.

## — A Prayer for Today —

Lord, I pray for an attitude that is Christlike. Whatever my circumstances, whether good or bad, triumphal or tragic, let my response reflect a God-honoring attitude of optimism, faith, and love for You. Amen

# Courage During Times of Change

*Therefore don't worry about tomorrow, because tomorrow will worry about itself. Each day has enough trouble of its own.*

*Matthew 6:34 HCSB*

Are you anxious about situations that you cannot control? Take your anxieties to God. Are you troubled about changes that threaten to disrupt your life? Take your troubles to Him. Does your corner of the world seem to be trembling beneath your feet? Seek protection from the One who cannot be moved.

The same God who created the universe will protect you if you ask Him . . . so ask Him . . . and then serve Him with willing hands and a trusting heart. And rest assured that the world may change moment by moment, but God's love endures—unfathomable and unchanging—forever.

Live for today, but hold your hands open to tomorrow. Anticipate the future and its changes with joy. There is a seed of God's love in every event, every circumstance, every unpleasant situation in which you may find yourself.

*Barbara Johnson*

## — A Prayer for Today —

Dear Lord, help me become the woman I can be and should be. Guide me along a path of Your choosing, and let me follow in the footsteps of Your Son, today and every day. Amen

# Choosing Wisely

*But the wisdom that is from above is first pure, then peaceable, gentle, willing to yield, full of mercy and good fruits, without partiality and without hypocrisy.*

*James 3:17 NKJV*

Because we are creatures of free will, we make choices—lots of them. When we make choices that are pleasing to our Heavenly Father, we are blessed. When we make choices that cause us to walk in the footsteps of God's Son, we enjoy the abundance that Christ has promised to those who follow Him. But when we make choices that are displeasing to God, we sow seeds that have the potential to bring forth a bitter harvest.

Today, as you encounter the challenges of everyday living, you will make hundreds of choices. Choose wisely. Make your thoughts and your actions pleasing to God. And remember: every choice that is displeasing to Him is the wrong choice—no exceptions.

Faith is not a feeling; it is action. It is a willed choice.

*Elisabeth Elliot*

## — A Prayer for Today —

Dear Lord, today I will focus my thoughts on Your will for my life. I will strive to make decisions that are pleasing to You, and I will strive to follow in the footsteps of Your Son. Amen

# His Infinite Love

*For I am persuaded that neither death nor life, nor angels nor rulers, nor things present, nor things to come, nor powers, nor height, nor depth, nor any other created thing will have the power to separate us from the love of God that is in Christ Jesus our Lord!*

*Romans 8:38-39 HCSB*

Christ's love for you is personal. He loves you so much that He gave His life in order that you might spend all eternity with Him. Christ loves you individually and intimately; His is a love unbounded by time or circumstance. Are you willing to experience an intimate relationship with Him? Your Savior is waiting patiently; don't make Him wait a single minute longer. Embrace His love today.

I am Thine, O Lord; / I have heard Thy voice, / And it told Thy love to me. / But I long to rise in the arms of faith / And be closer drawn to Thee.

*Fanny Crosby*

## — A Prayer for Today —

Thank You, Lord, for Your Son. His love is boundless, infinite, and eternal. Today, let me pause and reflect upon Christ's love for me, and let me share that love with all those who cross my path. Amen

# God, Worship, and Marriage

*We love Him because He first loved us.*

1 John 4:19 NKJV

If you're married, you already know that it takes cooperation and commitment to build a life together. But something else is necessary as well: you and your husband should worship together. When the two of you sincerely embrace God's love, you will feel differently about yourself, your marriage, your family, and your world. When you and your husband embrace God's love together, your marriage will be transformed. And, when the two of you accept the Father's grace and share His love, you will be blessed here on earth and throughout eternity.

So, if you genuinely seek to build a marriage that will stand the test of time, make God the centerpiece. When you do, your love will endure for a lifetime and beyond.

Those who abandon ship the first time it enters a storm miss the calm beyond. And the rougher the storms weathered together, the deeper and stronger real love grows.

*Ruth Bell Graham*

## — A Prayer for Today —

Your love is a perfect love, O Lord. Let me accept Your love today, and let me share it with my husband. Amen

# The Battle Is Won

*Cast your burden on the Lord, and He will support you; He will never allow the righteous to be shaken.*

*Psalm 55:22 HCSB*

Christians have every reason to live courageously. After all, the ultimate battle has already been won on the cross at Calvary. But even dedicated followers of Christ may find their courage tested by the inevitable disappointments and fears that visit the lives of believers and non-believers alike.

When you find yourself worried about the challenges of today or the uncertainties of tomorrow, you must ask yourself whether or not you are ready to place your concerns and your life in God's all-powerful, all-knowing, all-loving hands. If the answer to that question is yes—as it should be—then you can draw courage today from the source of strength that never fails: your Heavenly Father.

What is courage? It is the ability to be strong in trust, in conviction, in obedience. To be courageous is to step out in faith—to trust and obey, no matter what.

*Kay Arthur*

## — A Prayer for Today —

Lord, sometimes, this world can be a fearful place, but You have promised me that You are with me always. Today, Lord, I will live courageously as I place my trust in Your everlasting power and my faith in Your everlasting love. Amen

## Solving Life's Riddles

*If you don't know what you're doing, pray to the Father. He loves to help. You'll get his help, and won't be condescended to when you ask for it. Ask boldly, believingly, without a second thought. People who "worry their prayers" are like wind-whipped waves. Don't think you're going to get anything from the Master that way, adrift at sea, keeping all your options open.*

*James 1:5-8 MSG*

Life presents each of us with countless questions, conundrums, doubts, and problems. Thankfully, the riddles of everyday living are not too difficult to solve if we look for answers in the right places. When we have questions, we should consult God's Word, we should seek the guidance of the Holy Spirit, and we should trust the counsel of God-fearing friends and family members.

Are you facing a difficult decision? Take your concerns to God and avail yourself of the messages and mentors that He has placed along your path. When you do, God will speak to you in His own way and in His own time, and when He does, you can most certainly trust the answers that He gives.

### — A Prayer for Today —

Dear Lord, today I come to you seeking guidance. I will trust You to show me the path that I should take, and I will strive, as best I can, to follow in the footsteps of Your Son. Amen

# Sensing His Presence

*Where can I go from your Spirit? Where can I flee from your presence? If I go up to the heavens, you are there; if I make my bed in the depths, you are there. If I rise on the wings of the dawn, if I settle on the far side of the sea, even there your hand will guide me, your right hand will hold me fast.*

*Psalm 139:7-10 NIV*

If God is everywhere, why does He sometimes seem so far away? The answer to that question, of course, has nothing to do with God and everything to do with us.

When we begin each day on our knees, in praise and worship to Him, God often seems very near indeed. But, if we ignore God's presence or—worse yet—rebel against it altogether, the world in which we live becomes a spiritual wasteland.

Today, and every day hereafter, thank God and praise Him. He is the Giver of all things good. Wherever you are, whether you are happy or sad, victorious or vanquished, celebrate God's presence. And be comforted. For He is here.

## — A Prayer for Today —

Heavenly Father, even when it seems to me that You are far away, You never leave my side. Today and every day, I will strive to feel Your presence, and I will strive to sense Your love for me. Amen

# Defeating Discouragement

*The Lord is the One who will go before you. He will be with you; He will not leave you or forsake you. Do not be afraid or discouraged.*

*Deuteronomy 31:8 HCSB*

When we fail to meet the expectations of others (or, for that matter, the expectations that we have set for ourselves), we may be tempted to abandon hope. Thankfully, on those cloudy days when our strength is sapped and our faith is shaken, there exists a source from which we can draw courage and wisdom. That source is God.

When we seek to form a more intimate and dynamic relationship with our Creator, He renews our spirits and restores our souls. God's promise is made clear in Isaiah 40:31: "But those who wait on the Lord shall renew their strength; They shall mount up with wings like eagles, They shall run and not be weary, They shall walk and not faint" (NKJV). And upon this promise we can—and should—depend.

## — A Prayer for Today —

Dear Lord, when I am discouraged, give me perspective and faith. When I am weak, give me strength. When I am fearful, give me courage for the day ahead. I will trust in Your promises, Father, and I will live with the assurance that You are with me not only for this day, but also throughout all eternity. Amen

# Decision-Making 101

*An indecisive man is unstable in all his ways.*

*James 1:8 HCSB*

From the instant you wake in the morning until the moment you nod off to sleep at night, you have the opportunity to make countless decisions: decisions about the things you do, decisions about the words you speak, and decisions about the thoughts you choose to think.

If you're facing one of life's major decisions, here are some things you can do: 1. Gather as much information as you can. 2. Don't be too impulsive. 3. Rely on the advice of trusted friends and mentors. 4. Pray for guidance. 5. Trust the quiet inner voice of your conscience. 6. When the time for action arrives, act. Procrastination is the enemy of progress; don't let it defeat you.

People who can never quite seem to make up their minds usually make themselves miserable. So when in doubt, be decisive. It's the decent way to live.

When we learn to listen to Christ's voice for the details of our daily decisions, we begin to know Him personally.

*Catherine Marshall*

## — A Prayer for Today —

Dear Lord, give me the insight to make wise decisions and the courage to act upon the decisions that I make. Amen

# Diligence Now

*Do not lack diligence; be fervent in spirit; serve the Lord.*
*Romans 12:11 HCSB*

God's Word reminds us again and again that our Creator expects us to lead disciplined lives. God doesn't reward laziness, misbehavior, or apathy. To the contrary, He expects believers to behave with dignity and discipline.

We live in a world in which leisure is glorified and indifference is often glamorized. But God has other plans. He did not create us for lives of mediocrity; He created us for far greater things. Life's greatest rewards seldom fall into our laps; to the contrary, our greatest accomplishments usually require lots of work, which is perfectly fine with God. After all, He knows that we're up to the task, and He has big plans for us; may we, as disciplined believers, always be worthy of those plans.

True willpower and courage are not only on the battlefield, but also in everyday conquests over our inertia, laziness, and boredom.

*D. L. Moody*

## — A Prayer for Today —

Dear Lord, You expect Your children to be diligent and disciplined. You have told us that the fields are ripe and the workers are few. Lead me to Your fields, Lord, and make me a disciplined worker in the service of Your Son. Amen

# Looking Before You Leap

*An impulsive vow is a trap; later you'll wish you could get out of it.*

*Proverbs 20:25 MSG*

Are you, at times, just a little bit impulsive? Are you a woman who sometimes looks before she leaps? If so, God wants to have a little chat with you.

God's Word is clear: as believers, we are called to lead lives of discipline, diligence, moderation, and maturity. But the world often tempts us to behave otherwise. Everywhere we turn, or so it seems, we are faced with powerful temptations to behave in undisciplined, ungodly ways. Yet God's Word instructs us to be disciplined in our thoughts and our actions; God's Word warns us against the dangers of impulsive behavior. As believers in a just God, we should act and react accordingly.

Sometimes, being wise is nothing more than slowing down long enough to think about things before you do them.

*Criswell Freeman*

— A Prayer for Today —

Lord, sometimes I can be an impulsive person. Slow me down, calm me down, and help me make wise decisions . . . today and every day of my life. Amen

# The Bread of Life

*I am the bread of life, Jesus told them. "No one who comes to Me will ever be hungry, and no one who believes in Me will ever be thirsty again."*

*John 6:35 HCSB*

He was the Son of God, but He wore a crown of thorns. He was the Savior of mankind, yet He was put to death on a roughhewn cross made of wood. He offered His healing touch to an unsaved world, and yet the same hands that had healed the sick and raised the dead were pierced with nails.

Jesus Christ, the Son of God, was born into humble circumstances. He walked this earth, not as a ruler of men, but as the Savior of mankind. His crucifixion, a torturous punishment that was intended to end His life and His reign, instead became the pivotal event in the history of all humanity.

Jesus is the bread of life. Accept His grace. Share His love. And follow in His footsteps.

## — A Prayer for Today —

Dear Jesus, You give me peace. Thank You, Lord, for the gift of eternal life and for the gift of eternal love. May I be ever grateful, and may I share Your Good News with a world that so desperately needs Your healing grace. Amen

# A Profound Love

*Pursue love and desire spiritual gifts.*

*1 Corinthians 14:1 HCSB*

As a woman, you know the profound love that you hold in your heart for your own family and friends. As a child of God, you can only imagine the infinite love that your Heavenly Father holds for you. God made you in His own image and gave you salvation through the person of His Son Jesus Christ. And now, precisely because you are a wondrous creation treasured by God, a question presents itself: What will you do in response to the Creator's love? Will you ignore it or embrace it?

When you embrace God's love, your life's purpose is forever changed. When you embrace God's love, you feel differently about yourself, your neighbors, your family, and your world. More importantly, you share God's message—and His love—with others. Your Heavenly Father—a God of infinite love and mercy—is waiting to embrace you with open arms. Accept His love today and forever.

## — A Prayer for Today —

Dear God, let me share Your love with the world. Make me a woman of compassion. Help me to recognize the needs of others. Let me forgive those who have hurt me, just as You have forgiven me. And let the love of Your Son shine in me and through me today, tomorrow, and throughout all eternity. Amen

# Mentors That Matter

*The lips of the righteous feed many.*

Proverbs 10:21 HCSB

Here's a simple yet effective way to strengthen your faith: Choose role models whose faith in God is strong.

When you emulate godly people, you become a more godly person yourself. That's why you should seek out mentors who, by their words and their presence, make you a better person and a better Christian.

Today, as a gift to yourself, select, from your friends and family members, a mentor whose judgement you trust. Then listen carefully to your mentor's advice and be willing to accept that advice, even if accepting it requires effort or pain, or both. Consider your mentor to be God's gift to you. Thank God for that gift, and use it for the glory of His kingdom.

It takes a wise person to give good advice, but an even wiser person to take it.

*Marie T. Freeman*

## — A Prayer for Today —

Dear Lord, thank You for family members, for friends, and for mentors. When I am troubled, let me turn to them for help, for guidance, for comfort, and for perspective. And Father, let me be a friend and mentor to others so that my love for You may be reflected in my genuine concern for them. Amen

# A Passionate Life

*Never be lazy in your work, but serve the Lord enthusiastically.*

*Romans 12:11 NLT*

Are you passionate about your life, your loved ones, your work, and your faith? As a believer who has been saved by a risen Christ, you should be.

As a thoughtful Christian, you have every reason to be enthusiastic about life, but sometimes the inevitable struggles of life may cause you to feel decidedly unenthusiastic. If you feel that your enthusiasm is slowly fading away, it's time to slow down, to rest, to count your blessings, and to pray. When you feel worried or weary, you must pray fervently for God to renew your sense of wonderment and excitement. Life with God can be—and should be—a glorious adventure. Revel in it. When you do, God will most certainly smile upon your work and your life.

Life is too short to spend it being angry, bored, or dull.

*Barbara Johnson*

## — A Prayer for Today —

Dear Lord, the life that I live and the words that I speak bear testimony to my faith. Make me a faithful and passionate servant of Your Son, and let my testimony be worthy of You. Let my words be sure and true, Lord, and let my actions point others to You. Amen

# Your Real Riches

*Naked I came from my mother's womb, and naked I will leave this life. The Lord gives, and the Lord takes away. Praise the name of the Lord.*

*Job 1:21 HCSB*

Martin Luther observed, "Many things I have tried to grasp and have lost. That which I have placed in God's hands I still have." How true. Earthly riches are transitory; spiritual riches are not.

In our demanding world, financial security can be a good thing, but spiritual prosperity is profoundly more important. Certainly we all need the basic necessities of life, but once we've acquired those necessities, enough is enough. Why? Because our real riches are not of this world. We are never really rich until we are rich in spirit.

I have held many things in my hands, and I have lost them all; but whatever I have placed in God's hands, that I still possess.

*Corrie ten Boom*

## — A Prayer for Today —

Dear Lord, all I have belongs to You. When I leave this world I take nothing with me. Help me to value my relationship with You—and my relationships with others—more than I value my material possessions. Amen

# Real Repentance

*I preached to those in Damascus first, and to those in Jerusalem and in all the region of Judea, and to the Gentiles, that they should repent and turn to God, and do works worthy of repentance.*

Acts 26:20 HCSB

Who among us has sinned? All of us. But the good news is this: When we do ask God's forgiveness and turn our hearts to Him, He forgives us absolutely and completely.

Genuine repentance requires more than simply offering God apologies for our misdeeds. Real repentance may start with feelings of sorrow and remorse, but it ends only when we turn away from the sin that has heretofore distanced us from our Creator. In truth, we offer our most meaningful apologies to God, not with our words, but with our actions. As long as we are still engaged in sin, we may be "repenting," but we have not fully "repented." So, if there is an aspect of your life that is distancing you from your God, ask for His forgiveness, and—just as importantly—stop sinning. Now.

## — A Prayer for Today —

When I stray from Your commandments, Lord, I must not only confess my sins, I must also turn from them. When I fall short, help me to change. Forgive my sins, Dear Lord, and help me live according to Your plan for my life. Your plan is perfect, Father; I am not. Let me trust in You. Amen

# A Wise Move

*Now if any of you lacks wisdom, he should ask God, who gives to all generously and without criticizing, and it will be given to him.*

James 1:5 HCSB

Do you seek wisdom for yourself and for your family? Of course you do. But, as a thoughtful woman living in a society that is filled with temptations and distractions, you know that it's all too easy to stray far from the source of the ultimate wisdom: God's Holy Word.

When you commit yourself to daily study of God's Word—and when you live according to His commandments—you will become wise . . . in time. So, as a way of understanding God's plan for your life, study His Word and live by it. When you do, you will accumulate a storehouse of wisdom that will enrich your own life and the lives of your family members, your friends, and the world.

Knowledge can be found in books or in school. Wisdom, on the other hand, starts with God . . . and ends there.

*Marie T. Freeman*

## — A Prayer for Today —

Lord, make me a woman of wisdom and discernment. I seek wisdom, Lord, not as the world gives, but as You give. Lead me in Your ways and teach me from Your Word so that, in time, my wisdom might glorify Your kingdom and Your Son. Amen

# Making Peace with Your Past

*Forget about what's happened; don't keep going over old history. Be alert, be present. I'm about to do something brand-new. It's bursting out! Don't you see it? There it is! I'm making a road through the desert, rivers in the badlands.*

*Isaiah 43:18–19 MSG*

Have you made peace with your past? If so, congratulations. But, if you are mired in the quicksand of regret, it's time to plan your escape. How can you do so? By accepting what has been and by trusting God for what will be.

Because you are human, you may be slow to forget yesterday's disappointments. But, if you sincerely seek to focus your hopes and energies on the future, then you must find ways to accept the past, no matter how difficult it may be to do so. So, if you have not yet made peace with the past, today is the day to declare an end to all hostilities. When you do, you can then turn your thoughts to wondrous promises of God and to the glorious future that He has in store for you.

## — A Prayer for Today —

Heavenly Father, free me from anger, resentment, and envy. When I am bitter, I cannot feel the peace that You intend for my life. Keep me mindful that forgiveness is Your commandment, and help me accept the past, treasure the present, and trust the future . . . to You. Amen

# The Futility of Blame

*People's own foolishness ruins their lives, but in their minds they blame the Lord.*

*Proverbs 19:3 NCV*

To blame others for our own problems is the height of futility. Yet blaming others is a favorite human pastime. Why? Because blaming is much easier than fixing, and criticizing others is so much easier than improving ourselves. So instead of solving our problems legitimately (by doing the work required to solve them), we are inclined to fret, to blame, and to criticize, while doing precious little else. When we do, our problems, quite predictably, remain unsolved.

Have you acquired the bad habit of blaming others for problems that you could or should solve yourself? If so, you are not only disobeying God's Word, you are also wasting your own precious time. So, instead of looking for someone to blame, look for something to fix, and then get busy fixing it. And as you consider your own situation, remember this: God has a way of helping those who help themselves, but He doesn't spend much time helping those who don't.

## — A Prayer for Today —

Dear Lord, when I make a mistake, I want to admit it. Help me not blame others for the mistakes that I make. And when I make a mistake, help me to learn from it. Amen

# Excellence, Not Excuses

*And now, children, stay with Christ. Live deeply in Christ. Then we'll be ready for him when he appears, ready to receive him with open arms, with no cause for red-faced guilt or lame excuses when he arrives.*

*1 John 2:28-29 MSG*

We live in a world where excuses are everywhere. And it's precisely because excuses are so numerous that they are also so ineffective. When we hear the words, "I'm sorry but . . . ," most of us know exactly what is to follow: the excuse. The dog ate the homework. Traffic was terrible. It's the company's fault. The boss is to blame. The equipment is broken. We're out of that. And so forth, and so on.

Because we humans are such creative excuse-makers, all of the really good excuses have already been taken. In fact, the high-quality excuses have been used, re-used, over-used, and ab-used. That's why excuses don't work—we've heard them all before.

So, if you're wasting your time trying to concoct a new and improved excuse, don't bother. It's impossible. A far better strategy is this: do the work. Now. And let your excellent work speak loudly and convincingly for itself.

## — A Prayer for Today —

Heavenly Father, how easy it is to make excuses. But, I want to be a woman who accomplishes important work for You. Help me, Father, to strive for excellence, not excuses. Amen

# Counting Your Blessings

*Finally, brethren, whatever things are true, whatever things are noble, whatever things are just, whatever things are pure, whatever things are lovely, whatever things are of good report, if there is any virtue and if there is anything praiseworthy—meditate on these things.*

*Philippians 4:8 NKJV*

How will you direct your thoughts today? Will you obey the words of Philippians 4:8 by dwelling upon those things that are true and honorable and right? Or will you allow your thoughts to be hijacked by the negativity that seems to dominate our troubled world? Are you fearful, angry, bored, or worried? Are you so preoccupied with the concerns of this day that you fail to thank God for the promise of eternity? Are you confused, bitter, or pessimistic? If so, God wants to have a little talk with you.

God intends that you experience joy and abundance. So, today and every day hereafter, celebrate the life that God has given you by focusing your thoughts upon those things that are worthy of praise. Today, count your blessings instead of your hardships. And thank the Giver of all things good for gifts that are simply too numerous to count.

## — A Prayer for Today —

Dear Lord, help me have an attitude that is pleasing to You as I count my blessings today, tomorrow, and every day. Amen

# Friends and Family

*As iron sharpens iron, a friend sharpens a friend.*
*Proverbs 27:17 NLT*

A loving family is a treasure from God; so is a trustworthy friend. If you are a member of a close knit, supportive family, offer a word of thanks to your Creator. And if you have a close circle of trustworthy friends, consider yourself richly blessed.

Today, let us praise God for our family and for our friends. God has placed these people along our paths. Let us love them and care for them. And, let us give thanks to the Father for all the people who enrich our lives. These people are, in a very real sense, gifts from God; we should treat them as such.

The best times in life are made a thousand times better when shared with a dear friend.

*Luci Swindoll*

## — A Prayer for Today —

Heavenly Father, thank You for my friends and family. Let me be a trustworthy friend to all, and let my love for You be reflected in my genuine love for them. Amen

# The Shepherd's Care

*Your righteousness reaches heaven, God, You who have done great things; God, who is like You?*

Psalm 71:19 HCSB

It's a promise that is made over and over again in the Bible: Whatever "it" is, God can handle it.

Life isn't always easy. Far from it! Sometimes, life can be very, very difficult. But even then, even during our darkest moments, we're protected by a loving Heavenly Father. When we're worried, God can reassure us; when we're sad, God can comfort us. When our hearts are broken, God is not just near; He is here. So we must lift our thoughts and prayers to Him. When we do, He will answer our prayers. Why? Because He is our Shepherd, and He has promised to protect us now and forever.

When considering the size of your problems, there are two categories that you should never worry about: the problems that are small enough for you to handle, and the ones that aren't too big for God to handle.

Marie T. Freeman

## — A Prayer for Today —

Dear Lord, when I obey Your commandments, I am blessed. Today, I invite You to reign over my heart. I will sense Your presence, Father; I will accept Your love; and I will praise You for the Savior of my life: Your Son Jesus. Amen

# The Gift of Grace

*For by grace you are saved through faith, and this is not from yourselves; it is God's gift—not from works, so that no one can boast.*

*Ephesians 2:8-9 HCSB*

God has given us so many gifts, but none can compare with the gift of salvation. We have not earned our salvation; it is a gift from God. When we accept Christ into our hearts, we are saved by His grace.

God's grace is the ultimate gift, and we owe Him the ultimate in thanksgiving. Let us praise the Creator for His priceless gift, and let us share the Good News with all who cross our paths. We return our Father's love by accepting His grace and by sharing His message and His love. When we do, we are eternally blessed . . . and the Father smiles.

God does amazing works through prayers that seek to extend His grace to others.

*Shirley Dobson*

## — A Prayer for Today —

Accepting Your grace can be hard, Lord. Somehow, I feel that I must earn Your love and Your acceptance. Yet, the Bible promises that You love me and save me by Your grace. It is a gift I can only accept and cannot earn. Thank You for Your priceless gift. Amen

# God Heals Us

*I have heard your prayer, I have seen your tears; surely I will heal you.*

*2 Kings 20:5 NKJV*

Women of every generation have experienced adversity, and this generation is no different. But, today's women face challenges that previous generations could have scarcely imagined. Thankfully, although the world continues to change, God's love remains constant. And, He remains ready to comfort us and strengthen us whenever we turn to Him. Psalm 147 promises, "He heals the brokenhearted, and binds their wounds" (v. 3). When we are troubled, we must call upon God, and, in His own time and according to His own plan, He will heal us.

God's peace is like a river, not a pond. In other words, a sense of health and well-being, both of which are expressions of the Hebrew shalom, can permeate our homes even when we're in white-water rapids.

*Beth Moore*

## — A Prayer for Today —

Lord, sometimes life is so difficult that I can't see any hope for the future. But with You, there is always hope. Keep me mindful that there is nothing that will happen today that You and I can't handle together. Amen

# A One-of-a-Kind Treasure

*Every word of God is pure; He is a shield to those who put their trust in Him.*

*Proverbs 30:5 NKJV*

God's Word is a roadmap for life here on earth and for life eternal. As Christians, we are called upon to study God's Holy Word, to trust its promises, to follow its commandments, and to share its Good News with the world.

As believers, we must study the Bible and meditate upon its meaning for our lives. Otherwise, we deprive ourselves of a priceless gift from our Creator. God's Holy Word is, indeed, a transforming, life-changing, one-of-a-kind treasure. And, a passing acquaintance with the Good Book is insufficient for Christians who seek to obey God's Word and to understand His will. After all, neither man nor woman should live by bread alone . . .

Weave the unveiling fabric of God's word through your heart and mind. It will hold strong, even if the rest of life unravels.

*Gigi Graham Tchividjian*

## — A Prayer for Today —

Heavenly Father, Your Holy Word is a light unto my path. In all that I do, help me be a worthy witness for You as I share the Good News of Your perfect Son and Your perfect Word. Amen

# Abundant Peace

*And the peace of God, which surpasses every thought, will guard your hearts and your minds in Christ Jesus.*

*Philippians 4:7 HCSB*

Are you the kind of woman who accepts God's spiritual abundance without reservation? If so, you are availing yourself of the peace and the joy that He has promised. Do you sincerely seek the riches that our Savior offers to those who give themselves to Him? Then follow Him. When you do, you will receive the love and the abundance that Jesus offers to those who follow Him.

Seek first the salvation that is available through a personal, passionate relationship with Christ, and then claim the joy, the peace, and the spiritual abundance that the Shepherd offers His sheep.

God has promised us abundance, peace, and eternal life. These treasures are ours for the asking; all we must do is claim them. One of the great mysteries of life is why on earth do so many of us wait so very long to lay claim to God's gifts?

*Marie T. Freeman*

## — A Prayer for Today —

Heavenly Father, You have promised an abundant life through Your Son Jesus. Thank You, Lord, for Your abundance and Your peace. Your blessings endure forever, Lord, and I will praise You today, tomorrow, and throughout eternity. Amen

# A Time to Rest

*Come to Me, all you who labor and are heavy laden, and I will give you rest. Take My yoke upon you and learn from Me, for I am gentle and lowly in heart, and you will find rest for your souls. For My yoke is easy and My burden is light.*

*Matthew 11:28-30 NKJV*

Sometimes, the struggles of life can drain us of our strength. When we find ourselves tired, discouraged, or worse, there is a source from which we can draw the power needed to recharge our spiritual batteries. That source, of course, is God.

God expects us to work hard, but He also intends for us to rest. When we fail to take the rest that we need, we do a disservice to ourselves and to our families.

Is your spiritual battery running low? Is your energy on the wane? Are your emotions frayed? If so, it's time to turn your thoughts and your prayers to God. And when you're finished, it's time to rest.

Life is strenuous. See that your clock does not run down.

*Mrs. Charles E. Cowman*

## — A Prayer for Today —

Dear Lord, when I'm tired, give me the wisdom to do the smart thing: give me the wisdom to put my head on my pillow and rest! Amen

# Joy and the Christian Life

*Light shines on those who do right; joy belongs to those who are honest. Rejoice in the Lord, you who do right. Praise his holy name.*

*Psalm 97:11-12 NCV*

God's Word makes it clear: He intends that His joy should become our joy. The Lord intends that believers should share His love with His joy in their hearts. Yet sometimes, amid the inevitable hustle and bustle of life-here-on-earth, we can forfeit—albeit temporarily—God's joy as we wrestle with the challenges of daily living.

Joni Eareckson Tada spoke for Christian women of every generation when she observed, "I wanted the deepest part of me to vibrate with that ancient yet familiar longing, that desire for something that would fill and overflow my soul."

If, today, your heart is heavy, open the door of your soul to Christ. He will give you peace and joy. And if you already have the joy of Christ in your heart, share it freely, just as Christ freely shared His joy with you.

## — A Prayer for Today —

Dear Lord, You are my loving Heavenly Father, and You created me in Your image. As Your faithful child, I will make Your joy my joy. I will praise Your works, I will obey Your Word, and I will honor Your Son, this day and every day of my life. Amen

# The World . . . and You

*Don't copy the behavior and customs of this world, but let God transform you into a new person by changing the way you think.*

*Romans 12:2 NLT*

We live in the world, but we must not worship it. Our duty is to place God first and everything else second. But because we are fallible beings with imperfect faith, placing God in His rightful place is often difficult. In fact, at every turn, or so it seems, we are tempted to do otherwise.

The 21st-century world is a noisy, distracting place filled with countless opportunities to stray from God's will. The world seems to cry, "Worship me with your time, your money, your energy, and your thoughts!" But God commands otherwise: He commands us to worship Him and Him alone; everything else must be secondary.

As we have by faith said no to sin, so we should by faith say yes to God and set our minds on things above, where Christ is seated in the heavenlies.

*Vonette Bright*

## — A Prayer for Today —

Dear Lord, I am an imperfect human being living in an imperfect world. Direct my path far from the temptations and distractions of this world, and let me follow in the footsteps of Your Son today and forever. Amen

# The Treasure Hunt

*For where your treasure is, there your heart will be also.*
*Luke 12:34 NKJV*

All of humanity is engaged in a colossal, worldwide treasure hunt. Some people seek treasure from earthly sources, treasures such as material wealth or public acclaim; others seek God's treasures by making Him the cornerstone of their lives.

What kind of treasure hunter are you? Are you so caught up in the demands of everyday living that you sometimes allow the search for worldly treasures to become your primary focus? If so, it's time to think long and hard about what you value, and why. All the items on your daily to-do list are not created equal. That's why you must put first things first by placing God in His rightful place: first place. The world's treasures are difficult to find and difficult to keep; God's treasures are ever-present and everlasting. Which treasures, then, will you claim as your own?

## — A Prayer for Today —

Heavenly Father, when I focus intently upon You, I am blessed. When I focus too intently on the acquisition of material possessions, I am troubled. Make my priorities pleasing to You, Father, and make me a worthy servant of Your Son. Amen

# At Peace with Your Purpose

*But now in Christ Jesus you who once were far off have been brought near by the blood of Christ. For He Himself is our peace.*

*Ephesians 2:13–14 NKJV*

Are you at peace with the direction of your life? If you're a Christian, you should be. Perhaps you seek a new direction or a sense of renewed purpose, but those feelings should never rob you of the genuine peace that can and should be yours through a personal relationship with Jesus.

Have you found the lasting peace that can be yours through Jesus, or are you still rushing after the illusion of "peace and happiness" that our world promises but cannot deliver? Today, as a gift to yourself, to your family, and to your friends, claim the inner peace that is your spiritual birthright: the peace of Jesus Christ.

Prayer guards hearts and minds and causes God to bring peace out of chaos.

*Beth Moore*

## — A Prayer for Today —

Dear Lord, let me accept the peace and abundance that You offer through Your Son Jesus. You are the Giver of all things good, Father, and You give me peace when I draw close to You. Help me to trust Your will, to follow Your commands, and to accept Your peace, today and forever. Amen

# Constant Praise

*Through Him then, let us continually offer up a sacrifice of praise to God, that is, the fruit of lips that give thanks to His name.*

*Hebrews 13:15 NASB*

The Bible makes it clear: it pays to praise God. But sometimes, we allow ourselves to become so preoccupied with the demands of daily life that we forget to say "Thank You" to the Giver of all good gifts.

Worship and praise should be a part of everything we do. Otherwise, we quickly lose perspective as we fall prey to the demands of the moment.

Do you sincerely desire to be a worthy servant of the One who has given you eternal love and eternal life? Then praise Him for who He is and for what He has done for you. Praise Him all day long, every day, for as long as you live . . . and then for all eternity.

God is worthy of our praise and is pleased when we come before Him with thanksgiving.

*Shirley Dobson*

## — A Prayer for Today —

Heavenly Father, I come to You today with hope in my heart and praise on my lips. I place my trust in You, Dear Lord, knowing that with You as my Protector, I have nothing to fear. I thank You, Lord, for Your grace, for Your love, and for Your Son. Amen

# God Is Here

*Draw near to God, and He will draw near to you.*
*James 4:8 HCSB*

God is constantly making Himself available to you; therefore, when you approach Him obediently and sincerely, you will most certainly find Him: God is always available to you. Whenever it seems to you that God is distant, disinterested, or altogether absent, you may rest assured that your feelings are a reflection of your own emotional state, not an indication of God's absence.

If, during life's darker days, you seek to establish a closer relationship with Him, you can do so because God is not just near; He is here.

The empty tomb proves Christianity. The empty church denies it.

*Anonymous*

## — A Prayer for Today —

Dear Lord, thank You for Your constant presence and Your constant love. I draw near to You this day with the confidence that You are ready to guide me. Help me walk closely with You, Father, and help me share Your Good News with all who cross my path. Amen

# Honoring God

*Honor GOD with everything you own; give him the first and the best. Your barns will burst, your wine vats will brim over.*

*Proverbs 3:9-10 MSG*

Whom will you choose to honor today? If you honor God and place Him at the center of your life, every day is a cause for celebration. But if you fail to honor your Heavenly Father, you're asking for trouble, and lots of it.

At times, your life is probably hectic, demanding, and complicated. When the demands of life leave you rushing from place to place with scarcely a moment to spare, you may fail to pause and thank your Creator for the blessings He has bestowed upon you. But that's a big mistake. So honor God for who He is and for what He has done for you. And don't just honor Him on Sunday morning. Praise Him all day long, every day, for as long as you live . . . and then for all eternity.

## — A Prayer for Today —

I praise You, Lord, from the depths of my heart, and I give thanks for Your goodness, for Your mercy, and for Your Son. Let me honor You every day of my life through my words and my deeds. Let me honor You, Father, with all that I am. Amen

# Enthusiastic Discipleship

*Don't work only while being watched, in order to please men, but as slaves of Christ, do God's will from your heart. Render service with a good attitude, as to the Lord and not to men.*

*Ephesians 6:6-7 HCSB*

With whom will you choose to walk today? Will you walk with shortsighted people who honor the ways of the world, or will you walk with the Son of God? Jesus walks with you. Are you walking with Him? Hopefully, you will choose to walk with Him today and every day of your life. Jesus has called upon believers of every generation (and that includes you) to follow in His footsteps. And God's Word promises that when you follow in Christ's footsteps, you will learn how to live freely and lightly (Matthew 11:28-30).

Jesus doesn't want you to be a run-of-the-mill, follow-the-crowd kind of person. Jesus wants you to be a "new creation" through Him. And that's exactly what you should want for yourself, too. Jesus deserves your extreme enthusiasm; the world deserves it; and you deserve the experience of sharing it.

## — A Prayer for Today —

Dear Lord, You have called me not to a life of mediocrity, but to a life of passion. Today, I will be an enthusiastic follower of Your Son, and I will share His Good News— and His love—with all who cross my path. Amen

# Living in an Anxious World

*Cast all your anxiety on him because he cares for you.*
*1 Peter 5:7 NIV*

We live in a world that often breeds anxiety and fear. When we come face-to-face with tough times, we may fall prey to discouragement, doubt, or depression. But our Father in heaven has other plans. God has promised that we may lead lives of abundance, not anxiety. In fact, His Word instructs us to "be anxious for nothing" (Philippians 4:6). But how can we put our fears to rest? By taking those fears to God and leaving them there.

As you face the challenges of daily life, you may find yourself becoming anxious, troubled, discouraged, or fearful. If so, turn every one of your concerns over to your Heavenly Father. The same God who created the universe will comfort you if you ask Him . . . so ask Him and trust Him. And then watch in amazement as your anxieties melt into the warmth of His loving hands.

## — A Prayer for Today —

Father, sometimes troubles and distractions preoccupy thoughts and trouble my soul. When I am anxious, Lord, let me turn my prayers to You. When I am worried, give me faith in You. Let me live courageously, Dear God, knowing that You love me and that You will protect me, today and forever. Amen

# Ultimate Accountability

*We encouraged, comforted, and implored each one of you to walk worthy of God, who calls you into His own kingdom and glory.*

*1 Thessalonians 2:12 HCSB*

For most of us, it is a daunting thought: one day, perhaps soon, we'll come face-to-face with our Heavenly Father, and we'll be called to account for our actions here on earth. Our personal histories will certainly not be surprising to God; He already knows everything about us. But the full scope of our activities may be surprising to us: some of us will be pleasantly surprised; others will not be.

Today, do whatever you can to ensure that your thoughts and your deeds are pleasing to your Creator. Because you will, at some point in future, be called to account for your actions.

There may be no trumpet sound or loud applause when we make a right decision, just a calm sense of resolution and peace.

*Gloria Gaither*

## — A Prayer for Today —

Dear Lord, let my words and actions show the world the changes that You have made in my life. You sent Your Son so that I might have abundant life and eternal life. Thank You, Father, for my Savior, Christ Jesus. I will follow Him, honor Him, and share His Good News, this day and every day. Amen

# Abundant Living

*I came so they can have real and eternal life, more and better life than they ever dreamed of.*

John 10:10 MSG

The familiar words of John 10:10 should serve as a daily reminder: Christ came to this earth so that we might experience His abundance, His love, and His gift of eternal life. But as every woman knows, some days are so busy and so hurried that abundance seems a distant promise. It is not. Every day, we can claim the spiritual abundance that God promises for our lives . . . and we should.

Christ is the ultimate Savior of mankind and the personal Savior of those who believe in Him. As his servants, we should place Him at the very center of our lives. And, every day that God gives us breath, we should share Christ's love and His abundance with a world that needs both.

## — A Prayer for Today —

Thank You, Dear Lord, for the abundant life that is mine through Your Son Jesus. In all that I say and do, let me share Your message of abundance with my family, my friends, and my community. Give me courage, Lord, to claim the spiritual riches that You have promised, and help me to share Your abundance with all who cross my path. Amen

# Life Eternal

*In a little while the world will see Me no longer, but you will see Me. Because I live, you will live too.*

*John 14:19 HCSB*

How marvelous it is that God became a man and walked among us. Had He not chosen to do so, we might feel removed from a distant Creator. But ours is not a distant God. Ours is a God who understands—far better than we ever could—the essence of what it means to be human.

God understands our hopes, our fears, and our temptations. He understands what it means to be angry and what it costs to forgive. He knows the heart, the conscience, and the soul of every person who has ever lived, including you. And God has a plan of salvation that is intended for you. Accept it. Accept God's gift through the person of His Son Christ Jesus, and then rest assured: God walked among us so that you might have eternal life; amazing though it may seem, He did it for you.

## — A Prayer for Today —

I know, Lord, that this world is not my home; I am only here for a brief while. And, You have given me the priceless gift of eternal life through Your Son Jesus. Keep the hope of heaven fresh in my heart, and, while I am in this world, help me to pass through it with faith in my heart and praise on my lips . . . for You. Amen

# Commissioned to Witness

*Go, therefore, and make disciples of all nations, baptizing them in the name of the Father and of the Son and of the Holy Spirit, teaching them to observe everything I have commanded you. And remember, I am with you always, to the end of the age.*

Matthew 28:19-20 HCSB

After His resurrection, Jesus addressed His disciples. As recorded in the 28th chapter of Matthew, Christ instructed His followers to share His message with the world. This "Great Commission" applies to Christians of every generation, including our own.

As believers, we are called to share the Good News of Jesus with our families, with our neighbors, and with the world. Christ commanded His disciples to become fishers of men. We must do likewise, and we must do so today. Tomorrow may indeed be too late.

Our faith becomes stronger as we express it; a growing faith is a sharing faith.

*Billy Graham*

## — A Prayer for Today —

Heavenly Father, every man and woman, every boy and girl is Your child. You desire that all Your children know Jesus as their Lord and Savior. Father, let me be part of Your Great Commission. Let me give, let me pray, and let me go out into this world so that I might be Your worthy disciple, today and every day. Amen

# Notes

## Notes

## Notes